THE
DAUGHTERS
OF JUÁREZ

THE
DAUGHTERS
OF JUÁREZ

A TRUE STORY OF SERIAL MURDER
SOUTH OF THE BORDER

TERESA RODRIGUEZ
DIANA MONTANÉ WITH LISA PULITZER

ATRIA BOOKS
NEW YORK LONDON TORONTO SYDNEY

ATRIA
BOOKS

1230 Avenue of the Americas
New York, NY 10020

Library of Congress Cataloging-in-Publication Data is available.

ISBN-13: 978-0-7432-9203-0
ISBN-10:   0-7432-9203-0

First Atria Books hardcover edition March 2007

Map courtesy of Chris Robinson

10 9 8 7 6 5 4 3 2 1

ATRIA BOOKS is a trademark of Simon & Schuster, Inc.

Manufactured in the United States of America

For information regarding special discounts for bulk purchases,
please contact Simon & Schuster Special Sales at
1-800-456-6798 or business@simonandschuster.com.

To the murdered women of Ciudad Juárez,
State of Chihuahua, México

To Victor, Julian, and Tony,
without whose love and support
this book would not have been possible

Contents

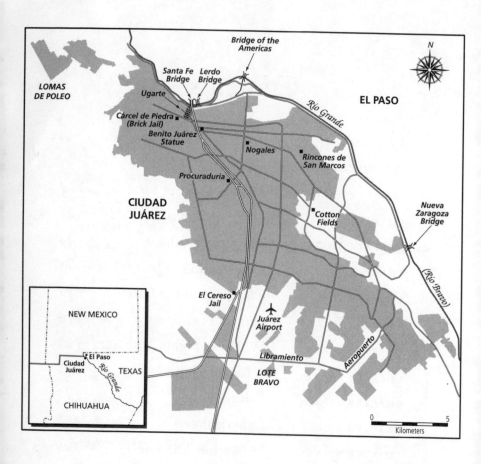

Bridge of the Americas

Santa Fe Bridge   Lerdo Bridge

LOMAS DE POLEO

Ugarte

Cárcel de Piedra (Brick Jail)

Benito Juárez Statue

Nogales

Rincones de San Marcos

Río Grande

EL PASO

N

Procuraduria

CIUDAD JUÁREZ

Cotton Fields

Nueva Zaragoza Bridge

(Río Bravo)

El Cereso Jail

Juárez Airport

Libramiento

Aeropuerto

LOTE BRAVO

NEW MEXICO

El Paso

Ciudad Juárez

TEXAS

Río Grande

CHIHUAHUA

0   5
Kilometers

Preface

In 1993, life in Juárez, Mexico, began to change for many young women. One by one, their violated and mutilated bodies began to appear in the vast desert areas that encircle the city. At the time of this book's publication, the killings continue and there remain dozens of unresolved cases. Although some say the dead can speak, the families of the victims ask themselves if anyone is listening.

Among the theories, insiders and advocates for the victims have suggested that a serial killer or killers may be on the loose; that members of Juárez's powerful drug cartel and a handful of prominent buisnessmen on either side of the border in conjunction with police may be responsible for a number of these crimes. They believe that some people in power are more interested in covering up the crimes and shielding the perpetrators than in resolving the cases in any way that can bring peace of mind to many bereaved families.

I am Teresa Rodriguez, anchor and investigative reporter for Univision, the largest Spanish-language television network in the United States. I traveled to Juárez, Mexico, on four separate occasions, both with my news production team and on my own, to carry out my investigations.

My own family emigrated from Cuba when I was nine months old. While I grew up with few luxuries, that fact never seemed to matter. My mother could sew, so I never lacked for new clothes. I was always told I could be anything I wanted to be if I just set my mind to it. The women I am going to tell you about are fighting for that same right, but their struggle is marked by a trail of blood and their abusers remain at large despite repeated calls for justice.

We expect fair trials in the United States of America. And yet even in our own country, we know that justice is not always served. However, as you read this book, you will see that in the state of Chihuahua and perhaps throughout Mexico, many of those rules that we take for granted don't exist. People are living in substandard conditions, and political corruption reigns.

In the following pages, you will read an incredible and disturbing account of serial murder, police corruption, and political indifference. Drawing from a variety of sources, including interviews with law enforcement personnel, civil rights leaders, victims' families, local journalists, and others, I bring you a firsthand account of the atrocities against women that are occurring just south of the U.S. border.

Among the dozens of interviews I conducted while in Mexico was an exclusive one-on-one sit-down with the alleged mastermind behind the murders, Egyptian chemist Abdel Latif Sharif Sharif, who died in jail proclaiming his innocence. His allegation that members of the Chihuahua State Police Department, working in concert with high-ranking government officials, narcotraffickers, and perhaps even wealthy business-men crossing into Mexico from the U.S. city of El Paso, are behind the killings is not without merit and, in fact, has been bolstered by inquiries conducted by representatives from the United Nations and Amnesty International.

Yet, despite the findings of these studies, the formation of numerous commissions, the appointment of federal special prosecutors, and the undying efforts by local women's rights activists to right the wrongs, the abuses against Mexico's young women continue seemingly unabated.

Introduction

THE HOWLING OF THE COYOTES is nothing compared to the stillness that falls on the desert once it swallows its prey; when the sun sets and one life stops in Juárez. And it isn't the coyotes that strike, with the ferocity and stealth of predators, nor any animal that inhabits the arid terrain. This marauder walks among his victims, examining their every move, perhaps even befriending them. And when she least expects it, he unleashes a deadly sting, like the venomous scorpion common to this parched region, violently raping, mutilating and slaughtering his prey, leaving her to die among the tumbleweed knowing her desperate cries for help will be pointless and trackless. No one will hear her in this barren wilderness. And when his job is done, the beast rejoices. In his warped and perverted mind he is confident that soon, she too will rot away, like the other daughters of Juarez becoming one with this desolate wasteland.

The area was once a deep chasm between two mountain ranges rising out of the desert. Spanish explorers baptized it El Paso del Norte, the Pass of the North. In 1821, when Mexico won its independence from Spain, El Paso del Norte and what is now the American Southwest became a part of the Mexican nation. Twenty-five years later, a treaty between Mexico and the United States would set the boundary between the two countries, creating two border cities: El Paso, Texas, on the north bank of the Rio Grande and Ciudad Juárez on the south side.

The Mexican border town was named after Benito Juárez, Mexico's revolutionary hero. In an autobiographical account entitled "Notas para mis hijos" that he left for his children, he tells he was born on March 21, 1806, in the village of San Pablo Guelato in the state of Oaxaca. Orphaned at a young age, he worked the fields. His uncle, who wanted him to study for the priesthood, the only venue left for poor people and especially Indians, taught him how to read. The young man left his home for the capital, where he studied theology. Eventually he became involved with the law-making processes of the country, rising to chief justice of the Mexican Supreme Court and later, the president of the republic. Today, the monument in his honor is a focal point in the middle of a large plaza in downtown Juárez.

Not too far from there, in neighboring El Paso, at a point where Texas, Mexico, and New Mexico meet, a massive monument of Christ on the Cross, stands atop a 4,576-foot summit. This image of Cordova cream limestone was to be one of the first I would see as I looked out from my hotel window in El Paso. I couldn't help but wonder how many women had died looking up toward that Christ, their bodies broken, pleading for mercy.

As I embarked on my assignment, I asked myself if city planners ever envisioned the crime and violence that the maquiladoras might bring as the growing job market lured thousands to the area making this border town a gold mine.

Now, as I stood before the statue of the Mexican leader in downtown Juárez, where many of the girls were last seen transferring from bus to bus to go home or to work, I wondered if this Mexican visionary ever fathomed that his beloved city would become such an abyss of murder and injustice. Perhaps that's why some swear that they've seen Benito Juárez weep.

THE
DAUGHTERS
OF JUÁREZ

CHAPTER ONE

A Corpse in the Sand

I don't feel safe because once I step out on the street,
I don't know if the second step I take will be my
last.

—GUILLERMINA GONZÁLEZ,
VICTIM'S SISTER

RAMONA MORALES hurried from her small concrete house in Juárez, Mexico, just after 8:30 p.m. on July 11, 1995. She was determined to be at the bus stop when her daughter, Silvia, arrived after a long day of school and work.

In the last thirty-six months, there had been a series of brutal sexual attacks against young women in and around the Mexican border city, all of them fatal. Ramona wanted to make sure her teenage daughter didn't become the next victim.

She had noticed short stories about the killings in the newspaper. Many of the victims had disappeared on their way to or from work, often in broad daylight; their lifeless remains were found weeks, sometimes months later, in the vast scrublands that rim the industrialized border city. What the newspapers hadn't reported would have frightened her even more. The victims bodies exhibited signs of rape, mutilation, and torture. Some had been bound with their own shoelaces. Others were savagely disfigured. One young girl endured such cruelty that an autopsy revealed she had suffered multiple strokes before her assailant finally choked the life from her.

The victims were young, pretty, and petite, with flowing dark hair and full lips. All had been snatched from the downtown area, while waiting for a bus or shopping in stores. An alarming number were abducted en route to their jobs at the assembly plants, known locally as *maquiladoras*, that made parts and appliances for export.

The once unremarkable border town was fast becoming the fourth-largest city in Mexico with the opening of hundreds of these export factories. Locked behind towering gates and manned security booths, these contemporary assembly plants, many with neatly tended greenery and lush lawns, seemed a stark contrast to the prickly cacti and blowing tumbleweed indigenous to the arid region. Eighty percent of the factories were American-owned and produced goods for major U.S. corporations including Lear, Amway, TDK, Honeywell, General Electric, 3M, DuPont, and Kenwood. They had been built in response to NAFTA, the North American Free Trade Agreement, signed by the United States and Mexico in 1993.

The plants, which looked just like the ones constructed by those same companies north of the border, were drawing tens of thousands of laborers from across Mexico each year with the promise of work. The constant influx of people was rapidly creating a booming metropolis. Indeed, the city of Juárez was growing so fast that it was nearly impossible to map.

The city's roadways were a hodgepodge of paved and unpaved streets, some marked, others anonymous sandy paths that led to the shantytowns and squatters' villages continually springing up on the outskirts of town. When viewed from north of the border, Juárez appeared a vibrant and major metropolis, but on closer inspection the city seemed to be El Paso's poor, depressed relative, more reminiscent of a third world country.

The one- and two-story buildings crowding the narrow streets just off the Santa Fe Street Bridge from El Paso were dilapidated, their pastel colors dulled by a layer of brown dust from the sandstorms and car fumes. There were no emissions laws in Mexico, and pollution continued to be a problem.

In addition to car exhaust, road debris was a major concern in the city. Ramshackle tire shops—little more than wooden huts—dotted almost every corner, offering motorists a quick fix for the innumerable blowouts caused by such debris. American-built cars and trucks from the seventies and eighties dominated the landscape, many of them looking like they'd been resurrected from junkyards.

After dark, loud music blared from the nightclubs and cantinas that lined the streets of the red-light district, frequented by local street gangs, drug traffickers, and those who wanted to dance and party. Bars stayed open all night on Mariscal and Ugarte Streets, magnets for those eager to cross the border and indulge under the veil of anonymity.

Driven by a desire to maximize profits, the city's factories also operated on a twenty-four-hour schedule. Even some of the schools held two sessions each day to accommodate the ever-growing student population.

Getting a job on one of the hundreds of assembly lines meant a chance at a better life for the impoverished and often untrained laborers flooding into the Juárez area from throughout the region. Construction and forestry jobs had all but dried up in other parts of the country. Juárez was one of the few places in Mexico that was experiencing a growth in the job market.

The truth, in fact, was that there were plenty of employment opportunities in the factories of Juárez—so many that entire families could expect to find work there in a fairly short period of time. Girls in their early to mid teens were especially sought after because they didn't expect much money for their labor and could rapidly perform detailed assembly work. Many were under the legal age of sixteen and had lied about their ages on their job applications to secure a paycheck, most with the dream of earning enough to buy a pretty dress or a fashionable pair of shoes.

Silvia Elena Rivera Morales was just seven years old when her family relocated to Juárez in the mid-1980s from La Laguna, a region in Coahuila, the third-largest state in Mexico. The construction industry was on the decline, and Silvia's father could no longer find steady work. The family's eldest son, Domingo, was employed as a teacher in one of the local elementary schools. But his salary was not enough to provide for the family of seven, so the Moraleses decided to try their luck in Juárez.

As in other Latin American cities, there are extremes of

wealth and poverty in Ciudad Juárez. While the Mexican city is literally within walking distance of El Paso, Texas, the two cities couldn't be more different.

Ciudad Juárez is located in the northern state of Chihuahua, one of thirty-one states that make up Mexico. By 1990, its population of 1.5 million was nearly triple that of the state capital of Chihuahua City.

Crossing into Mexico costs little more than twenty-five cents for pedestrians. Vehicles pay a nominal fee in each direction, except at the Bridge of the Americas, which is free. U.S. and Canadian citizens need only show a valid identification, such as a driver's license, to enter Juárez. In contrast, citizens of Mexico and other countries need a passport and a multiple entry visa to come to the United States.

Prior to the Mexican-American War of 1846, El Paso and Juárez constituted one large metropolis, its people divided only by the Rio Grande. But when the Treaty of Guadalupe Hidalgo was signed in 1848, the two nations agreed to split the city, with the area south of the river falling to Mexico. Four bridges with pedestrian and motor vehicle access connect the twin cities, as they are often called. The United States and Mexico now share the waters of the Rio Grande through a series of agreements overseen by the joint U.S.-Mexico Boundary and Water Commission.

But the river has all but dried up in many parts, due to drought and overuse. For much of the year, it is little more than a sandy ditch filled with household refuse and other trash. From its riverbanks, Mexican locals watch the steady stream of vehicular and pedestrian traffic crossing into their city. Many have set up camp in small cardboard boxes there. They use the area as a way station until they can execute their escape from the poverty of their native land for what they hope will be a better life in the United States of America.

Ironically, most of the job opportunities in the El Paso/Juárez area are on the southern side of the border, in Mexico. The U.S.-owned factories provide the majority of income for residents of El Paso, who cross daily to work as managers and other middle-level employees at the maquiladoras.

The lower-paying assembly-line jobs are what the young Mexican girls and their families travel hundreds of miles to fill. These jobs pay little more than three to five dollars a day, enough to put food on the table but not always enough to put a roof over the worker's head.

An increase in the number of factories in Juárez and along the northern border came in 1982 with the devaluation of the Mexican currency, the peso. By 1986, 94 percent of maquiladora employment was in the border states of northern Mexico. The shift in jobs to the industrial sector came after the cancellation of the Bracero Program, a U.S. government program started in the early 1940s to bring a few hundred experienced Mexican agricultural laborers to harvest sugar beets in the Stockton, California, area. The program soon expanded to cover most of the United States to provide much-needed farm workers for the booming U.S. agricultural sector. But the program was halted in 1964 in response to harsh criticisms of human rights abuses of the Mexican laborers. The following year, the Mexican government implemented the Border Industrialization Program (BIP), better known as the Maquiladora

Program, to relieve the resulting high unemployment rates in northern Mexico. The new program used low-wage Mexican labor to entice U.S. manufacturing to the region, allowing companies to move production machinery and unassembled parts into Mexico without tariff consequences, as long as the assembled product was returned to the United States for final sale. In exchange, Mexican laborers would receive salaries that they wouldn't otherwise be able to obtain.

By 1991, there were almost seven hundred maquiladoras located in the Mexican border cities, with more than three hundred in Ciudad Juárez, as compared to ninety-four in Matamoros and eighty-two in Reynosa, just across the border from Brownsville and McAllen, Texas.

Juárez underwent a second transformation in the mid-1990s under the North American Free Trade Agreement (NAFTA), between Mexico, the United States, and Canada, that established the world's largest free trade zone.

On December 17, 1992, in three separate ceremonies in the three capitals, President George H. W. Bush, Mexican president Carlos Salinas, and Canadian prime minister Brian Mulroney signed the historic pact, which eliminated restrictions on the flow of goods, services, and investment in North America. The U.S. House of Representatives approved NAFTA by a vote of 234 to 200 on November 17, 1993, and the U.S. Senate voted 60 to 38 for approval on November 20. The agreement was signed into law by President William Jefferson Clinton on December 8 and took effect on January 1, 1994.

Under NAFTA, the tax breaks enjoyed by the maquiladora industry would no longer be confined to the border area but would be available throughout Mexico. The U.S. and Mexican governments anticipated that the provision would entice manufacturers to leave the overstressed border area and expand into Mexico's interior.

Instead of relocating deeper into the country, however, the maquiladoras of the northern region increased employment dramatically.

While Tijuana had the largest number of assembly plants, Ciudad Juárez had the largest maquiladora workforce, totaling in excess of two hundred thousand by 1994. The numbers were growing at an uncontrollable rate with tens of thousands of workers pouring into the city annually with hopes for a better life.

But there was no thought or planning for the influx of workers. The treaty exempted foreign companies from paying any local taxes, so the city had no funds for basic residential infrastructure. That meant that workers whose wages were already low had to fend for themselves in every way, from housing to child care to garbage disposal.

Many set up what resembled temporary camps in the arid foothills surrounding the city. Families crammed into single-room wooden shacks and makeshift homes of cardboard. They lived with dirt floors, no indoor plumbing or electricity, and badly rutted roads that wound through oppressive, dusty communities without parks, sidewalks, or sewers. There was no one to pick up the garbage, so it was dumped indiscriminately and scattered on nearby hillsides. Most of the shantytowns were springing up on land accessible only by foot.

To get to work, young girls had to travel alone, often late at night or in the wee hours of the morning, on treacherous unlit terrain to the nearest bus stop miles away. Neighborhoods changed from one block to the next, with sections of paved streets regularly giving way to dirt roads and rough, rocky terrain. Tire repair shops were plentiful along the main roadways and the dusty desert paths.

In many ways, Ciudad Juárez had become like Tijuana. The downtown cantinas stayed open late and attracted college students and thrill seekers in search of cheap liquor and a good time. The district had also become a haven for drug dealers and prostitutes. Prostitution was legal in Mexico for women over the age of eighteen. Many of the clubs hired pretty young girls to dance and serve alcohol. The jobs at the bars often paid more than the three or five dollars a day at the maquiladoras.

The Moraleses believed their living conditions would dramatically improve when in 1986, they packed their belongings and set off for the northern border city, leaving their roots and their small village behind. Ramona and her husband had grown up in La Laguna, where they met and married. She was sixteen when she wed Angel Rivera Sánchez Morales, four years her senior and the son of a family friend. The two had dated less than four months before exchanging vows. They had five children when they picked up and moved to Juárez. In addition to Silvia and her eldest brother, Domingo, there was Juan Francisco, who was twenty, sixteen-year-old Angel Jr., and Javier, who had recently turned thirteen.

Angel immediately found work as a machinist in one of

factories, as did three of his sons. His eldest boy, Domingo, who was then twenty-two, was elated when he found a teaching job at one of the local schools.

The family rented a small house with plumbing and electricity in the modest community of Nuevo Hipódromo, a treeless neighborhood or *colonia* on the outskirts of the city that was densely packed with unfinished cinder-block houses. It was a short bus ride away from the downtown district and the factories that dotted the landscape.

Within a year, the family had earned enough money to purchase a small lot across the street from an abandoned field owned by the Mexican national oil company, Pemex. This property was one of the last pieces of habitable vacant land in the colonia.

With the help of friends, Angel built a small, boxy house with a cement patio for his family in the working-class neighborhood. It was simple, with concrete floors and two bedrooms. There was a kitchen with running water and a bathroom with a toilet and shower. He painted the house a pale pink and erected over the front patio a simple grape arbor, which he tended with care.

Ramona enjoyed the arbor's shade during the stultifying summer months and idled away the hours chatting with friends and family under its protective cover. Next to the front door, the family hung a colorful placard that read "Rivera Morales Family. Anything is possible with Christ."

Unlike many of her peers, Ramona Morales's daughter had shied away from the topless bars and seedy downtown clubs, where other girls her age had found work as dancers, wait-

resses, and barmaids. There were more than 6,000 cantinas operating in Juárez, in contrast to just 624 schools. Working at
the clubs was an easy way to make money. Silvia had also
shunned the assembly-line jobs of the maquiladoras, where
shifts were ten and twelve hours long and women were often
subjected to sexual harassment.

She didn't have to work in a maquiladora. Silvia had op-
tions because her father was a machinist, and her brothers all
brought income into the house. She was able to take a job in a
decent neighborhood at a popular shoe store, Tres Hermanos
(Three Brothers), on Avenida 16 de Septiembre, the city's
main shopping strip.

Silvia was concentrating on her studies, determined to
someday find work as an administrator or a teacher like her
brother Domingo. With her wavy black hair, full lips, and
almond-shaped eyes, a rich shade of cocoa brown, she bore a
striking resemblance to her musical idol, Selena, the Texas-
born singer who had risen to stardom both in Mexico and the
United States. Silvia too loved to sing, and she possessed a
powerful voice for her slight five-foot-two frame. She had
taught herself the lyrics in English to the pop star's hit "I
Could Fall in Love with You" and liked to belt out the words
as she went about her early-morning routine. It was clear she
preferred them to the religious hymns of her Sunday choir
group.

Ramona enjoyed listening to her daughter's melodic voice
but grew upset each time she heard Silvia purring the seductive
Spanish verses of Selena's love songs. The lyrics were too sexually charged for a girl of such a tender age, she thought.

On the morning of July 11, 1995, Silvia's eldest brother, Domingo, gave her a ride to school. He was now living in a house he and his father had built on their small property. The two residences shared a common driveway, where Domingo kept his car.

Domingo spotted his sister just before ten that morning, hurrying to the bus stop with a neighborhood boy. He yelled out to her from the car window. He and his wife, on their way downtown, offered Silvia a ride.

It was supposed to be an easy day for Silvia. She had a light schedule at school, just one exam, because it was summer, so she was leaving the house much later than usual. Her normal routine was to leave before 4 a.m. to get to school by six. By 1 p.m. she was to be on her way to the shoe store, where she worked until closing.

Domingo noticed that Silvia was unusually quiet during the twenty-minute car ride. He wondered if maybe she'd gotten into an argument with their mother that morning. Not one to pry, he just let it go.

It was nearing 11 a.m. when he let his sister out in front of the Universidad Iberoamericana, a private high school where Silvia was taking classes in business administration. She was to sit for an exam that morning and then go straight to work at the shoe store downtown. Her shop was located in a touristy part of the city, adjacent to the historic Our Lady of Guadalupe Mission. The white adobe structure was the municipality's oldest surviving church. Completed in 1668, it was the first house of worship erected on the border between Mexico and the United States. In the same square is a second house of worship, the breathtaking Juárez Cathedral, with its neoclassical façade and striated towers. It was constructed in the early part of the twentieth century as an annex to the Guadalupe Mission to accommodate the rising number of worshippers. An ornate iron fence encircles the two buildings, which are among the few tourist attractions of historical note in the otherwise industrial city.

It was already dark when Ramona set out to meet Silvia's bus that Tuesday night; there were few street lamps illuminating the way. Pebbles crunched beneath her feet as she hastened along the unpaved roads, virtually breathless as she neared the stop.

Ramona was no youngster. At fifty-one, she was slightly overweight for her five-foot frame. Her short dark hair was streaked with gray and her wrinkled hands were a testament to years of washing dishes and doing laundry for five children. In recent months she had begun to suffer from back pain that often radiated to both her knees. Still, she was cheerful and quick to smile.

Ramona hastened her pace as a bus rumbled by, its directional signal flashing the driver's intent to pull over beside the solitary tree that marked the local bus stop. It was 8:45 p.m. Silvia would be arriving soon. She had told her mother to expect her on the next bus, the one that arrived just after nine. Her shift at Tres Hermanos would end at eight that evening.

Ramona was forever worrying about her pretty child because, at sixteen, Silvia was far too trusting and possessed a naïve confidence in her ability to protect herself.

"Take care," Ramona had repeatedly admonished the teen. "Girls are disappearing."

"They can't do anything to me," Silvia always replied; it was the typical response of a sixteen-year-old girl who believed she was invincible.

It was just after 9 p.m. when Ramona stepped up to the door of the arriving bus, a blue and white version of the bright yellow school buses ridden by children in the United States. She watched the weary passengers get off, waiting to see her daughter. But as the last traveler descended the steps, there was no sign of Silvia.

She must have stopped to chat with friends while waiting for her connection at the bus transfer site downtown, Ramona thought. Most of the city's buses stopped at the site, marked by an enormous statue of Benito Juárez García, the Mexican revolutionary war hero and former Mexican president for whom the city was named. The eight-foot-tall statue, which stood atop a large pedestal base, was made of white Carrara marble, black Durango marble, and stone quarried from Chihuahua. It stood at the center of a four-city-block park dotted by grassy patches and a few benches. Teens gathered there to play ball and bus passengers waited there for connections; it was there that Silvia made her daily transfer from one bus to another. The Moraleses lived along the Route 30 line, which traveled between the downtown district and the Juárez Airport.

Standing alone on the dark, deserted road, Ramona watched as the nine fifteen bus came and left. So did the nine thirty and ten o'clock buses. With each passing bus, Ramona's heart raced a little faster. Wild thoughts were flashing through her mind as she tried to talk herself into staying calm. She didn't want to think about danger. She didn't want to think of the newspaper articles about the missing girls. She just wanted to see Silvia's face.

By 10:30 p.m., she was in a panic. Frozen with fear, she continued to stand at the bus stop. Silvia would show up, Ramona told herself.

At 1 a.m., the last bus for the night made its stop—the final trip on the line. Silvia was not among the passengers descending the steps. Ramona watched helplessly as the driver shut the empty bus's doors and pulled away. She felt dizzy from the dust and diesel fumes; she couldn't seem to catch her breath as she raced home. Once there, she tried to wake her husband. But Angel was not well. Diagnosed with a tumor in his lung, he was growing increasingly weak and was not easily roused from sleep.

After pacing the bedroom for several minutes debating what to do, Ramona ran out the front door and down the street to a neighbor's home. Her friend Sandra lived a few houses away; she had a brother-in-law who was a captain in the Juárez Police Department.

Oblivious to the time, Ramona banged on Sandra's door. She had barely blurted out the words before Sandra was on the phone to the local hospitals and then the Red Cross. Next she dialed her brother-in-law, the police captain.

"Silvia Morales is missing," Ramona heard her friend speak into the receiver. Could he please mobilize some forces?

The captain knew Silvia from the neighborhood and from the popular shoe store where she worked. Believing he would take immediate action, Ramona returned home and nervously sat by the phone for hours thinking she would hear from the police. But no one called.

The official alerts were rarely given much attention by local officers, who seemed to place little value on the lives of the missing young women, in part because so many of them were not natives of the city but members of a transient population that had come to Juárez in search of work.

Another reason officers were so dismissive of the reports was that their pay was among the lowest of all municipal jobs and attracted some of the city's most undesirable candidates. Only an elementary school education was required to join the Juárez police force, which had no investigative powers and was strictly preventive in nature. It was widely believed that many officers accepted bribes to make ends meet or had taken the job to earn the extra side money assisting drug dealers and other unsavory criminals.

Those with an honest heart were often forced out or quit in frustration.

It was daylight and the sun was coming up over the mountains as Ramona paced the living room, remembering the morning Silvia left for school. The temperature had already climbed into the eighties when her daughter departed just after ten. Ramona recalled that Silvia had barely touched her breakfast: tortillas, beans, and diced tomatoes Ramona had prepared from the small vegetable garden she tended in the side yard. Perhaps Silvia had been nervous about the exam she was to take at school that morning.

Ramona couldn't stay idle another second. Determined to find her daughter, she began an amateurish investigation of her own. That morning she set out for the shoe store to find out if Silvia had reported for work the previous afternoon. In spite of his illness, her husband insisted on accompanying her downtown. Angel was deathly afraid for Silvia and could not stay at home and wait for answers. She was his only daughter. The couple arrived before the store was even open and stood on the sidewalk anxiously waiting for the shopkeeper to arrive.

The store manager told the couple that Silvia had been in but had asked permission to leave at 12:30 p.m. to take a second exam at school. Silvia said she would be back by three. But the teen never returned to the shoe store that day.

Confused, Ramona checked with school administrators and was told by the principal that there was no other exam scheduled for that afternoon. The story was not making sense. Silvia had never lied before. She was a good girl.

Ramona returned home to wait for her daughter, while Angel and her friend Sandra went to the police station to file a report.

It was Election Day in Juárez, and many of the local offices were closed. Police were of no assistance. They were busy dealing with voting logistics. Besides, authorities required a waiting period of seventy-two hours before taking a missing persons report. The officer behind the window at headquarters sneered at Angel and Sandra when they suggested that Silvia had met with foul play, telling them she had probably run off with a boyfriend and would eventually turn up.

Ramona was furious when she heard what police had told her husband. Undeterred, she continued with her own primitive investigation. Walking to two local nightclubs, La Cueva and El Barko, she talked to friends and neighbors to learn if anyone had seen Silvia. Her daughter had been to the dance

clubs several times in the past with a woman in the neighborhood who took young girls dancing. The woman had three
daughters of her own and encouraged other young girls to join
them on evenings out. Silvia had also been to the local
nightspots a few times with her brother Domingo. No one recalled seeing Silvia that night.

Ramona next questioned her daughter's friends in the
neighborhood.

One young girl who lived on the same block as the Morales
family remembered seeing Silvia that Tuesday afternoon at the
monument of Benito Juárez, ready to take a bus. The neighbor
was walking with a friend from class when she spotted Silvia
standing a few feet away from the bus stop by a tree.

Silvia was not herself that day, the girl recalled. "She didn't
greet me like she always did. I talked to her and she didn't talk
back. She was very pensive, like distracted."

The girl reported that Silvia was standing next to a *chero*, a
cowboy. Clothed all in black, he was speaking English. It was
not unusual to see men in cowboy attire in Juárez. Many of the
city's male population sported cowboy hats and pointed-toe
boots, attire left over from the days when horses were a means
of transportation. Now such clothing had become fashionable.
What was unusual was to see a man dressed all in black in the
middle of summer and speaking English.

"I wouldn't be able to tell you if he was really a friend," the
teen told Ramona. "Or if he was with her, because, like I told
you, she looked like she had a lot on her mind and she was very
distant. She wasn't talking to me at all.

"But the man seemed to be speaking to Silvia," she said.

Ramona learned that another bus had arrived at the stop that afternoon—not the one that Silvia normally took home but one that was marked Valle de Juárez, or Valley of Juárez. That bus took passengers out to Juárez Porvenir Highway, which ran through a much more prosperous residential area. The girl said Silvia got on it, and so did the man standing next to her.

The day after Silvia disappeared, Ramona's phone rang. Racing to answer it, she found no one on the other end of the line.

"Is it you, my daughter?" she spoke into the receiver. "If you left with a boy, we forgive you, just come back." There was no response.

It was July 14 when Ramona went to the *procuraduría* or state attorney general's office on Eje Vial Juan Gabriel to speak with officers about Silvia's disappearance. Her friend Sandra gave her a ride to the downtown headquarters, which also housed the State Police Department. Three days had passed and there had been no word. Her heart raced as she climbed the cement steps to the mirrored-glass building, which was just off a four-lane roadway and several miles from the downtown shopping district.

Since local police were not trained to conduct investigations of a criminal nature, all missing persons were to be reported to Chihuahua state police.

The overhead fluorescent lights in the lobby exaggerated the wrinkles of Ramona's tired, weatherworn complexion as she waited for someone to take her report. It was chaotic inside with people milling about or queued up in various lines waiting to be helped by the few uniformed officers standing behind walk-up windows and seated at tall wooden desks. The marble floors were a sickly green, and grimy from the continuous foot traffic in and out of the building. Dust from the desert collected on just about everything, including shoes, and made it difficult to keep buildings clean. Ramona was given a number and told to wait on one of the wooden benches.

The methodic ticking of the second hand, on the wall clock above, nearly sent her into hysterics as she listened for her turn. Finally her name was called.

The uniformed officer behind the window barely looked up as Ramona described the circumstances of Silvia's disappearance.

"My daughter never returned, not from the shoe store, not from school," the visibly shaken woman blurted out. "She said she was going to school to take a test, and then she was going to the shoe store to work. She'd be home some time between nine and nine twenty."

"Does she have a boyfriend?" the officer asked.

Ramona didn't like the officer's attitude. But eager to get help, she provided the name of the young man from the neighborhood whom Silvia had been dating.

"Does she go to bars frequently?"

"No. Not my Silvia. She is a good girl. She is a girl who goes from her school to home. She is a very happy girl."

"How does she dress? Does she wear miniskirts?"

Ramona was growing angry at the officer's derisiveness. "My daughter was wearing jeans, a rose-colored blouse, and white tennis shoes when she left the house on Tuesday morning."

"She probably went with some *cholo*, some guy, a boy-friend," the policeman snickered.

Neighbors and friends had told Ramona about the offensive, obnoxious attitude of the state police. While its officers were better educated than those of the local Juárez force—a high school degree was mandatory—their salaries were still considered low on the pay scale, and corruption was rumored to be rampant among their ranks.

Women's rights activists had begun voicing their outrage that detectives were faulting the victims, implying that they willingly went off with a man or were leading double lives, sneaking off after work to dance at the city's bars and discos. In fact, a majority of the dead girls had disappeared on their way to or from work and were wearing long pants and sneakers, not miniskirts and spiked heels, as police were insinuating.

In this male-oriented culture, girls out on their own were frowned upon and often assumed to be promiscuous. Activists believed it was this mind-set that had prompted officials to overlook the growing number of poor Mexican girls whose violated, butchered bodies had been turning up in the desert.

There was growing speculation among residents of Juárez that officers from both the state and municipal police forces were somehow involved in the murders—or that they were covering up for the guilty party or parties.

Ramona watched as the uniformed policeman slid her a form and instructed her to fill it out. With Sandra's help, she completed the paperwork, believing it was a preliminary step to a meeting with detectives from the Chihuahua State Police Department, which carried out all investigations of a criminal nature. Instead, they told her to commence an investigation and keep them apprised of any new developments.

"Perhaps she has run away with her boyfriend, or maybe she is with some friend," the officer suggested. "Wait to see if she returns."

"That's not the kind of girl my daughter is!" Ramona snapped, her voice rising as she glared at the man behind the window. "My daughter would never do that. She would have told me, 'I'm gonna stay with a friend.' She's not like that. She's a good girl.

"Silvia only went to school, and from there she went to work. From her home to school and from school to work," she said over and over in a tearful mantra.

Frustrated, confused, and worried about her daughter's whereabouts, Ramona left the police station with no help and no answers.

In the days that followed, there were more anonymous calls to the Morales home. One male caller claimed to know where Silvia was being held and provided Ramona with an address. Jumping into a car, she and her husband, along with her son and daughter-in-law, raced to the residence. Domingo went inside but found only an elderly couple who knew nothing of Silvia. The family reported the lead to police, along with a second tip from a man claiming that a factory worker named Alejandro knew the teen's location.

Police assured the family they were following these and several other, more promising leads. But as the days turned into weeks, the Moraleses heard nothing of Silvia.

Then, on August 19, Ramona learned that a body had been

found not far from her home on Casas Grandes Highway. It was that of a young woman with long dark hair. She had been raped and strangled, her ravaged remains dumped beside the vacant lot that belonged to Pemex.

Ramona fell to her knees and recited a prayer to the Virgin of Guadalupe, Mexico's patron saint, when she learned that it was not Silvia; for a moment she experienced a renewed faith that her daughter was still alive and would be returning home soon.

In early September, nearly two months after Silvia Morales disappeared, a local rancher was scouting a secluded stretch of desert east of the airport called Lote Bravo for wild horses when he stumbled upon the remains of a young woman hidden beneath some brush. She was partially naked; her blouse and bra were pulled up over her head, exposing what remained of her mutilated breasts. Carefully placed just beside the body were a pair of white panties and white tennis shoes, later identified as belonging to the Morales girl.

Startled, the rancher raced back to his truck and sped off in search of a telephone to notify police.

Uniformed officers encircled the scene with yellow crime scene tape and began a perfunctory investigation. Already more than forty women had been murdered, many with the same modus operandi. Yet police had few leads and no real suspects.

Donning a surgical mask, forensic pathologist Irma Rodríguez of the Chihuahua State attorney general's office arrived on the scene to collect evidence from what little was left of the young woman with the cinnamon skin who sang like Se-lena. Dr. Rodríguez was dismayed by the growing number of young women turning up dead in Juárez. While forensic sci-ence enabled her to determine the cause of their deaths, she had been unable to identify their killers.

"She has several small cuts on her right arm," one uni-formed officer standing over the mutilated body remarked. The multiple surface wounds appeared to indicate that the vic-tim had struggled fiercely with one or more assailants.

Authorities subsequently determined that the remains were those of Silvia Morales. She had been raped and then strangled with her own shoelaces. Her right breast had been severed and her left nipple was bitten off. Sand was found em-bedded underneath her fingernails, raising the possibility that Silvia had been alive after the attack and was left in the desert to die.

It was just before 10 a.m. on Saturday, September 2, when Ramona Morales spotted the blue and white patrol car pulling up to her house. She and her husband were outside on the porch, sipping coffee and enjoying some fruit, when two uni-formed policemen got out of the vehicle and strode to the chain-link fence that encircled their property.

"Ma'am, we've found your daughter," one of the men said, pushing open the gate and stepping onto the porch.

Ramona sprang from the white plastic armchair, overjoyed that Silvia had finally been located. "How did you find her?" she asked the officer. "Tell me, tell me."

Even after the men asked to see one of Silvia's shoes, she continued to remain optimistic.

Puzzled, she led the officers inside, leaving them to wait in the small, rectangular living room, hung with ornately framed photographs of Silvia posing in the lacy white quinceañera dress she had worn to mark her fifteenth birthday, as part of the Latin American tradition symbolic of a young woman's coming-of-age.

The officers stood with their arms folded behind their backs as Ramona disappeared into a back bedroom and then emerged moments later, breathless and clutching a single white shoe. The officers exchanged glances.

"Ma'am, we need you to come with us," the same officer directed. His response should have telegraphed to Ramona that something was amiss. But her mind was not going in that direction.

Ramona wondered why the policemen had asked to see one of Silvia's shoes when they didn't even bother to take it with them. They had simply looked at the size and put it down.

Francisco, the couple's second-oldest son, was in the kitchen. Hearing a commotion, he poked his head into the living room in time to see the officers leading his mother from the house.

"I'll come with you," Francisco volunteered, racing after the trio. His father was not anxious to accompany them. Angel looked fearful of what he might learn.

Yet Ramona was certain that Silvia was alive and waiting for her at the police station. The officers had given her no reason to believe otherwise.

"No!" one of the officers retorted. "She will go alone."

For a moment there was complete silence on the patio as the Moraleses exchanged fretful looks.

"Come on, señora," the officer directed, motioning Ramona to the police car. He assured Francisco he would return his mother home in a few hours.

Ramona Morales collapsed to the floor of the morgue after authorities showed her the bleached white skull that had been recovered from beneath some brush in Lote Bravo. She could not reconcile this parched, skeletal remnant as having belonged to her beloved daughter.

Even after police showed her the pretty rose-colored blouse they had found hiked up over her daughter's breasts, the one that Silvia had been wearing on the day she disappeared, Ramona clung to the hope that Silvia was still alive. The ugly reality was simply too painful for the mother to accept. Instead, she convinced herself that somehow there had been a terrible mix-up. Ramona maintained that the remains she had been shown were not those of Silvia, and that her daughter was still alive, studying and singing in some far-off place, happy and well.

Despite their promise, the police didn't drive Ramona back home that afternoon but left her to fend for herself outside the morgue. The despairing mother was forced to beg in the street for bus fare back to Colonia Nuevo Hipódromo, where her husband and sons confronted the horrible reality.

Grief numbed Ramona's senses and robbed her of her will to live. The family buried Silvia in a cemetery nearby. Ramona made daily visits to the tomb of her dead child, and nightly she prayed to the Virgin of Guadalupe, the patron saint of Mexico, that the same fate didn't happen to another daughter of Juárez.

But it did.

Eight days after Silvia Morales's forsaken body was discovered in the desert, another one was found in Lote Bravo: that of a twenty-year-old woman whom police later identified as Olga Alicia Pérez. She had been raped and stabbed; her hands had been tied with a belt and her neck was broken. As with Silvia, her right breast had been severed, and her left nipple bitten off.

Ramona's blood ran cold when she read of the grisly finding in the newspaper—and of the discovery of the bodies of six more teens in the days ahead. By the winter of 1995, nineteen young women had been killed, bringing the total, over three years, to forty-five.

Juárez, it seemed, was the perfect setting for a killer or killers. The victims were plentiful, poor, and trusting, and the crimes seemed to go unpunished.

And yet the question remained, who was killing these young women and why?

CHAPTER TWO

A Bag of Bones

They showed me a slab of bones. The only thing I
could see was her little severed head.

—IRMA PÉREZ
MOTHER OF VICTIM OLGA ALICIA PÉREZ

IT WAS SEPTEMBER 9, 1995, when police showed Irma Pérez all
that remained of her daughter—a bag of bleached bones. Olga
Alicia Carrillo Pérez had disappeared about one month before
on August 10, after working the afternoon shift at a downtown
shoe store not far from the one where Silvia Morales had been
employed.

Her disfigured corpse was found not by police as part of an
organized search, but by a passerby, some distance off the Airport Delivery Highway in a remote area of Lote Bravo known
as Zacate Blanco. Olga Alicia was one of eight young girls recovered in that same lonely stretch of desert in the four-month
period between August and November of that year.

Like those of earlier victims, Olga Alicia's remains were
not buried but simply left out in plain sight for others to find,

as if the killer or killers felt immune to detection or capture. Indeed, corpses would quickly decompose once exposed to the harsh elements of the desert: in summer, temperatures rose well above 110 degrees, enough to rapidly increase the rate of decay. And in winter, coyotes, mice, and rats fed on the human flesh.

Olga Alicia had been missing barely one month, yet her skull was so badly deteriorated that the pathologist had to hold it together for her mother to look at the jaw. With no fleshy tissue to soften its appearance, the jaw and teeth appeared frighteningly large. Irma Pérez nearly passed out from the gruesome sight, and after only a few seconds, begged the medical examiner to halt the identification process. She could not bear to look at what authorities insisted were the remains of her only child.

It took several minutes for Irma to regain her composure, enough to acknowledge that the pretty blouse that had been found near the body belonged to Olga. Still, she was skeptical that this decomposed corpse was once her daughter. The bones were so badly decayed they appeared as if they had been exposed to the elements far longer than thirty days.

Authorities told Irma there was not enough material to conduct a DNA test on the body; she was asked to simply go on the word of officials that this was Olga Alicia. With no financial means to hire an outside party to investigate the findings, she had little alternative but to accept this bag of bones as proof of her daughter's death.

Irma Pérez eked out a measly but honest living cooking and selling hamburgers and sodas from a stand on the narrow sidewalk in front of her tiny stucco house. Like so many other parts of the city, the busy, characterless district where Irma lived had its own square, a local church, and storefronts scrawled with graffiti. The clatter of the passing motorbikes, cars, and trucks was audible even after she closed her front door at night.

Irma was a single parent. She had spent hour upon hour manning the hot grill to scrape up the money to pay the bills each month. The smell of burger grease was forever embedded in her clothes.

Her life changed significantly with her daughter's death. She suffered a stroke and was not well. The only thing that seemed to bring a faint expression of joy was talking about Olga and looking at her pictures. She lived surrounded by photographs capturing moments from Olga Alicia's short and tragic life.

Beneath her bed were shoeboxes filled with more pictures, and stacks of newspaper clippings about the murdered women of Juárez. Ever since her daughter disappeared, she'd been obsessively collecting clippings about every missing girl in the city. At night, she spread them out on the frayed bed coverlet and read them over and over, looking for any similarities, clues that might lead her to her daughter's killer.

Like Ramona Morales, Irma Pérez had quickly alerted authorities to her daughter's disappearance. She, too, was told to wait seventy-two hours to file an official report, and even then it took police six days to send an officer to the location where Olga Alicia was last seen. By then Irma, just like Ramona, had commenced an investigation of her own. She learned that her daughter had gone to the local headquarters of the reigning political party, the National Action Party, or Partido de Acción Nacional (PAN).

The regional government, which controlled the state of Chihuahua, was currently in the hands of the National Action Party under the governorship of Francisco Barrio Terrazas. Barrio was in office when the killings in Juárez first began in 1993, and his administration had been charged with looking into the murders. Now, in 1995, Barrio's six-year term was nearing completion and members of Mexico's opposing Institutional Revolutionary Party, or Partido Revolucionario Institucional (PRI), led by Patricio Martínez, were campaigning hard to overtake the governorship in elections scheduled for later that year. The PRI party held the presidency and had been in power in Mexico for more than seventy years.

To attract support for the local PAN candidate, members of the regional headquarters had been hosting a series of dances. A woman had come to the Pérez house some months earlier to invite Olga Alicia to accompany her to the social gatherings. She would act as Olga's chaperone.

The story was eerily familiar. Ramona Morales spoke of a local woman who chaperoned young neighborhood girls to local dances. Silvia had wanted desperately to go with her in the days before she disappeared, but their night on the town was canceled when one of the woman's daughters misbehaved and everyone got punished.

At first Olga had refused to go the PAN dances. She wasn't interested in going out. She was serious about her studies and was about to begin classes at a prestigious local university, where she had been granted a partial scholarship. But Irma had insisted that her daughter have a little fun and pushed her to go out.

August 10, a Thursday, was supposed to have been a short workday for Olga. At the request of her mother, she was quitting the job at the shoe store to seek employment closer to home. But she had agreed to come in for several hours on her day off to help her boss train some new employees. Olga told her mother that she would be home by six. When Olga did not show up, Irma went out looking for her.

People in the neighborhood said that Olga was among a group of youths at the political headquarters on Avenida 16 de Septiembre, where a rally was going on. Irma knew that her daughter was interested in a young, junior member of the political party. She'd met the young man at a PAN-sponsored dance.

Since attending that first dance, Olga and the chaperone had become regulars at the social gatherings.

Officers laughed at Irma Pérez when she went to police headquarters that Sunday to file the missing persons report.

"How old is your daughter?" one of the uniformed officers asked.

"Twenty," Irma responded, furious when the officer glanced at his coworker and started to snicker.

"She'll be back," the two chuckled in unison. "She's probably running around with some boy."

Irma was horrified at their jokes—and at the way the police had dismissed her. To them, her daughter's disappearance was just another domestic case that would eventually resolve itself.

Determined to get help, Irma found a legal aide adviser named Rogelio Loya to accompany her back to headquarters. It was clear to her that authorities paid attention only when someone with clout was representing the family of the missing person.

Still, Irma was so frustrated she wanted to scream at the officers to get them to do something to find Olga Alicia. She asked her sister to try to locate the phone numbers of the families of the other missing girls. But when she dialed the families, she learned that most had found their daughters—deceased. "Yes, I found mine, but she is dead," one mother told her.

"Yes, I found my daughter recently, but only her body," said another.

Uncertain what else to do, Irma sought help from the young people at the PAN headquarters who had been friendly with her daughter. But the group was not cooperative. The political community shunned Olga, pushing her away when she tried to learn more about her daughter's involvement.

While members of PAN were uncooperative, Irma found some help in the night watchman. The hired security guard was crying the night he told Irma that her daughter had been brought to the PAN offices that Thursday night by a female employee of the shoe store. He told her that he thought it strange that the employee would drive so far out of her way to drop off the young woman. She lived more than forty minutes away on the opposite side of town.

The night watchman resigned shortly after Olga Alicia disappeared, and the legal aide who had been helping Irma was refusing to take her calls. It was said he had been threatened.

Irma had no idea by whom, and was too ill to follow up on any more leads.

As in the case of the Morales teen, several days after Olga vanished, Irma got an anonymous call from someone claiming to know the whereabouts of her daughter. The caller provided an address. Irma's sister volunteered to investigate. Posing as a social worker, she rang the bell of the two-story residence on Fraccionamiento Almita. She found a house full of children as if a nursery school or day care center was in session. There was no sign of Olga Alicia.

Still, Irma continued her search. She paid regular visits to the morgue as part of her vigil, waiting in the reception area to learn if there had been any news. The notification she'd been dreading finally came one Saturday morning, when she arrived at the medical examiner's office for her daily update. Shocked that no one had called her, Irma listened as authorities told her there was not sufficient material to conduct DNA testing. But they assured her the body was that of her only daughter.

To console Irma, officials explained that many of the victims had been leading double lives—lives that they kept hidden from their mothers. They insinuated that the dead girls had been furtively working as prostitutes or dancers in the seedy downtown clubs of Ugarte Street. Perhaps Olga Alicia had been one of those girls leading a secret life, they suggested.

Irma fumed. She was well aware that a number of the dead girls were very young—nine, ten, eleven years old. How could officials possibly fabricate a double life for those girls?

The authorities had an answer for that too. They blamed the victims' mothers. They were lazy, uncaring; they didn't take proper care of their children. That's why the girls turned to strangers for care and attention.

Irma later learned that the female chaperone who'd been taking her daughter to the political dances was a friend of the detectives assigned to investigate Olga Alicia's case.

Interestingly, there had been a number of stories circulating of women befriending young girls, enticing them with a chance to socialize at dances with other young people. These women were purportedly acting as agents for various men, selling these unwitting young girls for sex.

There were also reports of women disappearing while waiting in line for a job at the city's maquiladoras. Several prospective employees related stories of managers snapping their pictures, purportedly as part of the job interview process. Various accounts reported that a number of these women had either vanished or were turning up dead.

Ramona Morales was told by some of her neighbors that a man had been driving the streets of her colonia, taking pictures of the young girls who lived there.

The accounts were frightening, yet officials were unable to substantiate any of the stories. Nor were they able to stop the murders. From August to November of 1995, the bodies of seven young women were recovered from the vast wastelands in Lote Bravo not far from where the bodies of Silvia Morales and Olga Alicia Pérez were found.

Four of the corpses, including that of Silvia Morales, conformed to a precise pattern: each one had been raped, stabbed, and strangled. All of them were found with a broken neck, a severed right breast, and the left nipple bitten off.

Even more telling was an apparent link between the bodies
of two more young women discovered in December not far
from Lote Bravo in the fields behind the Pemex property, just
off the Casas Grandes Highway. One belonged to a fourteen-
year-old girl, who was later identified as Isela Tena Quin-
tanilla. Police noted that the child's hands had been bound
together with a rope that was knotted in the exact fashion as
one found on an earlier victim, a seventeen-year-old student
and maquila worker named Elizabeth Castro. Castro had disappeared on her way home from her factory job that past August. Her mutilated remains were found four days later in Lote
Bravo, not far from the corpses of the other dead girls.

With no real answers from authorities, wild theories were
being floated. Was organized crime part of the equation? Were
police looking at one or more than one serial killer? Were
there copycat murderers taking advantage of the situation?
Was this a case not of serial murders but instead of a sophisticated organ-trafficking ring? Was someone or some group
using these women as leading ladies for cheap snuff films and
later disposing of them so as to leave no evidence? Or perhaps
the killings were the work of a satanic cult, sacrificing these
women as part of a ritual?

Though record keeping was shoddy at best, and it's unclear
when the first crime may actually have occurred, authorities
believed that the first of the murders took place in 1993.

State police said the first victim was discovered on January
23 of that year, in a vacant lot in the Campestre Virreyes district of the city. An autopsy revealed that the young woman,

later identified as Alma Chavira Farel, had been raped, both anally and vaginally, and had died as a result of strangulation. Bruises on Farel's face indicated she'd been savagely beaten during the assault that claimed her life.

Another young woman was found on May 13, lying on her back in an expansive hilly region about five miles off the city's main highway, known locally as Cerro Bola. Authorities observed puncture wounds and abrasions on her left breast. It was determined that she too had been brutally raped and strangled to death. Her identity remains unknown.

Subsequently, nine more bodies exhibiting the same sorts of injuries and mutilations turned up in the desert. In all, at least fifteen other girls were found murdered in 1993.

Ten more young bodies were discovered in 1994, their deaths just as grisly. Eleven-year-old María Rocío Cordero's pathetic corpse was found on March 11, in a drainage pipe that ran alongside the Casas Grandes Highway. She had been abducted on her way to primary school, raped anally and vaginally, and then strangled to death by an unknown attacker.

Another teen was found tied to a stake in her middle school playground. An autopsy revealed she had been beaten and raped before she was strangled to death and left to be found by students returning to class the following day.

Oscar Maynez Grijalva, a young and talented staff criminologist with the Chihuahua state attorney general's office, or Procuraduría General de Justica del Estado de Chihuahua, had noticed distinct similarities among several of the homicides soon after joining the agency earlier that year.

Maynez found no forensic evidence to suggest that organs

were being harvested from the dead women. Such a procedure would require careful removal by someone with medical training, refrigeration, and rapid transport to some facility where the organ could be used. Instead, the criminologist was convinced there was another kind of serial killer on the loose in Juárez.

Born and raised in Juárez, Maynez was also a professor of forensics at the Chihuahua State Police Academy in south Juárez and held university degrees in both psychology and criminology. Determined to make the coursework interesting to the young cadets, he decided to use real homicide cases to demonstrate the steps involved in piecing together a criminal investigation. While browsing state police files for material, he noticed two cases that were eerily similar. The victims were both young women who shared identical physical characteristics and had been raped and killed in a very methodical fashion.

Because of the similarities, Maynez decided to use the two cases in his training of the new police recruits. He also took the step of drafting a three-page report that included a psychological profile of the perpetrator and an argument that there could be a serial killer on the loose in the city.

In mid-1994, Maynez presented his findings to his superior, thinking that they could be of help in the ongoing investigation. But the young criminologist was taken aback when State Police Academy Chief Jorge Ostos simply thanked him for being diligent in his work but did nothing more. When Maynez tried to hand Chief Ostos a copy of the report, his boss pushed it back at him and told him to keep it.

While he had known the quality of investigative work was

substandard when he first signed on with the attorney general's office, he was hoping he could make a difference. It was soon after NAFTA was signed, and there was international pressure to make the police more professional, to institutionalize a respect for human rights in Mexico. Maynez saw an opportunity to help, to contribute, and he happily accepted the challenge. But he was quickly faced with a number of obstacles and almost immediately began to question the investigative techniques of members of the state agency.

Time and again investigators asked that he falsify his findings on a wide variety of cases. In an interview, Maynez later admitted to a naïve belief that the investigators were just trying to take the easy way out. He said that he routinely declined their requests in the hopes they would go out and do a thorough investigation. And for a time, they did. As time went on, however, he realized that the officers were being told by their superiors whom to target in investigations regardless of where the evidence pointed.

In addition, he was bewildered by his superior's response to his belief that a serial killer was at work in the city, but continued to follow the cases on his own. He knew from his training that serial rapists and killers were often acting out a fantasy and that if left unchecked, they would continue to replay their fantasy time and again—until someone stopped them. He feared that without an aggressive investigation, the murders would continue. He also worried that many of the workers in Juárez's maquiladoras were young, uneducated, and highly vulnerable.

No matter what was going on around them, the young girls still had to make their way to the factories at all hours of the day and night, sometimes on foot. The reality was that they needed to keep working, no matter what the danger, because of their dire financial predicaments.

Just as he predicted, Maynez found more murders during 1995 that followed the same pattern he had described in his report. He observed that nearly all of the victims were poor, young, and slender, with dark flowing hair and warm, reddish brown complexions. An alarming number were employees of Juárez's assembly plants. At least four, including the Morales teen, were found with a severed right breast and the left nipple bitten off.

While authorities put the number of homicides against women at nineteen that year, several nongovernmental organizations (NGOs) and local women's groups reported it was actually higher, with more than forty-two homicides against women that year alone. According to the women's organizations, more than half of the female victims showed signs of rape and torture.

Oscar Maynez was frustrated. In addition to Chief Ostos, he had also told then Deputy Attorney General Jorge López Molinar and Chief Homicide Investigator Javier Benavides that the murders warranted special attention because the deaths would continue if they didn't act quickly. But Maynez claims his warnings went unheeded.

Soon the total number of unsolved cases of rape and murder since 1993 would top one hundred.

CHAPTER THREE

The Juárez Ripper

Corruption, incompetence and incapacity, those
are the three things causing the murders of the
women.

—ABDEL LATIF SHARIF SHARIF,
ACCUSED OF MURDER

JUST ONE MONTH AFTER THE BODIES of Silvia Morales and Olga Alicia Pérez were recovered in September 1995, authorities got an apparent break in the case. A young woman identified only as "Blanca" came forward claiming she'd been kidnapped, brutalized, and raped over the course of three days at a home in Rincones de San Marcos, an upscale neighborhood on Juárez's northwest side.

The address was along the same bus route Silvia Morales had traveled the day she disappeared, the one marked "Valley of Juárez," which runs along the busy Calle de Insurgentes to a section of the city dotted with multilevel, single-family houses with private garages, sidewalks, and telephone service.

Blanca led officers to a comfortable Spanish-style villa with arched windows and a terra-cotta roof, just off the Casas Grandes Highway. A roomy white sedan was parked in the carport. Inside, officers found the homeowner, forty-nine-year-old Egyptian scientist Abdel Latif Sharif Sharif, an engineer in one of the city's American-owned maquilas.

Blanca told authorities he'd held her captive in his home for three days, during which time she was beaten and raped repeatedly. Local news accounts identified Blanca as a prostitute and reported her claim that Sharif had threatened to kill her if she tried to get away. She said he warned that he'd bury her corpse in the vast, cactus-strewn desert south of the city called Lote Bravo, where the bodies of many of the murdered women of Juárez had been found.

Blanca said that after three days of torture, she finally managed to escape from a first-floor window and staggered to a nearby home, where residents alerted police.

Based on her claims, police arrested Sharif that October and charged him with rape, an accusation he vehemently denied.

The Egyptian told authorities the woman was a prostitute and had actually beaten him after he refused to get her more drugs.

Sharif was quickly released when Blanca suddenly recanted her story and then disappeared without a trace. Rumors circulated that the Egyptian had paid her off, but no proof of such a transaction has ever materialized.

Blanca's disappearance may have gained Sharif his temporary freedom, yet her claims prompted police to look deeper into his criminal past. They learned that he'd been in trouble in the United States for sex-related crimes and that he'd fled to Mexico on October 14, 1994, to escape certain deportation back to Egypt.

It seemed remarkable that U.S. authorities had agreed to let the dangerous sex offender with two felony convictions on his record quietly move south of the border, without alerting Mexican officials.

In fact, authorities had been advised of the Egyptian's crossing by a former business colleague of Sharif's, who cautioned Mexican officials of his impending move across the border in 1994. But his warning had gone unheeded, allowing the dangerous felon unrestricted entry into Mexico.

Even after the charges were dropped, Sharif remained under intense scrutiny by Chihuahua state police, women's activists, and others in the Juárez community. Mexican authorities learned that Sharif was a two-time convicted sex felon, and his criminal history in the United States made him a logical suspect for many of the murders that had taken place since 1993.

An investigation into Sharif's activities in Juárez led police to the red light district, where, it was determined, he was a regular. There they found a woman named Erika Fierro. Fierro worked as a stripper at a club on Ugarte Street and reportedly used drugs. She told police she had met Sharif at a bar called Joe's Place in the spring of 1995. She claimed to have introduced him to nine of her girlfriends.

At some point Sharif supposedly admitted to engaging in sex with the nine women and then told Fierro something that stunned her—that he had murdered the girls and buried their corpses in desert areas south of the city. Fierro told Sharif she could no longer introduce him to her friends, but she later claimed she did not dare alert police to his story under a threat of death.

The ongoing police investigation into the Egyptian yielded witnesses who alleged they had seen him in the company of several of the dead women of Juárez, including Silvia Morales and the seventeen-year-old student and maquila worker Elizabeth Castro. A slender brunette, Castro was last seen alive boarding a factory-run shuttle bus to downtown Juárez on August 15, 1995.

In response to the ongoing murders, some of the factories had added shuttle bus services for their employees that took girls like Elizabeth Castro to the downtown district after their nine- and ten-hour shifts. There they would connect with public buses for their long rides home. Many of the factory-run buses were old and rickety. They were owned and operated not by the factories but by private citizens who contracted their services to the maquiladoras. Anyone could operate a bus, as long as they had the appropriate driver's license and no criminal record on file.

Castro's corpse was found on August 19, along the Casas Grandes Highway in Lote Bravo—not far from Sharif's upscale neighborhood. Officials said her body exhibited bite marks like those found on the body of Olga Alicia Pérez. An autopsy revealed she had been raped and strangled, her hands bound with her own shoelaces in a manner similar to prior victims.

Castro was a memorable girl with high cheekbones, a regal nose, and a charming space between her front teeth. Witnesses

who worked at the rough-and-tumble bars of Ugarte Street recalled seeing the pretty, dark-haired teen in the company of
the Egyptian Sharif Sharif that past summer. The polished
older man was a standout in fine silks, leather shoes, and pock-
ets full of money. He was well over six feet tall, and his expensive wardrobe stood in stark contrast to the typical
patrons—cowboys in worn jeans and pointed-toe boots, puffing on Marlboros.

The couple was reportedly spotted cruising the strip in
Sharif's shiny white sedan, and later seated at a corner table in
one of the local watering holes, kissing and laughing.

Based on this new information, authorities rearrested
Sharif in December of 1995 and charged him with Castro's
murder. They also suggested that he had been linked to at least
a dozen other murders.

While they had no proof, officials successfully dubbed him
"the Juárez Ripper" and hailed Sharif's capture as a major development in the case.

Even though authorities were claiming that Sharif Sharif
was tied to as many as a dozen of the city's murders, he was officially charged with just one homicide—the murder of Elizabeth Castro.

Still, headlines boasted of the capture of the "serial killer of
Juárez," and residents of the border city breathed a collective
sigh of relief.

In the days following his arrest, Sharif called a press conference at the sprawling cement-and-stone jail where he was
being held in solitary confinement.

El Cereso sits isolated on a vast stretch of dry, sandy earth just south of the city at the intersection of Eje Vial Juan Gabriel and Barranco Azul. Behind a tall, menacing barbed-wire fence, uniformed guards act as sentries manning the security booths and the observation towers of what has been inaccurately labeled "an adult rehabilitation center." In fact, El Cereso is more a maximum-security prison, a kind of way station for the city's most dangerous criminals. Inmates are locked three in a cell; some of those already convicted await transfer to a more permanent prison setting. Others are there to serve out their time.

The facility, with its peeling paint and rust-colored stains, was originally designed to house a maximum of 832 inmates when it was built in 1980. It was now grossly overcrowded with more than 2,000 inmates—more than double its intended number. State officials, not interested in managing the jail, had placed its operations in the hands of the local government.

Among those incarcerated inside El Cereso were 500 alleged murderers. Sharif was now counted among them.

For members of the local media, this would be their first look at the man authorities were calling "the Juarez Ripper." Though it was highly unusual for an alleged murderer to call his own press conference, Sharif had been granted permission to do so by the facility's warden.

With the jail in the hands of city officials, state police had no control over the facility or its warden. The director of El Cereso, Abelardo González, had a history of being sympathetic to requests from inmates.

The crowd in the small conference room on the main floor

of the jail fell silent as two uniformed guards brought in the inmate, who stood at least a foot taller than the officers. Sharif had an aquiline nose, thick mustache, and arched eyebrows.

Removing the steel cuffs from his powerful-looking hands, the officers led Sharif to a long wooden table, where the media's microphones had been set up. Journalists noted that he looked confused and exhausted. It was clear that Sharif had no idea that authorities were pointing the finger at him for the serial murders.

"Don't you know that you are being accused as the multi-homicidal killer?" one reporter yelled out in English. To which Sharif appeared dumbfounded. The cameras were rolling when the Egyptian slammed his fist on the table, looked out at the journalists through narrow black eyes, and declared his innocence. His enormous hands flailed as he charged that authorities had manipulated witnesses into making false statements against him.

"They lie, they even go to extremes to fabricate evidence like lying, manipulating, kidnapping people, beating up people," Sharif told reporters in a high-pitched, almost nasal rant. He was speaking about Chihuhuan state police official Francisco Minjares, later described as the architect of the case against Sharif.

The local media disregarded Sharif's claims, joining authorities in painting him as the Juárez Ripper. The nickname El Monstruo, or the Monster, appeared beneath his picture in morning newspapers. Local residents were scared to even look at the accused killer's image on television, saying he looked like the devil.

In the months ahead, state officials tied "the Egyptian," as he was popularly tagged, to at least a dozen of the city's murders, including the homicides of Silvia Morales and Olga Alicia Pérez.

News accounts stated that witnesses had come forward alleging that Sharif had paid five hundred pesos, about fifty American dollars, to the boyfriend of Olga Alicia Pérez to have sex with her. The young man was reportedly paid his fee upon delivering Pérez to Sharif's residence in Rincones de San Marcos.

Police had questioned Olga Alicia's boyfriend and claimed to have found nothing to link him to her death.

Sharif, meanwhile, was insinuating that government officials were holding him unjustly and without evidence to deflect public criticism in an election year.

Sharif had come to the United States in the early 1970s, first settling in the New York metropolitan area before transferring to the Miami-based headquarters of the U.S. oil company Cercoa, Inc., where he worked as an inventor and engineer.

There are reports that Sharif had been in trouble with several women there, but no charges were ever filed against him. The Egyptian was living in Florida only a short time when a beautiful young woman who lived several floors below him accused him of rape. In a television interview, the alleged victim, who identified herself as "Tracy," told a reporter that Sharif had invited her to a dinner party at his apartment in May of 1981.

The two were barely acquaintances, but she said Sharif had eased her mind when she learned that several of her friends would be among his dinner guests. When she arrived at the apartment, however, she was the only guest there.

Uncomfortable, she stayed just long enough to have a few sips of a drink that Sharif had mixed for her and then quickly returned to her own apartment, telling her host that she would come back when the other guests arrived. In the elevator, she began to feel dizzy, and once inside her apartment, she phoned her boyfriend for help.

Some time passed, and there was a knock at the door. Believing it to be her boyfriend, Tracy said, she answered it and was suddenly pushed into the living room by her now-crazed neighbor. She told authorities that Sharif had brutally raped her. She was later treated at a nearby hospital, where it was established that she had, indeed, been raped. Sharif was later arrested and charged with the assault.

Executives at Cercoa were sympathetic when their star employee came to them with his plight. Insisting that the sex was consensual, he asked for help. The company agreed to cover his legal expenses and even gave him a raise.

After pleading guilty to a lesser offense, Sharif received probation for the crime.

But soon he was in trouble again. In August of 1981, a second woman in North Palm Beach told police Sharif had brutally raped her in his car after she agreed to accompany him to his home for just a moment so that he could pick up something at his residence. The woman claimed she finally managed to break free by repeatedly striking the brutish man in the head with the heel of one of her shoes. Her clothes soaked in blood, she somehow jumped out of the moving vehicle and ran to a roadside gas station for help.

Executives at Cercoa were again sympathetic, and again they funded Sharif's defense. The brilliant chemist had reportedly earned millions of dollars for the company with his inventions, and it appeared they did not want to lose their precious employee. Sharif remained on the payroll while serving a sentence of forty-five days in the Palm Beach County jail for the attack, and then returned to work.

According to news accounts, the following year Cercoa bought out Sharif's contract—apparently because he had racked up substantial legal bills for the company. But that did not stop investors from offering to fund him and a fellow Cercoa employee, Tom Wilson, in a partnership of their own.

In a subsequent interview with the A&E Network about Sharif, Wilson admitted that at the time, he had had some reservations about the scientist and had even questioned him about his criminal conviction. But Wilson had felt satisfied by Sharif's explanation that the sex had been consensual.

It was a decision Wilson would later regret. The two were not in business for long when Wilson began to notice that his new partner had a drinking problem. He'd also observed that Sharif was abusive toward women while under the influence of alcohol. The revelation was troubling to Wilson, who was no longer certain he wanted to continue his business partnership with the Egyptian chemist.

While in Gainesville, Sharif reportedly married, but the union quickly ended after he supposedly beat his new wife until she fell unconscious.

In the spring of 1983, Sharif was arrested again. This time he was charged with the brutal rape of a twenty-year-old nursing student he had lured to his home with an ad in the *Gainesville Sun* seeking a roommate.

The vicious attack took place on the night the woman moved into the tidy green ranch house at NW 35th Street in Alachua County. According to a police report, it was just before midnight on March 16, 1983, when she heard Sharif entering her bedroom. She said he grew enraged when she turned down his advances. He then began pounding her in the head and face with his fists before forcing himself on her in her own bed.

During the attack, the woman later told authorities that Sharif grabbed the bedside lamp and threw it at her, shattering it against the wall and breaking the bulb. He then stepped on the glass and cut his foot, leaving a trail of blood on the carpet. He also attempted to hit her with a glass she kept on the nightstand and with a statue of W. C. Fields that the victim kept near the bed.

During the hours-long assault, the woman said Sharif smashed her head against a wall and threw her into a window. He then threatened to kill her and said he intended to bury her body in the woods behind his home.

Then, in a bizarre turn of events, he suddenly apologized to her and rushed her to a local hospital for treatment.

There he lied to officials, telling them that the young woman's injuries were the result of a lover's quarrel, not a rape. But her wounds were so severe that his words could not explain the physical harm he had inflicted upon her.

Sharif was taken into custody by members of the Gainesville Police Department on March 18, 1983, and ordered held without bail. During a search of his home, police found evidence to corroborate the victim's story.

On the floor of her bedroom lay a smashed statue of the comedian W. C. Fields. They observed a large crack in the plaster of one wall, a broken lightbulb on the left side of the bed, and bloodstains on the floor. A glass by the bedside was also shattered, and semen stains were found on the sheets. A gun was also confiscated during the search.

In January of 1984, while awaiting trial, Sharif managed to escape from the Alachua county jail, but was quickly recaptured. On the thirty-first of that month, he was sentenced to twelve years in prison for the rape and attempted murder of the young nursing student.

At the sentencing, the prosecutor vowed that Sharif would be met at the prison gates upon his release and immediately deported to his native Egypt. But it was not to be. After serving only five years, Sharif was granted early release and paroled. The prosecutor's letters to officials at the Immigration and Naturalization Service requesting immediate deportation had no effect; there were no federal agents to meet the olive-skinned ex-convict when he strolled through the prison gates in 1989.

Instead, there was a job waiting for him in Midland, Texas, with Benchmark Research and Technology, an oil company that also ran a factory in Juárez, Mexico. Midland, a city of one hundred thousand located halfway between Dallas/Fort Worth and El Paso, is about a five-hour drive to the Mexican border.

Sharif was well liked by his peers at Benchmark, and his work was hailed as exemplary. Nearly two years passed before he had another run-in with the law. This time, the offense was minor, a drunk driving arrest.

But word of Sharif's arrest sparked his former business partner into action.

Tom Wilson was now living in Texas. When he learned that Sharif had been released from prison and had escaped deportation, he was horrified. He felt partially responsible for what had happened to the young nursing student back in Gainesville. He was wracked with guilt that his partnership with the foreign-born scientist had provided Sharif with the means with which to continue his violent escapades; wanting to ensure that no one else would fall prey to his former business partner, he set out to make things right.

Wilson made a series of phone calls, including one to the Gainesville police. A lieutenant named Sadie Darnell took the call. While Darnell had not worked Sharif's rape case, she was outraged to learn that the forty-two-year-old chemist had been permitted to remain in the United States with two felony arrests on his record.

Darnell was incredulous when told the ex-con appeared to be winning over the judge presiding over his ongoing deportation hearing in Texas.

During the lengthy proceeding, Sharif had used his intellect and charm to persuade the court that he was remorseful, and he even begged the magistrate to give him one more chance.

Darnell's background check on Sharif revealed that he had

five aliases and three dates of birth on file—hardly the profile of someone likely to change his ways. In a subsequent letter to the court, she lobbied for his deportation.

"Sharif has been given the unique privilege of being able to reside in the United States," Darnell wrote to the judge. "He has abused this privilege time and time again. His behavior has demonstrated him to be a predator of women. . . . The victims have been irreparably damaged. Please consider them."

It was Darnell's strong letter to the court that finally moved the El Paso judge to commence proceedings for deportation in 1993.

Remarkably, while awaiting word on the deportation proceeding, Sharif allegedly abducted a woman, held her captive in his home, and raped her over and over again before she finally escaped. Charges were filed, but Sharif's deportation lawyer struck a deal with the government: his client would leave the country of his own volition if the case against him was dismissed.

The American oil company for which he worked in Midland, Texas, kept him on the payroll, allowing him to continue his work as an engineer from an assembly plant they operated in Juárez. A company lawyer had even represented him when he was first arrested and charged with the alleged rape and kidnapping of Blanca.

For a short while, it appeared Mexican police had done their job. The first four months of 1996 passed without a single murder. But April brought a grisly discovery.

As the alleged serial killer of Juárez, Sharif Sharif, sat in the city's central jail awaiting trial on twenty-six counts of murder, the decomposing bodies of seven young women were uncovered within yards of each other amid discarded potato chip bags and beer bottles in a desolate area of fine, powdery white earth called Lomas de Poleo, on the very northwest edge of the city. The makeshift burial site was about twenty minutes outside of the city of Juárez, just off the Casas Grandes Highway. The location was in the complete opposite direction of Lote Bravo, where many of the earlier bodies had been recovered.

Among the corpses were the remains of a ten-year-old girl whose identity is still a mystery. The child stood just three feet, nine inches tall. The discovery of eight deep cuts on her tiny frame led authorities to conclude that her final hours on this earth had been brutal. Another of the victims had been bound with her own shoelaces; the teenager had been stabbed and mutilated in a similar fashion to the other dead girls found nearby.

The findings sent a wave of terror through the city and raised questions about Sharif's involvement. Nine more bodies would be found by year's end.

Medical examinations of the victims revealed that their murders had occurred at different times. Yet it was reported that all of the young women had been sexually assaulted and brutalized by one or more killers.

Residents and activists soon began to question whether police had the right man in custody and were looking to the state's new attorney general, Arturo Chávez Chávez, for answers. In March, Governor Francisco Barrio had appointed Chávez to the state's top law enforcement post, and already the state official was in the hot seat.

The gruesome discoveries sparked angry protests in the border city, with hundreds of women taking to the streets to demand justice. Among those marching were the mothers, grandmothers, sisters, and cousins of the victims, waving banners and clutching crude wooden crosses they'd painted black to symbolize the loss of their loved ones.

As the questions surrounding Sharif's involvement grew, Ramona Morales and Irma Pérez began to wonder if the Egyptian scientist truly was responsible for killing their daughters.

Authorities even found that one of their own was raising questions about their claims. Contrary to what many believed, Oscar Maynez, the criminologist, was also convinced that Sharif Sharif was not the culprit. Maynez was aware of "El Egipcio's" criminal past and his status as a violent sex offender. And while he shared the widely held belief that Sharif Sharif deserved to be behind bars, he was not convinced that he was responsible for the Juárez murders. For one thing, Maynez pointed out, the murders had begun before the Egyptian even moved to Juárez. Secondly, Sharif was a relative newcomer to Juárez. Based on his investigation, Maynez had concluded that the bodies were being dumped in a very organized and methodical fashion in little-known areas outside the Juárez city limits that were extremely inaccessible: a car wouldn't go there.

In addition, a forensics examination of Blanca, the local prostitute who first brought Sharif to the police's attention, had determined the woman to be lying. She was not the victim of a rape, as she claimed, but had gotten into an argument with the Egyptian that turned violent, resulting in her injuries.

Even more startling was a forensics report on Elizabeth Castro, the young maquila worker Sharif was charged with killing. The body recovered by police couldn't have been Castro; it was that of a woman nearly four inches taller. In addition, the skin tones were different. Castro had an olive complexion while the corpse had fair skin and freckles. In addition, an autopsy determined that the young woman police had identified as Castro had been dead well over a month. Castro, meanwhile, had been missing just four days when the body, identified as hers, was recovered in the Pemex field.

"She's alive . . . because the corpse of the woman that the authorities say I killed is that of a tall woman, a woman with freckles, and more important, she is a white woman, totally different from the description in the file of Señorita Elizabeth Castro," Sharif insisted in an interview with Univision.

Mounting public pressure on authorities to get to the bottom of the latest string of murders prompted police to conduct a massive raid on the bars and nightclubs of the red light district, where several of the dead women had been seen in the weeks before their disappearances. Nearly two hundred youths were rounded up during the sting operation in April 1996, among them nine members of a local street gang known as Los Rebeldes, or the Rebels. The raid was ordered in response to a tip police had gleaned from a man named Héctor Olivares Villaba.

To calm the frazzled nerves of the residents of the border

city—and to save face in light of the ongoing crimes following the arrest of Sharif Sharif—police had questioned a number of suspects, including Olivares, an alleged member of the Los Rebeldes street gang, in connection with the rape and murder of an eighteen-year-old maquila worker named Rosario García Leal, whose battered body had turned up on April 8, in a remote area outside of the city.

Leal was still wearing her factory identification tag from the Philips assembly plant when her corpse was recovered. An autopsy revealed that she had been brutalized and stabbed during the violent assault that had claimed her young life.

During an interrogation of Olivares, the gang member reportedly confessed to participating in Leal's murder, which he said took place in December 1995. Police said that Olivares claimed he had committed the crime in concert with other gang members, including its supposed leader, Sergio Armendáriz Díaz, also known as El Diablo, or the Devil. Perhaps this new lead would prove Sharif's claims of innocence.

Acting on this new information, officers stormed the clubs of Mariscal and Ugarte Streets, including the one where Armendáriz was employed as a security guard. Over the next several days, investigators interrogated the detainees. While they released a majority of the young men and women, at least ten of the gang members, including Armendáriz, were held and subsequently charged with some of the murders, raising questions about Sharif's role in the murders. But his culpability would soon be solidified with a startling revelation by state officials.

In the days ahead, police claimed that during subsequent

interrogations, Armendáriz and his cohorts confessed to the killing of at least eight women under orders from the jailed Egyptian, Sharif Sharif. That the clever foreign-born scientist could have hatched such a plot from his jail cell seemed unthinkable. Yet authorities said the gang members had provided intimate details of their arrangement with the Egyptian.

According to police, Sharif had agreed to pay in the neighborhood of one thousand pesos for the murders of two women a month. The killings were to be carried out in a similar fashion to those of which he was accused—to prove police had the wrong man in custody and to leave the public with the impression that the "real" killer was still on the prowl.

The money was allegedly exchanged during prison visiting hours, with Sharif slipping an envelope of hard currency across the table. The first installment was said to contain the equivalent of three thousand dollars. The cash payments were reportedly delivered to a local pool hall, where they were handed over to Armendáriz.

Based on their confessions, police subsequently indicted ten members of Los Rebeldes on at least seven of the homicides. The individuals were Sergio Armendáriz Díaz, Juan Contreras Jurado, Carlos Hernández Molina, José Luis González Juárez Rosales, Héctor Olivares, Fernando Guermes Aguirre, Luis Andrade, Carlos Barrientos Vidales, Romel Omar Ceniceros García, and Erika Fierro, the woman who had earlier claimed to have arranged "dates" for Sharif. In testimony given that April before ministers of the court, Fierro explained that she was at a bar called La Tuna with a female friend she called "Mausy," whom she described as the girlfriend of a man who sold hamburgers on the street near Joe's Place, when Sergio Armendáriz signaled her over.

"Sergio Armendáriz, El Diablo, the leader of the gang Los Rebeldes, said he wanted me to introduce her [Mausy] to him," Fierro reportedly testified. "She didn't want to talk to him. But I insisted and she went. Later, I didn't see her again. I knew he was going to kill her, but I couldn't do anything else because he had threatened to kill me."

Attorney General Arturo Chávez Chávez was pleased and appeared before the media that month to boast about the "FBI-style" investigation that had led to the arrests.

In the days ahead, news reports gave several versions of the alleged killings; one claimed that the gang members had tortured their victims on a sacrificial block of concrete before slaughtering them and dumping their corpses in remote locations outside the city. Other stories maintained that the girls were taken to cheap motels where they were raped and murdered and then cast in the desert. Forensic examinations showed that several of the corpses displayed bite marks over portions of their bodies, and a number of the young women were found to have crushed skulls.

Police later linked the jailed gang members to even more of the killings, a total of seventeen, claiming that Sharif Sharif had ordered all of the murders from the confines of his maximum-security jail cell. State police comandante Antonio Navarrete led the investigation that tied the gang to Sharif Sharif.

Gang members charged they had been beaten and tortured and ultimately forced to confess to crimes they didn't commit.

Their stories were corroborated by family members, who described debilitating and painful injuries, including the gang leader's claim that he'd been handcuffed to his cell for three days straight and struck in the head hard enough to leave him with a permanent scar.

To many, the alleged murder-for-hire plot seemed absurd. How could Sharif Sharif make contacts with these individuals, convince them to carry out a series of murders, and pay them for their work from his jail cell? The men had no apparent connection to Sharif Sharif and no serious criminal backgrounds.

Further questions arose after it became apparent that police were not able to establish any money trail between Sharif and his supposed gang of assassins. Indeed, Sharif spoke only a few words of Spanish and would have been hard pressed to communicate with the men—much less lay out a detailed modus operandi for crimes to ensure that all of the murders looked similar.

In his exclusive one-on-one interview in February of 1999, the Egyptian told Univision he believed he was being used as a scapegoat. That day, Sharif was in day twelve of a hunger strike. Supposedly he was refusing food to call attention to what he characterized as his "wrongful conviction."

Sharif was an imposing figure, taller and fairer-skinned than most of the inmates at El Cereso. He appeared ashen, no doubt from twelve days without food. He was only allowing himself Gatorade and water, nothing else.

"I am the perfect scapegoat because I don't speak Spanish!" he cried, his voice rising as he spoke to the camera. "I didn't even speak any Spanish until I got into prison! And I'm not from here. I am a foreigner. I don't have family to defend me on the outside!

"But I am a hardworking man. When I was on the outside, I worked very hard. As vice president of a company in Midland, Texas, I supervised all the communications via telephone, fax, and computers. And I also started a company here."

Leaning back in the chair, Sharif pulled out a pack of Marlboros from his shirt pocket and lit up. "*Mira*, look," he said, pointing to some of the documents as he exhaled the smoke. "Here are the forensic findings on the body of the woman they say is Elizabeth Castro. Her corpse was at least two weeks old, and the Elizabeth Castro they refer to is a woman whose body was found only four days before.

"They come here, they take impressions of my teeth, sperm samples, blood samples, hair from my head, pubic hair, urine, and my . . ." He stretched out a hand, tapping the tips of his fingers, alluding to his fingerprints. "But everything was negative! They don't want to announce the results so we can't use it for my behalf, but everything was negative."

Sharif was correct. Authorities did, in fact, take dental impressions, and the teeth marks on Castro's body did not match those of the Egyptian.

Like so many others in Juárez, Sharif alluded to police involvement in the crimes. "I am absolutely certain of one *policía*," he claimed. "And I believe more, but I have no proof. I have the proof about one, and I am sure about two other people. But they're not *policías*. They're rich, they're drug traffickers . . . *ricos, narcotraficantes, mafia.*"

Mexican mafia? This seemed entirely too far-fetched for such ritualistic crimes against the poor. Why would they waste their time with these girls? Could there be much more to this convoluted plot? Could the killers be raping the girls to satisfy their sexual whims, later murdering them so no one could identify them?

Sharif insisted that "incompetence, corruption, and ineptitude" were behind the murders in Juárez. "There is one *policía* who is very powerful and he is always everywhere, handling things no matter where he is, hiding, and fabricating lies."

According to the Egyptian, the officer was "short of stature." He pointed out that all of the victims had been "slender and petite." "It's the type of woman he likes, a woman he can control and overpower." He grinned.

When asked about his alleged ties to members of Los Rebeldes, Sharif almost cut in, as if expecting the question.

"I never saw Los Rebeldes, *nunca en mi vida*. Never in my life, before I came here to El Cereso, had I even heard of Los Rebeldes, never. It's all fabricated. The police tortured them, put guns to their heads; they received death threats so they would make incriminating statements against me.

"What do I have in common with the gangs? I don't like gangs." He grimaced. "They hurt and kill people. I am an educated person, I am an intelligent person, but I don't speak Spanish! You hear how I speak Spanish, and I taught myself in prison. How am I going to manage a Mexican gang, *una ganga mexicana?*"

When asked when he intended to reveal the identity of this

corrupt police officer, Sharif smiled. "When I get out of here," he said. "Dead or alive, I will get out of this place."

Sitting back in his seat, Sharif began to blow smoke rings and break them with his long fingers. "I'm not fasting to pressure a judge," he said in conclusion. "My fast is to God. It's been twelve days since I've eaten anything. I want the people to listen to me. What I'm saying is the truth and I have proof.

"Meantime I'm here. I may even die here, who knows? I take it one day at a time, one Gatorade at a time."

Sergio Armendáriz, aka "El Diablo," also denied any role in the killings when he spoke to Univision that day. "They forced me to sign a confession," the broad-shouldered inmate insisted. "And they signed my name with a X, saying I'm illiterate. That's not true! I've been to school."

Armendáriz's dark eyes narrowed as he recalled the police interrogation that had landed him in jail. "They grabbed my right arm to make me sign a document, a confession," he began. "And what do they know? I'm left-handed! And look, look at this scar on my forehead. They did this to me with a gun butt, because I wouldn't sign!

"Not only that! They cuffed me! I was handcuffed for three days inside the jail!

"I didn't sign and I didn't confess because I didn't do anything. I will not accept a guilt that is not mine."

While his nickname sounded sinister, like a title he had acquired because of his alleged gang activities, Armendáriz insisted it was actually a pet name given to him by his mother when he was a young boy because he was so devilish. He further claimed there wasn't even a gang called Los Rebeldes.

"There's an area, a barrio, a sector of the city where people like to have all kinds of fun," he said. "What's wrong with that? They congregate in that part of the city. . . . And that's an area where people can have fun.

"In other words, an area where you can go and dance and where you can get anything you want. So how can we call a gang by the name of that area, Los Rebeldes? I don't know who Los Rebeldes are. When they talk about that in here, they talk about those of us who are detained in here. I can't believe anything else, because like I've told the authorities, everything else, including the girls they're accusing me of murdering . . . is a fabrication!"

Armendáriz swore that he had never met Sharif. But authorities maintained they had proof that the gang leader had committed at least one of the murders. An odontological profile revealed that a bite mark found on the breast of one of the murdered women matched the teeth of Sergio Armendáriz, they said.

"According to the DA's office, the first set of tests on my teeth correspond to the bite marks on the body, to the marks that are on the breast," Armendáriz acknowledged. "But then my attorneys hired a dentist and that dentist's tests indicate the contrary. Then they did further testing and that's what we're waiting for now.

"And once they prove it isn't true, that they aren't my teeth marks, then, with the grace of God, I'll be able to get out.

"Furthermore, the authorities said they had video that showed me murdering a woman, and when we demanded to see that video, they never showed it to us. If they were shooting a video, how come they didn't stop me from committing the crime they thought I was committing before I supposedly murdered her?"

When questioned by members of the media, Mexican officials produced no video and no proof of any meetings taking place at the jail between alleged gang members and their supposed leader, Sharif Sharif, nor did they offer any evidence of financial transactions between the parties.

Still, authorities insisted Armendáriz and the others were behind the killings, and for a time the city was quiet once again.

The discovery of twenty-five more bodies in 1997 plunged the residents of Juárez into a panic anew—and raised even more questions about police claims that Sharif Sharif and the gang members were responsible for all the murders.

Even after authorities claimed to have linked Sharif Sharif and gang leader Sergio Armendáriz to at least two of the killings through bite marks found on the women's breasts, the murders were continuing, leaving open the real possibility that the culprit or culprits were still at large.

Charges had been dropped against five of the ten gang members who had first been taken into custody. Ceniceros, Guermes, Hernández, Olivares, and Fierro had all been freed for lack of evidence. Still, five, including Armendáriz, remained incarcerated at El Cereso for the murders.

As in previous cases, the latest victims were petite and pretty, with long dark hair and full lips. Many worked in the factories and, like the earlier victims, had been snatched from the downtown district in broad daylight. Their bodies exhibited signs of rape and mutilation when they were found rotting in remote locations around the industrial city.

Among the latest fatalities was a twenty-two-year-old mother named Silvia Guadalupe Díaz, who vanished without a trace on March 7, after having gone to a local maquiladora to ask for work.

As with earlier victims, Díaz's disappearance was never investigated by police. Officers disregarded her husband's repeated pleas for help in locating his young bride. Silvia had left him with their three-month-old baby boy and toddler girl when she left that morning in search of a job to help feed her family. Yet authorities didn't appear concerned over the young mother's failure to return home that day, even as corpses continued to pile up like cordwood.

In the days after Díaz's disappearance, the bodies of several more victims were recovered. On March 11, a rancher out riding his horse came upon the skeletal remains of a ten-year-old girl who had been raped, beaten, strangled, and partially buried in a barren stretch of land south of the city.

Three days later, the body of an eleven-year-old girl was discovered in Cerro Bola, the same stretch of desert where the first of the serial killer's victims was found in January 1993. Police said the child had been raped after she was murdered. An autopsy revealed she had been stabbed fifteen times in the neck and chest and died of excessive bleeding.

Then, on March 21, two more young victims were found.

One was sixteen, the other eighteen. Both women had been sexually assaulted and dumped in remote areas outside the city. The eighteen-year-old had five puncture wounds on her neck.

On March 29, agricultural workers finally came across the naked and battered body of the twenty-two-year-old mother, Silvia Díaz. Her mutilated remains had been dumped in an irrigation ditch about 820 yards west of the Juárez Porvenir Highway in Lote Bravo. Her undergarments and a uniform, similar to the ones worn by maquila workers, were found nearby. It appeared that Díaz had found work and had been toting the new smock her employers had given her home in preparation for her new job.

According to her mother-in-law, Díaz was last seen at a factory in one of Juárez's many industrial parks. An autopsy revealed she had been raped and strangled. The body showed signs of having been dumped soon after her disappearance on the seventh, left for the coyotes and rats roaming the desert sands.

The new wave of killings sparked more angry protests, with relatives of the murdered women joining local activists in once again demanding justice. That the women of Juárez were organizing and taking a stand against the authorities was groundbreaking. This would mark the first time in Mexican history that women were putting women's issues on the agenda of government.

It was an anomaly that Mexican women were finding jobs by the thousands in these maquiladoras along the border. In the past, they rarely would have considered leaving the home to work. Now these women were an important part of the workforce. They were suddenly out of the home and making a living just like men.

Maquiladora managers were anxious to hire women because they could be paid a lower wage than men. They were also preferred because the managers believed they had superior manual dexterity and were better suited to perform the repetitive and often physically debilitating tasks required of assembly-line workers. Production rates were higher with female employees, they said, because women were able to perform the jobs more effectively and at a quicker pace.

Pioneer women's activist Esther Chávez Cano charged that by employing mostly women, these foreign companies were unwittingly sparking a clash over gender roles in Mexico. Perhaps the murders of the young maquila workers were somehow linked to that conflict.

A slender wisp of a woman, with short auburn hair and rimless eyeglasses, Chávez had long been urging authorities to take aggressive action to track down and apprehend whoever was responsible for the murders. She had even started a local women's group, 8 de Marzo, named for March 8, International Women's Day, to push for more public action against the continuing crimes.

Her interest in the murders dated back to 1993, when she began to notice short news items reporting the killings buried inside the local newspaper, almost like footnotes, and one after the other. The crimes never seemed to capture the front pages, no matter how grisly they were or how many girls were disappearing.

With news of each new homicide, the fiery activist sought

to learn as much as she could about the circumstances surrounding the murder. As part of her research, she even went to the crime scenes. Chávez found that many of the girls had been snatched from the downtown area while waiting for a bus; their slight, mutilated bodies were cast into the desert lands encircling the city with little regard. A majority of victims were slender and petite, weighing between ninety and one hundred pounds, with long dark hair, plump lips, and olive complexions.

For the most part, the dead girls were poor and their families had little if any money to track down the culprits or raise awareness of the crimes. With no phones and no means of transportation, relatives of the missing women had to travel for miles on foot just to file a missing person's report or to check for news. Often they were turned away, told to come back in seventy-two hours to speak with an officer. By then it was too late.

Chávez was outraged that in spite of the growing body count, authorities were continuing to blame the victims for bringing on the sexual assaults by walking the streets unescorted in short skirts and shoes with high heels—provocative attire that investigators insinuated had led to their murders. She pointed out that a majority of the dead women had been dressed in slacks or blue jeans when they disappeared.

"If you want to rape and kill a woman, there is no better place to do it than in Juárez," Esther wrote in an op-ed column that appeared in the fall of 1995 in the same newspaper in which Dr. Irma Rodríguez published her autopsy findings on the Morales girl.

By mid-1997, Chávez was publicly demanding the resignation of the state police official overseeing the investigations, charging that the department hadn't done its job and that new investigators needed to be brought in on the case. Her request prompted authorities from the Chihuahua State Police Department, who normally were mum about the status of the investigation, to comment publicly.

In June, Julián Calderón Gutiérrez, first commander of the state police, insisted his officers were making solid progress. On June 2, Calderón told the *Las Vegas Sun*, one of a number of newspapers in the United States that were following the wave of murders, "We know many people believe we're not even investigating, but the fact is we have fourteen officers assigned to these cases alone, and we've cleared up a number of them and are progressing on others."

Still, mounting public criticism prompted Chihuahua state attorney general Arturo Chávez Chávez (no relation to activist Esther Chávez) in late 1997 to announce the creation of a new task force to investigate the growing number of murders in Juárez. The Special Task Force for the Investigation of Crimes Against Women (FEDCM) would operate out of the satellite office maintained by the attorney general in Juárez under the direction of a special prosecutor handpicked by Chávez himself.

Not surprisingly, the attorney general was quickly criticized for having waited more than three years to act. Arturo Chávez had been in office since 1994. Yet by the time the task force was formed, more than 170 women had been murdered in Juárez, and the number was continuing to climb.

Critics suggested the new unit was designed to quell citizen unrest before the election process heated up; state elections were to be held in July of 1998. (The municipal government of Juárez and the state government in Chihuahua City were both under PAN rule.) Chávez was also forced to respond to questions about missing evidence and incidents in which journalists and bystanders trampled the crime scenes, leaving empty soda cans and cigarette butts in their wake.

CHAPTER FOUR

The Devil Is in Juárez

I was looking for her, but I wasn't looking for her
among the dead, I was looking for her alive.

—JESÚS GONZÁLEZ,
FATHER OF VICTIM, SAGRARIO GONZÁLEZ

EVEN WITH THE ATTORNEY GENERAL'S newly created special task force, the murders of pretty, young Mexican women appeared to continue unabated, with thirty-eight more homicides in 1998—nearly half exhibiting signs of sexual assault and mutilation. Among them was a young factory worker named María Sagrario González Flores.

Like Silvia Morales, this young teen was last seen transferring buses in the center of the city on April 16. Her family maintains she was snatched in broad daylight, either while waiting at the bus transfer site or during her lonely walk home to the desert colonia of Lomas de Poleo, located northwest of the city.

For weeks Paula González Flores had been begging her seventeen-year-old daughter to quit her job at the downtown maquila, where she worked the assembly line, soldering electrical components for Capco Crane & Hoist, a New England–based crane manufacturer. Flores became concerned after managers at the plant insisted Sagrario change her shift from the overnight to the early morning, which began promptly at 6 a.m.

What plant managers may have failed to realize was that by changing the young girl's hours, they were putting her in grave danger. Sagrario had been commuting by van to work each day with her father, Jesús, and older sister, Guillermina, who also worked at the plant on the overnight shift but in different departments.

Now Sagrario was on her own, traveling the desolate route from the family's makeshift residence to the factory alone. To be on time for work, she needed to wake at three o'clock in the morning, shower in the dark, and be on her way by four.

The González family lived in one of the more marginal areas of the city, where the architecture was as harsh as the landscape. Some houses had literally been fabricated from rubbish; they were erected from pieces of cardboard, wood, and metal cobbled together with screws driven through bottle caps. The buildings were frightening and odd-looking structures on the outside, but the laughter of the children playing and the ranchera music emanating from the radio told a different tale. There was love here, and hearth and warmth inside.

The Gonzálezes' home had been hastily slapped together with tar paper and wood and then painted a pale pink with a forest green shingle roof. There was a series of smaller shacks that the family used to store farming tools and animal feed encircled by a fence of wooden stakes and barbed wire. The barrier was intended to keep farm animals from wandering away. There was no running water. The outhouse stood behind the dwelling, and a small well dug by hand provided fresh drinking water. The home had just one large room, divided into separate living spaces by pieces of fabric. Odd sections of rug and carpet covered areas of the dirt floor and helped to hold the warmth inside during the dry, cold winter nights.

A colorful floral curtain divided the living room from the family's cramped sleeping quarters. The parents' double bed was pushed against one wall, and two sets of bunk beds hugged the other. There was barely room to walk between them.

Paula and Jesús González had moved with their seven children to Juárez in 1996, from the state of Durango, after the forestry industry in their tiny village had begun to falter and jobs grew scarce. The family constructed their house almost overnight and illegally tapped into utility lines to obtain power for several lightbulbs and a small television.

A number of the city's residents pilfered electricity by stringing common household extension cords together until they reached a home. A tangle of crisscrossing wires through the neighborhoods made it impossible to determine who was connected to whom. Many of the live wires ran along the ground, and even across the dirt roads, making them hazardous to the children playing outside or walking with friends.

For miles there was nothing but parched sand, sagebrush, and bristly, pencil-thin saguaro cacti. There were no traffic sounds, only the clucking of roosters roaming the hills.

Jesús González was dismayed when his wife phoned him at

the factory just before 10 p.m. on April 16 to report that Sagrario had not yet reached home. Her shift had ended at 3 p.m., nearly seven hours earlier. But there was no sign of her.

At first Jesús believed his youngest child had left work with her boyfriend, a young man who was also employed at the Capco plant. Then he saw the boyfriend working, and his heart stopped. At that moment Jesús was overcome with panic and the horrible realization that he might never see Sagrario again. He knew what had become of the young women who disappeared on their way to and from work. His little girl was naïve and innocent. She sang in the church choir and spent many of her free hours rehearsing with her choir group. She was beautiful, with pale brown skin that was unblemished, dark wavy hair that fell to her waist, and plump lips. Like her mother, Sagrario had full, bushy eyebrows and long, thick lashes. She rarely wore slacks, opting for pretty dresses that fell to her knee.

Racing up to his supervisor, Jesús told him what had happened and obtained permission to leave—and to take his eldest daughter with him.

Guillermina burst into tears when she learned that her little sister had not made it home. Shaking, she ran to her locker to retrieve her purse, then met her father at the front of the building.

Their first stop was the local jail in downtown Juárez, where the municipal police were headquartered. The facility spanned four square city blocks and was reputed to be a place where inmates were treated harshly, not only by fellow prisoners but more often by the guards. Located in a dangerous section of the downtown area between Avenida 16 de Septiembre and Calle Oro, the jail was known locally as "the rock" because of a wall of white brick that encircled it like a fortress. It was also called "the brick jail."

Jesús was horrified at the officers' reaction to his concern over Sagrario's failure to return home that evening. It astounded him that with all the missing young women already found dead in the city, police were still trivializing a report of another missing girl. It was as if they were patronizing him when they told him they'd contact him if they found his daughter. While they didn't insinuate that she'd run off with a boyfriend, as they had with Ramona Morales and Irma Pérez, they snickered when he implored them to commence a search.

Jesús's eldest daughter tried to contain her emotions as she stood by her father listening to the officers belittling him with promises of help, knowing in her heart that these men didn't care at all about Sagrario's fate. Guillermina also didn't like the way the officers were leering at her. Like Sagrario, she too was slender with bright eyes framed by thick, dark eyelashes. Her long, shiny hair fell well past her shoulders.

Desperate to find Sagrario, Jesús and his daughter climbed into their van and rushed from the municipal police station to a friend's ranch. They knew the family had a cell phone and wanted to borrow it to call the emergency line in hopes of getting a better response from officials.

Guillermina watched as her father dialed 060 on the telephone keypad. She could tell by his posture the news wasn't good. Officials claimed that police wouldn't dispatch a patrol car unless there was a real emergency. That a missing seventeen-year-old girl in a city saturated with murders of young women wasn't an emergency seemed unbelievable to Guillermina.

Aware that his wife was worried, Jesús stopped at home to pick up Paula and their son, Juan.

It was pitch-black when the family arrived at the mirrored-glass building housing both the district attorney's headquarters and the state police, who were handling the investigation into the murdered young women. Surely the state police would be able to help, Jesús thought as he stepped up to the window and asked to report his missing daughter. Someone could be raping and killing his child at that very moment. He needed to rescue her. He could barely get the words out before the uniformed officer interrupted him.

"Sir, you need to wait twenty-four hours before you can file a formal report on a missing person," the officer advised.

"We are looking for her alive," Jesús shot back.

It all seemed surreal. His daughter was missing and the police were refusing to do anything to help. While the official wait time to report a missing person had been shortened from the original seventy-two-hour requirement—thanks to the efforts of local activists like Esther Chávez—a full day still seemed too long to wait to commence an investigation, given the ongoing criminal climate. Following a check of the local hospitals, Jesús and Juan next retraced the route Sagrario would take on foot if she were on her way home. A light wind stirred up the powdery sand of the desert as they yelled her name into the blackness. *"Sagrario!"* they shouted.

There was no answer, only the howls of the coyotes off in the hills.

Paula was outside, standing in front of the pretty lace curtain that served as the family's front door, when her husband and son came trudging up the dirt path to their farm compound.

Jesús looked weary and defeated, and Juan was sad, angry, and tired. Hearing the commotion, Guillermina rushed outside to learn if there was any news. The twenty-two-year-old was more assertive than her baby sister and had stronger physical features. She wore her thick, pencil-straight hair pulled off her face, accentuating her angular cheekbones and Clorox-white front teeth.

Collapsing into each other's arms, the four sobbed uncontrollably. It was clear that something terrible had happened to Sagrario.

With no help from the authorities, the family had done what little they could to look for Sagrario. There was one chance left—the local volunteers who routinely searched the desert for victims.

There was growing speculation among residents of Juárez that officers from both the state and municipal police forces were somehow involved in the increasing number of murders—or that they were covering up for the guilty party or parties. Concerned that authorities were doing little to protect the citizens of the poorest communities of the city, a team of volunteer ham radio operators was periodically checking the scrublands that bordered the city for any signs of foul play.

Many of these men couldn't afford to own cars, so they organized carpools to travel to the search sites, and then split up to conduct their own explorations on foot. The task was not without risk. The desert heat was often stultifying, and blinding sandstorms and poisonous rattlesnakes abounded. The majority of the searchers donned cowboy hats, heavy cowhide boots, and sunglasses to guard against the elements.

Paula and her husband joined in the searches.

Sagrario had been missing for a little more than two weeks when the family learned that a woman's body had been found in a trench in a desolate area of Lote Bravo called Loma Blanca.

Someone had notified the local police that there was a taxi on fire there. Some boys had been playing nearby when they noticed the flames and raced over to see what was burning. On their way back, they stumbled upon the dead body and ran to alert police.

Paula grabbed her son Juan and rushed to the police station on Friday, May 1, to find out if the dead girl was her Sagrario. There she was greeted by a group of mothers of missing or slain girls and several local activists who were holding a vigil in the hallway of the government building. The look on their faces told Paula what she didn't want to know.

Finally a reporter spoke to her. "Señora, they just found another girl," he said.

"Which one and where did they find her?" Paula asked, fearful of his response.

"All I can tell you is that this girl was wearing an overdress from Capco."

Paula's heart sank in her chest.

"Wait here, Mama, I'll go," Juan interrupted.

Paula's legs trembled as she watched her youngest son disappear inside the building, aware that the other mothers congregated nearby were avoiding her gaze. In her early forties, Paula González was still physically fit and had managed to retain her youthful, natural beauty. She wore no makeup, and her thick hair was tied loosely in a ponytail. Like many of the city's residents, she dressed casually in slacks and the colorful sweaters she knit by hand.

Minutes seemed like hours as she paced the sidewalk, ruminating over why authorities had waited nearly three days to tell the family about Sagrario. From what Paula had gathered, officials had discovered the teenager's body that past Wednesday but had failed to contact family members or alert them when she had come to headquarters the previous day to check for news.

Less than thirty minutes had passed when Paula spotted her son exiting the building. His face told her what she already knew: the dead child was her baby girl.

According to authorities, Sagrario had been strangled and stabbed, three times in the chest, twice in the back. The wounds were shallow and did not penetrate any vital organs. The police believed she had also been raped, but her body was too decomposed to determine for certain.

Officials said the teen was still wearing the white smock typically worn by female workers at the city's factories when her body was discovered. Paula had embroidered her daughter's name on the uniform the day she brought it home from the factory, never expecting that it would later serve as a tool for the family to identify Sagrario's disfigured corpse.

News accounts were reporting that about one-third of the murdered girls were maquiladora workers. Now Sagrario González had been added to the rising statistics. Her body was in such an advanced state of decomposition that it was difficult to know if it really was Sagrario.

For identification purposes, her brother Juan was shown the white smock found on the body and some items of underwear that he believed belonged to his sister. For humanitarian reasons, he was shown a portion of his sister's arm and a reconstruction of her skull, rather than Sagrario's actual head and face, which had decayed into an amorphous mass of putrid tissue.

To alleviate some of the horror of the identification process, authorities had begun creating reconstructions of a victim's skull and face. They used those reconstructions rather than a cleaned skull, as they had been doing in past cases. The new technology was not yet available when mothers including Ramona Morales and Irma Pérez were asked to identify their daughters.

Chihuahua was one of the first of the country's states to employ facial reproduction techniques. Using the bones of the face and cranial measurements, the state's pathologist, Irma Rodríguez, was able to "give a face" to a cadaver, which was often nothing more than a skeleton with some tissue that was bloated and black from decomposition when it was brought in. The process normally took fifteen days from start to finish.

Dr. Rodríguez had been working the cases of the murdered young women since the mid-1990s. A woman of about forty with a cherubic face and short styled hair, she had a direct, forthright manner that brimmed with efficiency. She had been summoned to dozens of crime scenes, including that of Ramona Morales's daughter, Silvia. Back then, the state's crime lab had not been as sophisticated, and the families were made to view the actual decaying body parts of their murdered children. In many cases, recovered skulls were in such advanced states of decomposition that they looked like scary Halloween goblins, with their mouths open wide as if they were screaming in fear, hardly a comforting image for a grieving relative. Worse, the field rats that roam the desert have a predilection for nasal and auditory cartilage and often devour them from the faces of the victims within twenty-four hours.

Advances in forensic technology had now made it possible for experts to reconstruct a face from skeletal remains. Once the body was received at the morgue, Rodríguez and her team evaluated all the facial characteristics in order to implement the technique of facial reproduction, or what experts in the field call "giving a semblance of a face." She kept meticulous records of the crime scenes in a binder with explicit drawings and notes about the forensic examinations of the bodies and the state in which they were found.

Sagrario González's image had been reconstructed from odontological profiling. The new technology was also making it possible to identify some of the more decomposed bodies through photographs of the facial reproductions published in the city's newspapers.

Ramona Morales's thirteen-year-old neighbor, Celia "Lupita" Guadalupe, had been identified after the girl's mother recognized the child from a photo of one of Dr. Rodríguez's facial reproductions in the city's newspaper *El Diario de Juárez*. Authorities believed the teen was abducted while walking home from school one December afternoon in 1997. Her family had intended to pick her up that day, as they normally did, but her grandmother arrived late to find the child had already started out on foot.

Lupita's remains indicated she had been beaten so savagely that the examination of them brought the medical examiner to tears. The young girl's body was in such a state of decomposition that it had been impossible to determine if she had been raped, but the fact that she had been found naked from the waist up led Dr. Rodríguez to believe that indeed a sexual assault had preceded the child's murder. That the forensics expert was able to help the family identify their missing daughter was her only consolation.

Sagrario González's brother knew little about the method of facial reconstruction. Standing in the crime lab that Friday, he carefully studied the replica being presented as his sister's, troubled over the appearance of the teeth. They looked much bigger than they had been when she was alive. But Juan, like many of the country's poor, was too fearful to question authorities about the discrepancy.

His reservations were not uncommon. Many of the victims' families shared the young man's confusion over the protruding teeth and jaw of the reconstructions, unaware that without the surrounding soft tissue, they appear larger than they had in real life. While the technique of facial reproduction was state-of-the-art, it was limited in its capability to accurately portray the fleshy parts of a human being, especially the areas around the gums and teeth. Dr. Rodríguez felt she was sparing the next of kin the horror of viewing the actual skeletal remains of their loved one, yet the families of the dead were complaining about the state's policy of substituting a facial reconstruction for the purposes of identification. Many of the relatives were suspicious of the practice, convinced that authorities were hiding important information by using the lifelike models.

Paula González knew from her son's face that the news was not good. Tears streamed down her face, some embedding themselves inside the deep wrinkles that time and suffering had left, as she watched Juan Francisco descend the cement steps and stride toward her. She listened as he delicately assured her that the clothing police had shown him belonged to Sagrario.

The young man, however, had chosen not to tell his mother of his doubts about the size of his sister's teeth. Only later did he disclose his incredulity.

As if the day weren't difficult enough, Paula González grew even more upset that afternoon when police claimed that Sagrario had been killed while living a secret life. Officers told the family the teenager had been earning a second salary as a prostitute, selling her body to the men of Juárez.

The pronouncement enraged Sagrario's older sister, Guillermina, who found it unbelievable that investigators would make such a statement. The two girls were especially close, even wearing each other's clothes. Furious, Guillermina fought with officers, vowing to disprove their claims and to keep her sister's case in the headlines.

Her mother, meanwhile, was unable to contain her emotions. Upon learning the news, Paula González collapsed in the street outside police headquarters that day.

"Murderers!" she shouted at the uniformed officers entering and exiting the building. "You are all murderers!"

Sagrario would have turned eighteen on July 31, just three months after her brutal murder.

The González family was too poor to afford a casket or a headstone for Sagrario; a proper burial cost $150 in Mexico. Instead, they laid the young girl to rest in a desert cemetery reachable by a one-lane road of serpentine curves and harrowing switchbacks that led into the mountains behind their home. A mound of brown dirt and dozens of colorful plastic flowers marked the gravesite, which sat amid rows of aboveground tombs adorned with the plastic bouquets. Few flowers grow in the Sororan desert. Plastic reproductions are used in their place.

Crouching down, Paula caressed the ground, as if touching her lost daughter. Closing her eyes, she rocked back and forth.

"*¿Eres tú, mi reina?*" she whispered in a gentle tone. "Is this you, my queen? Is this you buried here, my Sagrario, my daughter?"

An audible sob filled the air, followed by a flood of tears. Paula González was not convinced that the body that lay in the ground was, in fact, Sagrario.

In the months after Sagrario's death, authorities notified the family that a DNA test performed on the body had come back with negative results. Officials promised a retest, and Paula and Jesús were anxiously awaiting news.

Nevertheless, the circumstances surrounding her disappearance prompted Sagrario's elder sister to take precautions. Fearing for her life, Guillermina quit her factory job just two weeks after her sister's body was found to become a shampoo girl at a local Supercuts hair salon. But her fright didn't stop her from challenging authorities' mishandling of her sister's case or the cases of other murdered girls.

Guillermina would go on to found a small, grassroots organization she named Voces Sin Eco, Voices Without Echo, to seek justice for Sagrario and other murdered women of Juárez. The group was comprised of just six families, fifteen members in total. Its goal was to keep the killings in the headlines, through candlelight vigils, the erection of crosses throughout the city, and bimonthly searches for clues and evidence police may have overlooked. Among the members was Irma Pérez, the mother of slain shoe store worker Olga Alicia.

Over time, Guillermina would also become an outspoken activist for justice and a public critic of both local and state authorities.

Still, she refused to pray in the little white church that sat on the hill above the family's dwelling in Lomas de Poleo. The house of worship had been Sagrario's home away from home. She had spent hour upon hour there, rehearsing with her choir group and attending mass. She'd even tried to get the priest to allow guitar accompaniment at Sunday mass to give it a more modern beat.

Guillermina was now suspicious of everyone, including a

priest who had befriended her sister and then disappeared soon after Sagrario's murder. She wanted to return to the cathedral in the family's hometown of Durango to pray for her slain sister. Since the murder, she had told her mother that she no longer believed that God was in Juárez.

"The devil is in Juárez," Guillermina insisted.

CHAPTER FIVE

Changing of the Guard

It's impossible for a vote to be worth more than a life.

—Samira Izaguirre,
Ciudad Juárez radio host

In addition to the murders of the city's young women, Ciudad Juárez was also experiencing a rise in drug-related violence. Since the late 1980s, Mexico had been the main transit route for South American cocaine and a major source of marijuana, heroin, and methamphetamines.

Drug smuggling had steadily increased after the signing of the North American Free Trade Agreement, according to law enforcement officials patrolling the U.S.-Mexican border. In fact, a study conducted in 1998 by members of state and federal border patrol agents and obtained by the *Wall Street Journal* found that the free trade agreement was actually making it easier for drug smugglers to transport their goods into the United States, with dealers consulting with professionals in the foreign exchange trade on ways to operate under the NAFTA procedures. Many of the illegal drug shipments were being smuggled in secret compartments of trucks, trains, and even cargo planes.

Authorities reported that by 1998, there were some 450 known gangs in Juárez, most of them involved in drugs. Score settling among rival *narcotraficantes* had become expected and even commonplace in the border city. Officials in Juárez reported eighty drug-related killings and seventy disappearances related to the illegal drug trade from 1994 to 1998.

Juárez, after all, was home to the leader of Mexico's biggest drug cartel, Amado Carrillo Fuentes. Officials believed Carrillo was responsible for importing as much as 70 percent of the cocaine that entered the United States annually. Carrillo favored shipping the narcotics through the Juárez–El Paso area, using Interstate 10 and Interstate 25, according to authorities.

Once primarily limited to intergang violence, the bloodshed of the city's drug trade began spilling onto the streets of the border city in July 1997, when, at the age of forty-two, Amado Carrillo Fuentes died during a botched cosmetic surgery procedure in Mexico City, supposedly designed to change his appearance to evade law enforcement. Word of Carrillo's death sparked a fierce turf war for control of the country's lucrative drug trade, with warring factions using areas of Juárez as a backdrop for their battle for supremacy.

It had been widely reported that the notorious kingpin had been managing and mediating among the country's five major drug cartels for years. Once he was out of the picture, the situation quickly erupted into a fierce battle for supremacy. Within weeks of Carrillo's death, more than eighteen drug-related killings were reported in Ciudad Juárez, with executions now occurring in the streets in broad daylight.

The situation grew even more volatile in August 1999, when four armed gunmen burst into the popular downtown restaurant Max Fim and opened fire, emptying 130 rounds as terrified patrons screamed in horror. Remarkably, only six people were killed and four others wounded in the bloody drug hit that day.

News of the dinnertime massacre sent a wave of panic through the city. The message was clear. With Carrillo's passing, the drug war had escalated to a level not seen before in Juárez. In the past, the killings had been confined to individuals involved in the trade. Now innocent bystanders were being picked off if they got in the way.

Many residents were terrified to travel the streets of the downtown area, where much of the violence was occurring. Officials were reporting that drug-related murders appeared restricted to the two square miles where most of the city's commercial and tourism businesses operated, just steps from the Cordova International Bridge to El Paso. Warnings were being issued to Americans thinking of crossing the border for a night of fun or a day of shopping the tourist boutiques.

Residents took to the streets calling for the violence to stop. More than three thousand demonstrators marched through the city that September. Their angry cries for action against the escalating violence added yet another layer to the already volatile situation. Now the state attorney general's office was being bombarded from all sides, facing angry demonstrations both by the families of the murdered women and by local residents fearful of the warring *narcotraficantes*.

Attorney General Arturo Chávez Chávez likely got little sleep that night. After facing three thousand protestors, he learned that four more people had been gunned down in a local bar and that four doctors from hospitals in the nation's capital had been tortured, strangled, and left in a heap in a public park in Mexico City. It is not clear if the slaughtered doctors were members of the team that performed the bungled cosmetic surgery on Amado Fuentes Carrillo, but their grisly executions heightened anxieties in the capital city.

Four months after the billionaire trafficker's death, authorities announced murder charges against three of the surgeons who had operated on Carrillo. Interestingly, at the time of the announcement, two of the doctors were already dead. Their bodies had been found several days earlier encased in cement in sealed drums along a roadside, according to Mexican authorities. One forensic scientist told the *New York Times* that autopsies revealed the surgeons had been tortured. There was evidence that the doctors had been blindfolded and handcuffed, then burned and beaten before being strangled to death.

On February 2, police officials, speaking on the condition of anonymity, told *El Diario de Juárez* that the heightened violence in the city was the product of an internal war between two factions of the Cartel de Juárez, one led by alleged long-time narcotrafficker Rafael Muñoz Talavera, who had served time in a Mexican federal prison for a 1989 cocaine arrest in California, and the other by Vicente Carrillo Fuentes, the younger brother of the late Amado Carrillo Fuentes.

Later that month, the *New York Times* quoted a "United States government functionary" as confirming that Muñoz Talavera had emerged as the cartel's new leader. Muñoz, however, disputed reports of his victory, claiming in an open letter to the Juárez newspapers that "I am a simple working man." The *New York Times* reversed its earlier allegations two days after Muñoz's letter was published, stating that the same "government functionary" was now claiming that the victory had not yet been proven.

The U.S. Drug Enforcement Agency (DEA) maintained that the Juárez Cartel was importing cocaine, heroin, and marijuana as well as "high-quality methamphetamines" into the United States with alarming ease. In a report released in early 2002, the federal agency maintained that "large quantities" of the methamphetamines were being delivered to Phoenix, Arizona, through the cartel's western operations in Hermosillo, Sonora. The agency also disclosed the discovery of cargo shipments from the Cartel de Juárez in Oklahoma, Illinois, Georgia, and Washington State and divulged that the former Carrillo cartel, under the direction of the late Amado Carrillo Fuentes, had been shipping cocaine directly to New Jersey and New York City.

That same month, an anti-drug-trafficking sting conducted by U.S. Customs agents resulted in the seizure of three Texas safehouses and an El Paso trucking business owned and operated by an alleged Mexican drug trafficker, Eduardo González Quirarte, who was believed to be a ringleader in the Cartel de Juárez. U.S. authorities reported that agents found that trucks belonging to González's El Paso Trucking Center were outfitted with "secret compartments" that had likely been used to move illegal drug shipments into the United States.

The clampdown in Mexico's northern border region appeared one-sided, with U.S. federal agents conducting the majority of the raids on U.S. soil—until an unexpected revelation sparked federal authorities in Mexico to stand up and take action.

That February, it was learned that a slain federal judicial police officer who had been gunned down in January by assassins wielding AK-47s had ties to the Juárez drug cartel. Even more startling was the fact that he was also a member of the Chihuahua special task force investigating the Juárez serial killings. In an article that appeared in the *New York Times* on February 1, 2002, Mexican attorney general Jorge Madrazo Cuéllar confirmed that the office subcommander, Mario Héctor Varela of the Chihuahua state police, was a corrupt "narco-policeman" with ties to the powerful Juárez drug cartel. The Mexican attorney general also confirmed for the newspaper that Varela had been a member of Chihuahua's special police task force investigating the abductions and murders of the women of Juárez.

The revelation, while stunning, came as no surprise to the women, who had long been suggesting that police might be involved in some of the killings.

Mexico's attorney general Cuéllar reacted strongly to the disclosure. Standing before the media that February, he vowed to appoint new detectives and prosecutors to the special unit to investigate women's homicides.

Chihuahua attorney general Arturo Chávez agreed. "Perhaps some of our investigations were not done well," he told journalists that February. "Maybe they should have been done better."

In response to the ongoing public criticism, Chávez invited famed American criminologist Robert Ressler to Juárez in the spring of 1998 to work side by side with Mexican authorities on the homicides. As reasons for the invitation, Chávez cited Ressler's vast experience in the area of criminal profiling and his technical skills at piecing together small bits of information to glean a portrait of a killer. "We have no one with that kind of experience in Mexico," Chávez told reporters at a press conference that April.

Ressler was well known in the United States for his work at the FBI's National Center for the Analysis of Violent Crime in Quantico, Virginia. He'd left the bureau's famed Behavioral Analysis Unit, which inspired the spine-tingling Hollywood thriller *The Silence of the Lambs*, in 1990 and was working as a consultant to law enforcement and others. He first gained notoriety in the United States in the early nineties after the publication of his book *Whoever Fights Monsters*, an in-depth look at serial killers.

Officials in Juárez were hoping he could help shed some light on the ongoing murders. Ressler would be involved as an independent investigator, hired by Mexican government officials, not as a formal FBI operative, representing the United States government. The plan was to analyze all the aspects of the crime—time of disappearance, age of the victims, their social status, and the circumstances of their deaths—and to make recommendations for improving the state police department's investigatory skills, such as psychological profiling.

During the first of three trips to Juárez that April, Ressler spent one week reviewing the files of the unsolved homicides and accompanying police to the crime scenes. In an interview, local activist Esther Chávez said she found it curious that officials would ask the American profiler for help when he did not speak the native language and, therefore, could not converse with the families of the murdered girls.

Nevertheless, the Chihuahua state attorney general's office held a press conference in late June at which Ressler announced his findings. Dressed in a dark-colored suit and cowboy boots, and towering over Mexican officials at well over six feet, the fair-haired criminologist told journalists that of the more than 160 murders that had occurred in Juárez since 1993, he found that 76 conformed to a pattern. A majority of the dead girls ranged in age from seventeen to twenty-four, and a large number had been raped and strangled, he said. Like Sagrario González, at least twelve had vanished on their way to or from work at a local factory.

Based on his investigation, Ressler theorized that one or more serial killers were crossing the border into Juárez from the United States to commit the killings. He pointed to areas like Mariscal Street in *el centro*, close to the seedy bars, where maquila girls walk alone after dark on desolate streets and in alleyways to transfer to outbound buses, and to the constant influx of young women, many with no ties or families to report them missing.

In response to questions about the way authorities had been handling the investigations, Ressler told journalists that Mexican police were doing the best they could with what they had. He cited inadequate staffing and inexperience as reasons for the lack of progress but noted that their investigation had been carried out as well as, if not better than, many conducted on the U.S. side of the border.

"The Juárez police did not have adequate cars or adequate personnel working on the case," he told a producer from Univision during a lengthy interview conducted at his home in Fredericksburg, Virginia. "They did the best they could, and I'd say a very good job. I looked at seventy-six case files, and the investigation of those crimes in Juárez wasn't, to me, substandard.

"They needed more money, I think maybe from NAFTA, to bring the police services up to standard and to get them the equipment and the personnel."

Ressler claimed to have seen some "convincing" evidence against the jailed Egyptian Sharif Sharif and members of the street gang Los Rebeldes. While he failed to provide any real details, he pointed to bite marks found on several of the victims' bodies that officials maintained matched those of Sergio Armendáriz—a claim the gang leader vehemently disputed. While DNA results had initially been favorable to the prosecutor's office, a second test performed at the request of Armendáriz would later prove inconclusive.

Mexican criminologist Oscar Maynez disagreed with Ressler's assessment that a serial killer or killers were crossing the border into Mexico to murder the young women of Juárez. Maynez had served as a staff criminologist for the attorney general's office under Governor Barrio but had quit in disgust after only two years over the way authorities were handling the investigations. He had since been invited back as chief of the state's forensic department. In that capacity, he oversaw much of the evidence in the ongoing homicide cases.

Maynez believed the perpetrator or perpetrators were from Mexico and preying on their own kind. He pointed to Ressler's work with serial killers in the United States, particularly his theory that men who commit serial murder are most often Anglo-Saxon and hail from European roots. Maynez noted there had never been a comprehensive study of serial murder in Mexico to negate the possibility that a Mexican man could be a serial killer.

Maynez was also skeptical about whether state police had actually presented the former FBI agent with all the facts pertaining to the homicides, or whether Ressler had unknowingly based his assessment on incorrect or incomplete data. Maynez maintained that without accurate facts, it would be impossible to reach a proper conclusion.

Whether or not the killers were from Juárez, one fact was extremely clear: they stalked their victims, they knew the desert well, and they had the means to reach desolate areas where no one could hear these young women's desperate cries for help.

When the American profiler returned to the border city some six months later in September of 1998, he learned there had been a major political upset in the state of Chihuahua. Voters had sent a clear message to members of the state's ruling PAN party in the July elections, casting their ballots for Patricio Martínez, the gubernatorial candidate for the opposing PRI party, which had been controlling Mexico for more than seventy years.

As part of his campaign, Martínez had vowed to end violence in the region "in one month" and had focused particular attention on the murders in Juárez. His promise appeared to win him favor with the electorate and gain him the state governorship.

Martínez appointed PRI member Arturo González Rascón to be sworn in as the new state attorney general on October 4, when the change of power officially took place.

The new politicians welcomed Robert Ressler and appreciated the help he was providing to investigators in accumulating and analyzing their data. The famed criminologist had arranged to have the FBI's fifteen-page Violent Criminal Apprehension Program, known as VICAP, translated into Spanish so that state investigators could use it as a guide. He and other members of law enforcement in the United States used the form to record data such as the modus operandi and victim profile for analysis, and as a guide to cross-reference data with other law enforcement agencies. Ressler had invited the VICAP people from the FBI to become involved in the case. When they failed to join in, he had taken it upon himself to have the VICAP form translated into Spanish.

Though the Mexican police had come under attack from civic activists, the media, and others, Ressler defended them, saying that they were not "just these guys in big hats taking siestas." He insisted, "They had a pretty good operation and pretty good people in top spots. . . . What the women's groups are saying is that these macho guys didn't give a damn about the victims. . . . I disagree with that."

In early October, the new Chihuahua state attorney general, Arturo González Rascón, announced the appointment of a thirty-four-year-old lawyer named Suly Ponce Prieto to the role of director of the Special Task Force for the Investigation of Crimes Against Women. In that capacity, she would oversee the investigation of all women's homicides, including murders of a sexual nature.

Rumors quickly circulated that the tall, auburn-haired Ponce was selected because of her political ties to Rascón, and she was soon labeled a political lackey. She arrived on the heels of three other directors who had stepped down from the post within a six-month period for reasons that were never disclosed.

Ponce would be based out of the attorney general's satellite office in Juárez and report to the district attorney, Nahúm Nájera, in charge in the border city.

In interviews, Ponce said that when she reported for work that first week, she found a state police department ill equipped to handle the homicide investigations. To her amazement, she found that officers lacked even the most basic tools—equipment such as paper bags, latex gloves, and crime scene tape, all of which are essential to the proper preservation of a crime scene.

According to published reports, Ponce learned that police had burned more than one thousand pounds of evidence, the bulk of it clothing that had been collected from crime scenes.

In the days before she took over the directorship in October, members of the previous administration had also cleared her office of all files pertaining to prior investigations performed by experts, including Robert Ressler. Eager to bring about positive change in her new role, Ponce told Mexican journalists she had been left with "nothing" to work from.

Although she had held posts as a university professor, public defender, and local magistrate, Ponce had never worked as a prosecutor. But her lack of prosecutorial experience didn't concern Rascón, who praised his new director as a talented professional. However, the office she was expected to run was hardly up to the times. The small, stark white room with the brightly painted blue door was minimally equipped with a simple metal desk, two nondescript office chairs, a typewriter, and a telephone.

Standing in the doorway that first day, puffing on a cigarette, Ponce wondered if her new position had been created as a public relations exercise to give people the illusion that something was being done. If so, that would change soon after her name went on the office door.

Almost immediately, Ponce demanded a bigger office space, state-of-the-art computers, and an updated phone system. She also wielded authority over the crime scenes, denying admission to bystanders and news reporters who had once been given unfettered access—right up to the point of repositioning the body of a homicide victim in order to capture a sensational photo for the following day's paper.

Under Ponce's direction, crime scenes were to be cordoned off and preserved.

Ponce theorized that of the 180 femicides that had occurred in Juárez since 1993, 30 percent, or 55 of the crimes,
were of a sexual nature. The rest, she claimed, were violent
homicides such as random killings or executions unrelated to
the serial murders that officials had linked to Sharif Sharif and
the gang members.

Ponce's presence, and her belief that Sharif Sharif was responsible for at least some of the murders, made the Egyptian's
defense even more difficult.

In Mexico, unlike the United States, a person is considered
guilty or "probably responsible" until proven innocent. It is up
to the defense attorney to disprove charges brought by the
prosecution, and up to a judge, not a jury, to determine a
person's guilt or innocence.

Ponce was aware that Sharif Sharif and his attorney, Irene
Blanco, had been successful in having five of the six murder
charges lodged against him thrown out by a judge earlier in the
year for lack of evidence. Still, one charge remained—the murder of maquila worker Elizabeth Castro. And although the evidence in that case seemed to point in another direction,
authorities remained unwilling to set Sharif free.

For months the Egyptian had been demanding a meeting
with Ponce's superior, Governor Patricio Martínez. Martínez,
however, was not interested in meeting with Sharif, who had
also requested to sit down with Oscar Maynez, the state's
forensic expert, and several local activists, including Esther
Chávez. The Egyptian wanted to speak with Maynez about his
own findings, which he had gleaned from an investigation he
had commenced from his jail cell.

According to the criminologist, Shariff was of the belief that the son of a local cantina owner was behind some of the murders, claiming the man, Armando Martínez, had cut the throat of one of the dancers who worked at his father's establishment. Sharif was insisting that the cantina was linked to the drug-trafficking trade in Juárez, and that the murdered dancer fit the victim profile to a tee, Maynez said. Sharif's source was a police official named Víctor Valenzuela Rivera, who would later testify before state legislators and journalists that he was at the Safari Club, a local bar frequented by police and narco-traffickers. There, Valenzuela Rivera claimed to have over-heard Armando Martínez joking about the murders and assuring the men that they were "protected" by government officials and police.

The stunning declarations were not without bloody conse-quences. When Sharif's attorney, Irene Blanco, insisted that police investigate the accusations against Martínez, her own family came under fire. Blanco told local Juárez newspapers that she received a death threat from an anonymous male caller who said "they were going to hit me where it most hurts." The day after she made the statement, unidentified gunmen travel-ing in a gray van fired on her young adult son as he drove along La Raza Street in downtown Juárez.

News accounts reported that three of the more than ten bullets that were fired that day impacted the young man's body, and were it not for the fact that he continued driving to a local hospital, he would have died of his injuries, doctors said. One bullet penetrated his stomach, another hit him in the leg, and a third struck his arm.

"I never thought they would be daring enough to do something to my family," Irene Blanco confided to a news source. "For my own good, I have to decide whether to continue with this case. I have a daughter to take care of as well."

According to Blanco, the attack on her son occurred at 1:30 p.m., and by 3 p.m. Suly Ponce was before the media, explaining that the shooting was "due to a confrontation between narcotraffickers." "Not one agent went to the hospital to speak to my son," Blanco recalled. "And yet two hours after the shooting of my son, the DA is stating in a press conference that it was a settling of debt between narcos, and that furthermore, I was going to take advantage of the situation, because the incident favored Sharif.

"It is evident that the state law is broken here and this is the type of investigation that is carried out in Chihuahua."

Blanco ultimately chose to relocate to another part of Mexico, but she continued to represent Sharif from her new environs.

In his one-on-one interview with Univision, Sharif had suggested that someone with power was behind the murders and was being protected by a person or persons in a position of authority. He insisted that at least one high-ranking police officer was involved, as well as two powerful drug lords and perhaps one or more businessmen from El Paso who commuted daily into Juárez. When asked if he could reveal the names of those individuals, Sharif vowed he would go public when he gained his freedom. Apparently, he was too afraid of repercussions.

While he was a two-time convicted sex offender, Sharif's

claims were not without merit. In 1998, the Mexican Commission for the Defense and Promotion of Human Rights (CMDPDH), an independent human rights group based in Cuauhtémoc, reviewed the state police files and published a scathing report criticizing irregularities in the homicide investigation.

They found that some of the files lacked photographs of corpses or DNA tests to help in identification; others were mistaken as to where a body was found. In a number of cases, they reported, victims had even been misidentified.

One state official with firsthand knowledge of Sharif's case revealed that the Egyptian's repeated requests to review the DNA evidence in the case of Elizabeth Castro were denied by state officials, even as they prepared for trial in the homicide case. In addition, no family member was ever shown Castro's body for identification purposes. The parents simply accepted the police's word that the body was, in fact, that of their daughter. "There is a mother out there who will never know what happened to her child," Oscar Maynez said of Castro's case.

When questioned, state officials could not explain why police had almost immediately transported Castro's body to a state facility in Veracruz, some two hundred miles from Juárez, where it was inaccessible to family members. They also couldn't explain why the results of the autopsy performed on the body had described a woman whose height, physical characteristics, and clothing did not match Castro's. They were also at a loss as to why the body was in a state of decomposition consistent with someone who had been dead for at least a month or more. Castro had been missing only four days when the body authorities were claiming to be hers was found.

Nevertheless, Ponce stood by on March 29, 1999, as a Mexican judge found Sharif Sharif guilty of Castro's murder and sentenced him to thirty years in prison for the crime.

It is not clear who ordered that Sharif Sharif be transferred that same day from his jail cell at El Cereso to the state penitentiary in Chihuahua City, where he was placed in solitary confinement, no longer free to walk the facility or speak to reporters, although news accounts reported that state police were behind the command. While tighter security was the official reason given, there very well might have been another reason for the quick transfer. Perhaps the chemist was receiving too much publicity outside Mexico and officials were anxious to silence him. Once sentenced, Sharif was not even allowed to see his defense attorney. Irene Blanco was instructed she would have to wait nine months before visiting her client.

Interestingly, Sharif's transfer came soon after his one-on-one interview with Univision aired on March 3, 1999 in the United States, Mexico, Central America, and several Latin American countries.

During the interview, he pointed out that several of the bodies had been found near the Pemex installation, the Mexican petroleum company, and alluded to the possibility that one of the murderers could be an American businessman employed there who was crossing into Juárez each day from his home in El Paso. Sharif insisted that during his own investigation into the murders, he claimed to have identified a handful of victims whose bodies had turned up on properties owned by Pemex or vacant lots nearby. He also suggested that members of the Mexican police could be involved in the murders, either as willing participants or as paid protectors of the culprit or culprits.

According to news accounts, at least one of the homicides was linked to a member of the municipal police.

Perhaps government officials wanted to stop the Egyptian from raising questions about its ongoing investigation. Or perhaps it was because he was the linchpin of their case, the alleged architect of the killings, and officials needed the public to believe in his guilt.

While at El Cereso, Sharif had been afforded the use of a fax machine, a cell phone, and a computer. He had also earned the right to carry a key to his jail cell. The warden at the maximum-security jail, Abelardo González, rewarded good behavior with privileges such as keys that allowed inmates to protect their personal belongings while they were not in their cells.

During his incarceration at El Cereso, Sharif had talked with the prison warden of his border crossings while living in Midland, Texas. "He drove across from El Paso to come here to have a good time, yes. He himself has admitted it, that he's kind of a bohemian type, without any ties, who just wants to have a good time.

"He would then have encounters with some of the young women and everyone knows he likes the young women, *las jovencitas.*" The warden smiled. "So that was enough for him to be accused of the murder of one of them."

Suly Ponce offered her perspective on the case during an in-depth interview conducted in February 1999, just four months after she assumed the role of the director of the special task force in charge of women's homicides.

While some had speculated that the victims were held for days, Ponce said that she believed that in the cases of the sexually motivated homicides, the murders typically took place on the same day as the abductions or one or two days later.

"Everything indicates that it happens in rapid succession, the kidnapping and rape and murder," she said. "The killers probably take them [the victims] to an abandoned place which they have designated, and there they rape them and ultimately kill them."

Ponce claimed that what disturbed her most about the murders was the lack of professionalism on the part of the police and other members of the previous administration in the way in which they handled the families of the victims.

"The government authorities would say that many of the victims worked in local nightspots, and so it followed that something bad would happen to them," Ponce explained. "The families didn't accept this, that a woman is destined to die a violent death just because she works in a nightclub."

Authorities were now working to develop that sense of trust, although Ponce admitted that her team of investigators was no closer to solving many of the homicides. Her reason was both startling and troublesome. According to Ponce, the investigations had stalled because relatives of the victims were uncooperative. Fearing that a thorough interrogation might expose their daughters' private lives, they had withheld information that could be crucial to solving the case, she said.

Ponce confidently went on to suggest her office was on top

of the investigation. Her demeanor changed, however, when she was confronted with a videotape shot the previous day by a member of the Univision crew in which law enforcement personnel could be seen walking through an active crime scene and potentially destroying evidence. The tape also showed that investigators had left behind possible evidence, including a bloody blanket. Ponce seemed taken aback by the video and made it clear that she intended to improve the quality of the department. Though she'd only been in office for four months, she assured the news crew that she'd already started to implement changes, including several new security measures to deter the perpetrators. Among them was the posting of police units around the maquiladoras during hours when the women were changing shifts and the recruiting of taxi drivers to take female workers home, especially the very young ones who were most at risk.

In addition, Ponce said she had urged the women of Juárez to avoid putting themselves at risk. She recommended they not walk alone through abandoned, desolate places. If they had to, they should find a way of not going by themselves. She also warned that hitching a ride with a stranger could result in a possible rape or worse, and advised that young working women take a bus or a taxi whenever possible.

If the bus failed to show up, Ponce insisted the women wait for someone they knew who could drive them, or even call a patrol car.

Unfortunately, her advice seemed out of touch with the reality of being a poor, uneducated woman in Juárez, living on three to five dollars a day. Indeed, the wages were so low in the factories of Juárez that maquiladora workers had to be careful how they spent every dollar. Taking a bus or taxi home from work at night might mean the difference between eating and going hungry. Most of the women couldn't afford to carry a cell phone. And even if they could afford a phone, it was not likely to work in the shantytowns and desert areas outside the city.

The women of Juárez also didn't trust the city's taxi drivers and municipal police officers. There had been much speculation that some members of the Juárez police department were involved in the crimes.

In fact, one young mother claimed to have been gang-raped by members of the municipal police force while in their custody in early February of 1999. Her story had already circulated around the colonias where many of the victims lived, casting even more mistrust among the population. Many were asking themselves who was more dangerous, a taxi driver, a bus driver, a police officer, or a total stranger?

Judging by the rising number of murders and lack of response by the authorities, the answer appeared simple: no one could be trusted in Ciudad Juárez.

CHAPTER SIX

One and the Same

In this city, it is a disgrace to be a woman and
much greater of a disgrace to be a poor woman.

ESTHER CHÁVEZ CANO,
WOMEN'S ACTIVIST AND FOUNDER, CASA AMIGA

ONE OF THE MOST DISTURBING and highly publicized stories to
come out against the police was from María de Jesús Talamantes, who claimed to have been gang-raped by members of
the local police department while in their custody in early February of 1999. A medical examination subsequently confirmed
that María had indeed been raped, and guards were arrested,
but a judge threw out the charges because of a lack of evidence
against the men.

Talamantes, a pretty young woman with wavy long hair
styled with bangs, lived on the outskirts of the city in a small
brick house. The trouble began when a neighbor struck her
son and quickly escalated into a brawl in which her husband
was beaten and the police were called.

In an interview with María not long after the alleged attack, she told members of Univision of the events that had landed her in the city jail earlier that month. The Talamantes family lived on a dusty two-lane road that dead-ended at the family's residence. The brick house was sturdier than many of the homes in Ciudad Juárez; both María and her husband, Pedro, were employed and contributing to the household finances. As the news crew filed into the small living room to set up for the interview that day, one of the cameramen observed a marked patrol car hidden in some brush just outside the house. Who were the officers watching and why?

While the following account is hearsay, portions of María's story have been substantiated by a medical examination. María claimed that, angered over learning that her neighbor had hit her son, she had marched to the man's home to confront him. But the neighbor was with several other men who were intoxicated and began to insult her. The young mother raced home to get help from her husband, and together, they returned to the neighbor's home. It was then that the group attacked Pedro Talamantes and began to brutally beat him, María said. Horrified, she asked her son to call the police.

But when the officers arrived, they informed the group that they were all going to be detained. Talamantes claimed that her husband was so badly hurt that officers had to pick him up off the ground and carry him to the police car. They were taken to the nearby Cárcel de Piedra, "the brick jail," where they were given a perfunctory hearing before a judge. No one was allowed to speak. María and Pedro were then sent to a doctor at the facility, where her husband received treatment for his injuries and she was examined.

María claimed she was then taken into a bathroom by a female guard who said she wanted to check her for drug use. After ordering her to get undressed, the guard allegedly began sexually abusing her—kissing her, caressing her breasts, and fingering her vagina. When María objected, the guard angrily slapped her across the face, ordered her to put her clothes back on, and struck her again, this time in the stomach.

Talamantes said she and the guard then left the bathroom. When she approached a uniformed male police officer to tell him of the physical and sexual abuse, he made no effort to help but instead threw her in a jail cell along with other women, some of whom were trembling and vomiting.

María said she watched quietly as some of the women asked the guards for drugs, which were promptly provided. The young mother said she innocently took some too, after the guards told her the pills would help her sleep in the crowded and uncomfortable jail cell as they reviewed her case.

Hours passed as María lay in the cell, half sleeping and half awake. She listened as the guards made suggestive comments to the women around her. At some point, they entered the cell and moved her to another lockup in a less visible area of the jail by the kitchen. She claimed that the space was littered with women's garments—panties, bras, and dozens of articles of clothing.

When she asked what was going on, one of the guards grinned at her and announced, "You're going to give it to us!" The guard was no more than thirty years old, with sunken cheeks and leathered skin.

The officer's cold stare did not soften even as María began

to cry. She recalled that it was then that she began to realize the magnitude of her situation.

She claimed the officer next said something that shocked her. "You want us to take you to Lomas de Poleo?" were his words. He was referring to the uninhabited stretch of desert northwest of the city where many of the murdered women's bodies had been found.

María said she tried to appear tough, ordering the officers to leave her alone. She watched as one of them left the cell and returned a short while later holding a briefcase with a photo album inside.

Talamantes alleged that the album contained photos of "little girls" being raped and beaten. Other images showed the victims "when they bit their nipples off; when they burnt them." As the guards glared at her, she leafed through the pages. She said there were images depicting men dragging various young women through the bushes by their hair. In one, a girl was laid on the ground, encircled by a group of the men. Other pictures showed the same girl being raped time and again as others looked on and jeered.

It was clear from the photos that the girl was screaming and crying, María recalled. Other photos showed several other young women being raped, both anally and vaginally, she said.

"In the photos, the men were laughing—laughing at what they were doing," she recounted. In others, a man was seen dousing a young woman with gasoline, and then lighting her on fire.

"I cried and prayed to myself," María later remembered.

"And as if reading my thoughts, the guards said, 'Think of them. You've seen it all, and you can't stay alive.' "

María said that when she announced that her husband was also being detained at the jail and would alert authorities if something were to happen to her, one of the officers grabbed a camera and snapped her photo from several angles, threatening to "kill" her and her husband if she told anyone about their late-night exchange. They now had her image on film and could find her anywhere, they warned.

María admitted she could not fall asleep that night, worrying about her situation and thinking about the horrific photographs of the young victims. In the morning, there was a change of guards. Though she still had no idea what charges had been brought against her, the guards declared that she had finished her sentence. Hopeful that she would now be going home, María was then moved to another cell; she was the only one in the dank space.

When Talamantes asked one of the guards why she was still being detained, the guard in the blue uniform grinned. She said he traced her shapely form in the air with his hands and said, "Because I like you."

María trembled. Just wanting to sleep, she retreated to the corner of the cell, where she lay down on the floor in a ball and dropped off to sleep. The officer in the blue uniform woke her with a kick in the face, she remembered. She said he ordered her to get up, and as she rose, he began pulling at her clothes and kissing her.

María claimed her husband could hear the commotion

from his nearby cell and called to her. But there was nothing he could do to stop the violence. María recalled that when Pedro implored the guard to leave her alone, he answered with a stunning remark.

"I'm not a guard, I'm a police officer" is what María claimed the attacker yelled back. The Juárez municipal police department was housed in the same building as the jail, so it was entirely possible that the man was, in fact, a police officer.

María recalled that the officer raped her that day. Within minutes, two more guards appeared in her cubicle. They too raped her.

Before leaving, the men vowed to "kill her entire family" if she spoke up, she said.

Later, the terrified young mother was released from the jail and reunited with her husband. For two days, she dodged his repeated questions about what had happened to her during her forty-eight hours behind bars. At first she told him that the guards had only questioned her. But Pedro, suspecting that something was wrong, continued to probe. He had noticed that his wife seemed to be walking oddly, as if she had been in-jured, and he asked her about it repeatedly.

Time and again, María said, she declined to answer his questions and was even fearful of his caresses. She said she fi-nally blurted out her secret, as the two of them were getting ready for bed, several days after their release. Furious, Pedro vowed to press charges against the police. Initially, she begged him not to pursue the matter, fearing for the safety of them-selves and their two young children. But Pedro wanted justice, and he implored her to think of the other women who could fall victim to these officers.

The next morning, Pedro went directly to the Department of Internal Affairs to file a report. The officials there insisted that María be present to tell her story, but she didn't want to comply. She said she was too afraid to speak, remembering the threats from the officers who had snapped her photo.

In the days that followed, María began having nightmares, waking up with a start after seeing the faces of her assailants in her dreams. Even her husband's gentle touch triggered memories of the rape.

Upset over his wife's condition, Pedro returned to the Department of Internal Affairs. Again, he was told that María would have to join him, as she was the one who needed to make the statement to authorities. When he returned home, his wife and children were not there. María had taken their sons for a walk to try to clear her head. It was an inferno outside in the sweltering heat, but inside the house the temperature had grown unbearable.

As Talamantes walked the streets with seemingly no destination, she happened upon a friend. The woman immediately noticed María's frenzied state and invited her and the boys into her home for a snack. The kind invitation set María at ease, and suddenly she felt a need to share her painful story. Her neighbor listened intently and then urged María to follow her husband's advice.

That night, María promised Pedro that she would tell her story to the DA. His argument now made sense: she needed to file a report and stop these horrible men before they hurt other women.

This time, a lawyer from Internal Affairs and a psychologist were waiting for María and her husband when they arrived at the generic-looking glass and cement headquarters of the state district attorney. María was first asked to sit in the lawyer's office and make a statement, detailing what had happened to her during her incarceration. The meeting proved difficult for her, and the interview stopped each time a uniformed officer entered the room. At one point, she became so upset that she jumped under the attorney's desk and curled up in a fetal position.

Over the hours, she did manage to provide authorities with an accounting of her ordeal. Still, she didn't dare mention the grisly photographs she had been shown.

Part of filing an official complaint was the identification process. During María's visit to the office, she was asked to pick out the people who had allegedly assaulted her. The officers were lined up behind a thick glass window, and María said she immediately spotted one of her assailants.

As she pointed him out, her husband let out an audible sigh, flying into a rage. For a moment, it appeared he was going to break through the glass window and grab the man, María recalled.

María said she was also asked to undergo a medical examination. The exam determined that she had, indeed, been raped. One of her assailants had also allegedly given her a vaginal infection.

The police officers vehemently denied María's story.

The attorney representing the Internal Affairs division told María that he would open a file on her case but cited discrepancies in the times that she alleged to have been assaulted. Officials claimed too that she had contracted the infection before she came to the jail.

Fifteen days passed, and only one of her four assailants was under investigation. No semen or DNA samples were collected from any of the accused men—or the female guard that María had named—something that almost certainly would have happened if such an incident had taken place in the United States. Yet blood work and other tests were performed on María. The defendants were also permitted to continue to work at the jail while the investigation was under way.

In a bold and potentially dangerous move, María told the local press of her plight, bravely appearing in front of television cameras that spring with her husband by her side. Her story grabbed headlines and was the subject of nightly news programs. In response, the four guards were arrested and paraded before the TV news cameras.

For a while, María had hopes that the men who had allegedly raped her would be brought to justice. But it was not to be.

Special Prosecutor Suly Ponce later told Univision that her office had done what it could to ensure a positive outcome. She and members of her staff believed that María was telling the truth, but their hands were tied once the case went to court.

"We put pressure on the judge," Ponce said. "The arrest warrant was issued and was acted upon at once. Unfortunately, that was all we could do to help detain those responsible for the crime."

In the end, a Mexican judge dismissed the charges, citing "lack of evidence," and the officers were set free. Three of them returned to their jobs at the city's jail.

Meanwhile, María and her family received numerous threats. Upon their return home, the Talamanteses recalled, marked patrol cars began cruising through their neighborhood, with officers stopping at various homes, banging on doors and asking questions about María. At night, members of the police department parked their cruisers nearby and shone their headlights at the Talamantes house, she said.

At one point, María's husband traveled to Los Angeles, leaving María and her children home alone in Juárez. That night, María observed a black Lincoln Mercury Marquis with tinted windows pull up outside her house. As the children slept, she said, she watched as someone got out of the car, raised a gun in the air, and fired two shots into the night sky. She thought briefly of calling the police but quickly rejected the idea. To her mind, her tormentors and the police were "one and the same."

According to María, the man was dressed all in black—the same description that was provided for the "cowboy" seen waiting next to Silvia Morales at the Juárez bus stop several years earlier.

Not long after her ordeal, María Talamantes found employment on the assembly line of a local maquiladora. On her first day, she went to lunch at the cafeteria in the factory complex.

As she sat eating, she felt as if someone was watching her. Turning around, she recognized one of the officers from the jail standing behind her. He was the same skinny man who had shown her the photo album in the cell near the jail's kitchen. Frightened, she inquired about him the following day and learned from fellow employees that he had come to the factory seeking work as a security guard.

María had never made public her knowledge of the jailhouse photo album, the one depicting the young women being beaten, raped, and set ablaze. She said she was simply too scared.

In time, she confided in a local activist named Judith Galarza, head of the Venezuela-based Latin American Federation of Associations for Relatives of the Detained-Disappeared (FEDEFAM). Galarza urged her to take her story to Mexican officials in Mexico City, commonly referred to as *el DF*, el Distrito Federal. The activist was fighting for justice for the murdered women of Juárez and was anxious to expose what she believed to be a lack of professionalism on the part of Mexican authorities.

"We have not heard testimony about similar incidents in other places," Galarza said in an interview with a newspaper reporter. "The cases in Juárez are exclusive to the region, which borders the United States and whose main population is made up of campesinos and indigenous people who come from the south. A great number of them are going to work in the maquiladora industry."

María agreed to join Galarza in Mexico City, and there she told her story again, but this time to a much larger audience and one she thought would carry more political clout. She hoped her efforts would bring about justice for the girls she had viewed in the photos.

María later admitted that she had mentioned the photos she had seen to government officials, who had flatly discouraged her from coming forward.

"I was afraid," María recalled in an interview with award-winning documentarian Lourdes Portillo. "Even the *licenciada* [district attorney] said not to say anything!

"I was told, 'We interviewed those cops, and the psychologists interviewed them, and they're dangerous, *están locos!* You should be very afraid.' "

Two years later, in mid-2001, Talamantes was again thrust into the limelight when a television crew tracked her down in Juárez after being asked not to by activist Esther Chávez. María was already struggling to earn enough money to feed her five children after her husband left her, forcing her to fend on her own with the kids.

Esther was worried that any additional emotional demands would throw the woman into a tailspin. She had already come to Chávez seeking help. Like many rape survivors, María was refusing counseling. Still, the crew showed up at María's doorstep insisting she grant them a taped interview on camera about her allegations of gang rape by police, which she did.

The story soon aired. Afterwards, police went to María's house, threw her up against a wall, and severely beat her, according to Chávez. The activist was in Spain on holiday when the incident occurred. Chávez first heard of the alleged attack when a staff member of her recently founded rape crisis center,

Casa Amiga, phoned her overseas to say that María de Jesús Talamantes had shown up at the shelter, battered and hysterical. It took more than four hours for the staffers to calm her down, and still she was refusing to speak with a therapist.

Even today, María continues to struggle to keep her family together and contain her anger at authorities for failing to properly punish her alleged rapists.

To compound matters, María felt ashamed over what her children were thinking. Her elder children had begun raising questions about the ordeal, explaining that classmates were saying ugly things about their mother. Not only had the attacks taken their toll emotionally and most certainly had driven her husband, Pedro, away, now they were negatively impacting her children as well.

There are some in the border city who have raised doubts over María's claims of rape and the existence of the grisly photo album she contended the jailers had shown her. In light of all that happened to her, there are also questions as to why she chose to remain in Juárez after all that she endured. But those who raise those questions do not understand the difficult conditions under which the people of Mexico live. Even if María wanted to leave Juárez, where would she go? She was a single mother caring for five children. Much of the country's economy was now in Juárez, as industry in other parts of Mexico had all but dried up. Many of the country's villages and towns were abandoned, with families traveling north in search of work.

Juárez was home, and the only place María's children had ever known.

There, at least, the family had a house, albeit a small one.

CHAPTER SEVEN

Whoever Fights Monsters

Whoever fights monsters should see to it that in the process he does not become a monster.

FRIEDRICH NIETZSCHE, GERMAN PHILOSOPHER

ON MARCH 8, 1999, four profilers from the Federal Bureau of Investigation's Behavorial Analysis Unit in Quantico, Virginia, arrived in Ciudad Juárez. The invitation had come after months of discussion between Chihuahua state officials and authorities from the El Paso bureau of the FBI. News reports indicated that then Mexican president Ernesto Zedillo had initiated the visit by first contacting U.S. president Bill Clinton to request the agents in the ongoing homicide investigation.

Outfitted in a brightly colored suit, her carroty red hair neatly styled, Ponce had stepped before the microphones that March to answer questions about the agents' impending arrival. The prosecutor explained that the team would provide investigatory training to members of the Chihuahua state police force and help to create a psychological profile for the serial killers or criminals who might be behind the murders.

During the press conference, Ponce blamed the previous administration for its negligence and mishandling of the investigation and maintained that she and her staff would receive much-needed assistance from the FBI agents in organizing and updating their files.

"It is now possible to do this right," she told the media that day. "To make any more mistakes would be unjust to the families of the victims and society in general."

The city's residents were optimistic. "We wholeheartedly welcome the FBI's help," said local activist Vicky Caraveo Vallina, a lawyer who was also director of Mujeres Por Juárez, or Women for Juárez, an advocacy group she had recently founded to raise public awareness about the murders. "Maybe they will prove what we've been saying all along, the authorities are doing an unsatisfactory job."

Caraveo, who was also the wife of a wealthy local businessman, was outraged over the ongoing killings of the city's poorest young women and had started the nongovernmental group to raise public awareness about the crimes. Attractive and educated, and a member of the city's elite, Caraveo seemed an unlikely advocate to take up the fight for the impoverished victims. Vicky's grandfather was a former official for the state of Chihuahua, and the family had made a name for itself in the banking industry in Mexico.

Young Guillermina González's grassroots organization, Voices Without Echo, was also putting itself on the map. Since members did not have any money to rent a space, the only way to contact them was by calling Guillermina's cell phone. She and her small group of volunteers had been painting bold black crosses against a pink backdrop on the city's utility poles to call attention to the murders. Soon poles in nearly every community bore the sobering symbol. In addition, billboards and posters affixed to the city's public buses preached the words "Be Careful, Watch for Your Life."

Caraveo, González, and other local women were being credited with bringing the injustices perpetrated against the city's women to the forefront. Some felt that if it weren't for them, many of the murders would have simply been swept under the rug by authorities anxious to close cases—either because of incompetence or more sinister motives. There was continuing wide speculation that members of the police department were involved in the killings, or were covering up for those responsible.

Remarkably, since January 1999, at least five more women had been murdered in the border city; some news agencies were putting the number as high as ten. Ponce insisted that only one of the murders was sexually motivated. But a review of the files revealed that at least two showed no apparent motive beyond psychosexual rage.

The most disturbing of the crimes was the brutal murder of a twelve-year-old maquila worker named Irma Angélica Rosales Lozano. (Sixteen is the legal age for girls to begin working at the maquiladoras in Mexico.) While local news outlets reported her age as thirteen, she was actually five months shy of her thirteenth birthday when her body was discovered on February 16, in a vacant lot on the southwest side of the city. She had been raped, vaginally and anally, and suffocated with a plastic grocery bag.

An investigation revealed that the killing had occurred in broad daylight, just hours after Angélica's shift ended at the Electrocomponentes de México, a nearby maquiladora where she had worked her usual nine and a half hours on the assembly line testing color-coded wires for new refrigerators.

Earlier that month, Irma had traveled twelve hours by bus from the parched farmlands of Durango; she was staying in Juárez with her older brother Miguel Angel García and his young wife. Her parents were both ill. They had used their savings to buy their only daughter a false ID so that she could find work and send money home to their tiny village, where young girls did not stray far from their mother's watch.

In Juárez, a fake birth certificate usually costs about twenty dollars, the price Miguel García paid a local forger for Irma's ID. It was all that was required to obtain work in one of the now nearly seven hundred maquiladoras. Even with the tens of thousands of workers arriving each year, assembly-line jobs were plentiful, with some factories employing two thousand workers per shift. Banners advertising jobs hung from the modern industrial complexes, boasting amenities including air-conditioning, showers, changing areas, and a cafeteria that served free meals to its staffers.

Suly Ponce had been in office for a little more than three months when Irma's tiny, violated corpse was found tossed in a ditch that February. Like that of Sagrario González, her death had followed an event at work that had resulted in the young girl being forced to commute alone.

Ironically, Irma and her sister-in-law, Yadira, had interviewed at two other factories before finding a workplace that had openings for both of them on the same shift. Electrocomponentes de México had previously been owned by General Electric but had been sold to the International Wire Group of Saint Louis, Missouri. The Juárez-based assembly plant was enormous and employed nearly 2,000 workers.

Like many of the young girls employed at the factories, Irma was a talker. Some of the workers in her group or "cell" complained when she didn't return from lunch on time; too busy chatting, she was hurting their chances of winning the special monetary bonus given to those who were most productive. Speed was rewarded at the International Wire Group. The women in Irma's cell knew they would never make their quotas, given the rambunctious girl's endless socializing.

Irma received a warning that first week from her supervisor. She was talking too much and would be moved to a different area of the 200,000-square-foot factory when she returned to work after the weekend, in hopes that she would perform better. Clutching the twenty-one dollars she had earned that first week, Irma and her sister-in-law excitedly headed to downtown Juárez that Friday afternoon for some shopping.

Wanting to look stylish and grown-up, Irma bought her first pair of high-heel shoes and a dress with a floral print. She would wear the new shoes to work that Monday, and in spite of the blisters she got during the nine-hour shift, she vowed to wear them again on Friday when she joined the other girls for a night of dancing downtown.

On Tuesday, February 16, Irma's supervisor confronted her about her performance in the new position. Published reports claimed the young girl had disappeared for a portion of her shift that Monday and was questioned the following day and ultimately fired for leaving her post.

It would be the first time that Irma would travel home by herself. Irma's home, in the neighborhood of Colonia México 68, was just on the other side of a scrolling fence that separated the manicured industrial park from the rows of crude houses of cardboard and tin that made up the expansive squatters' community, named for the anarchistic protests of 1968 in which members of the Mexican Army in Mexico City killed scores of demonstrating students.

Her sister-in-law Yadira could not leave her post. She simply called after the child to be careful on her way home. Irma should look for the number 5 or number 7 bus; either would take her close to their house, a cement hovel they shared with several people and that cost about fifty-five dollars a month to rent. More than three thousand people inhabited their impoverished village.

When Yadira arrived home that evening, she was shocked to learn that Irma was not there. She and Miguel raced back to the factory to search for the girl, then to the local jail, the hospitals, and even the police station. It was nearing 9 p.m. when a news report on television related the grim news that another murdered girl had been found.

Miguel was trembling when he dialed the local precinct to find out if the dead girl was Irma.

"Yes, we have a little girl here," the female dispatcher told him, referring to a young girl who was alive but jailed. She went on to describe the girl's clothing. The description fit what Irma was wearing, right down to her white tennis shoes. The operator claimed the child had been picked up for stealing and was incarcerated on the charges.

Miguel said he would be right down to collect his sister. Hanging up the receiver, he breathed a sigh of relief. At least she was alive, he thought.

A uniformed official greeted Miguel when he arrived at the office of Suly Ponce later that Tuesday evening. But the news he was given was not at all what he expected. There was no young girl being held for stealing, just the body of a young girl who had been raped, murdered, and then dumped in a ditch.

It was Irma, his baby sister, lying in the morgue that night.

Irma Angélica Rosales Lozano's death came on the heels of several other murders of young women, including that of thirteen-year-old Celia Guadalupe Gómez, a technical student who was raped, strangled, and left to die in a vacant lot, where her body was found two months earlier on December 10, 1998. Then in January 1999, the body of a second young girl, who has yet to be identified, was found tossed in an abandoned field. She too had been raped and strangled.

It was on the heels of these murders that the FBI agents would be touching down in Juárez.

There was no showy display to hail their arrival on March 8, International Women's Day, and it is not clear if their visit was orchestrated to coincide with the important date. In fact, there was no public announcement to mark their arrival; authorities wanted to keep the team's visit quiet and allow the men to conduct their investigation under a veil of anonymity, although a written report of their findings would later be presented to authorities. Though it was routine for members of the bureau to assist Canadian investigators with domestic criminal matters, this was the first time U.S. agents had been invited to Mexico to aid in that country's internal affairs.

During their five-day visit to Juárez, the FBI agents toured the crime scenes and reviewed photos and evidence of seventy-eight of the city's homicides. With few answers and mounting pressure to solve the cases, the residents were left to speculate about potential motives for the crimes. A serial killer on the loose, organ traffickers harvesting body parts to sell on the black market, women being abducted to be used as satanic sacrifices or sold into prostitution were among the rumors running rampant.

In fact, there had been several news accounts pointing to the possibility that the murders were part of a satanic ritual being carried out by members of a local religious sect or gang. One story that appeared in *Texas Monthly* detailed how one group of amateur searchers out scouring the desert in 1996 for possible victims had stumbled upon a wooden hut. Members of the search team claimed that inside were red and white candles, several pairs of women's undergarments, and fingerprints in fresh blood. They also described a number of disturbing images that had been sketched on a long wooden board. There was a drawing of a scorpion, the symbol of Juárez's drug cartel, and one of three naked women with flowing dark hair being watched by a fourth who wore a mournful expression. In that same drawing was a handful of soldiers gathered around what appeared to be a marijuana plant. Fingernails in the form of swords were scrawled across the top of the picture.

The group described another drawing that depicted naked women with their legs spread-eagle surrounded by nails in the shape of sledgehammers, and a male figure who appeared to be a member of a gang at the center of the image.

The profilers were in town to make an assessment and help calm growing anxieties. Oddly, their findings conflicted with those of former FBI profiler Robert Ressler, who was then considered to be America's foremost expert on serial murder. While Ressler believed that the murders were the work of two or three serial killers operating in Juárez, the FBI agents concluded that the crimes were most likely not linked.

"The team determined that the majority of the cases were single homicides," according to a statement released by the FBI field office in El Paso that summer. "It's too premature and irresponsible to state that a serial killer is on the loose in Juárez."

The agents concluded that in the seventy-eight cases they reviewed, there was more than one killer roaming the city. In fact, the team suggested that the only real serial murders to have occurred in the city were perpetrated by Sharif Sharif.

Yet Sharif had been charged and convicted of just one of the city's homicides, the murder of seventeen-year-old maquila worker Elizabeth Castro, which hardly qualified him as a serial killer. In 1999, a Chihuahua state judge cleared Sharif of all the charges connected to the Los Rebeldes gang. In fact, just three days before the team arrived in the city, that same judge had convicted the Egyptian on the single murder count and sentenced him to thirty years in prison. While the case against Sharif was based solely on circumstantial evidence, the judge who presided over the trial had been presented with a forty-page legal report outlining the accused's alleged murder plot, and his ties to the street gang supposedly led by Sergio Armendáriz.

Armendáriz and five other members of the Los Rebeldes street gang had been in jail for three years when the profilers arrived in Juárez. The men were each facing seventeen counts of murder. Yet there had been little movement in their cases and little mention of their involvement in the murders in the agents' subsequent report.

Frank Evans, the FBI special agent who had coordinated the team's visit to Juárez, told a Texas newspaper after his retirement in 2002 that Chihuahua state investigators had dismissed his team's findings "as not fitting with the established theory of the case."

In other words, the FBI's conclusions, based on two visits to the city and a review of the state police files, differed from the official theory that Sharif Sharif had committed the original killings and once in jail had orchestrated a string of copycat murders to make it appear that the true killer was still at large. "Sharif is a psychopath who should be locked up for life," Suly Ponce told a radio talk show host during an on-air interview. "His Egyptian culture contributed to his aggressive conduct against women."

Less than two weeks after the FBI agents left town, a fourteen-year-old factory worker named Nancy (whose last name is being withheld because of her age and the nature of the crime), was brutally raped, strangled, and left for dead in a remote desert area of Ciudad Juárez. The vicious assault occurred in the early morning hours of March 18, 1999. By then, an estimated 172 women had been murdered in Juárez.

Miraculously, Nancy, a reed-thin girl with dark eyes and a complexion blemished by teenage acne, had survived her ordeal and provided details of the attack to police.

The young worker told authorities that when her shift ended at 1 a.m., she immediately walked to the curb outside Motores Eléctricos, the maquiladora at which she was employed, to wait for the factory-sponsored shuttle bus toward her home in one of the garbage-strewn slums that rimmed the city. She had been assembling parts for the Milwaukee-based A. O. Smith, a manufacturer of glass-lined water heaters, for less than three weeks when the attack occurred. She'd started work on March 1.

The low-paying assembly-line job was the only position she could find. Nancy was under the legal age of sixteen and had no more than a sixth-grade education. Her exposure to city living had stirred dreams of a better life, one with fine clothes and a closet of her own to keep them in. Her mother was sympathetic but unable to help. She told her youngest daughter that if she wanted to add new fashions to her wardrobe of well-worn hand-me-downs, she'd have to earn the money to buy them.

Nancy's family was dirt poor and she had six siblings. They lived in a rickety lean-to, no larger than an outdoor shed, in a colonia of shacks beside some railroad tracks. Children played amid the skeletal remains of dead dogs and other animals and the human waste that washed from the hills each time it rained.

Nancy's neighbors pilfered electricity by threading electrical cords together until they reached a power source.

Aware that the export factories required their employees to be at least sixteen, Nancy told police that she had lied about her age on her job application, using falsified documents like so many of the young maquiladora workers did.

The Mexican government, like many third world economies, adhered to a strict policy of suppressing wages in order to draw foreign investment. What was unique to Juárez was the contrast between work life and home life for many of the assembly-line workers. Maquila workers like Nancy and young Irma Rosales were working in twenty-first-century conditions, enjoying central air-conditioning, state-of-the-art machinery, and access to sparkling indoor showers, private changing areas, and complimentary hot and cold meals served in a modern cafeteria.

While the young girls were assembling sophisticated circuit boards in these contemporary plants, they were facing illnesses like cholera and tuberculosis at home. Many, including Nancy, were surviving in seventeenth-century conditions, confronting life without plumbing and electricity in cardboard and tar-paper hovels with no floors or foundations. Typically, the bathroom was literally a hole dug in the ground that was surrounded by odd pieces of wood topped by the base of a fifty-five-gallon drum, probably taken from the garbage of one of the local maquiladoras. In some cases, colorful Mexican blankets were used as privacy curtains for these primitive toilets and showers.

Nancy's was the last stop on the bus route. She told authorities that on March 18, she watched as other passengers got off and then rose in preparation for her stop. Suddenly she realized the bus was heading in the wrong direction. She began to worry as it rolled past towering power lines and thorny cacti, and into the desert beyond her neighborhood.

The bus driver explained that he was experiencing "mechanical problems" and was simply looking for a gas station. Then he broke into sinister laughter.

"Are you afraid?" he asked.

Nancy felt the bus rumble onto some rocky terrain and come to a halt in a remote section of Lote Bravo.

"Have you ever had sex?" the driver demanded, grabbing at her throat. The last thing she recalled were his thick hands tightening around her neck. When Nancy came to, she was lying on her stomach in the middle of the desert; it was pitch-black and she was bleeding all over. She was completely unfamiliar with her surroundings.

Nancy recalled little of the attack—only that the bus driver had threatened to kill her if she told anyone. Under the cover of darkness, she somehow crawled along the brush, in the direction of a small house illuminated by a dim porch light. There she found help from two local men who answered her knock.

They later reported that the young woman was lying on the ground outside their house horribly injured; she was bruised and beaten, partially naked, and missing one sneaker.

Nancy identified her assailant as the shuttle bus driver who had picked her up at the end of her shift. An investigation commenced with rapid results.

The driver, Jesús Manuel Guardado, also known as "El Tolteca," was already in trouble with the law. His pregnant young wife had recently filed charges of domestic abuse against him. She told police that during one of her husband's tirades, he'd boasted of killing several women and said he'd kept trophies, items of their clothing, as proof. One news account reported that Guardado's wife also told police her husband had come home on several nights clutching a bloodied kitchen knife, but she had not dared ask any questions.

When police arrested Guardado on March 29, 1999, in Durango, Mexico, he reportedly divulged the names of four other men—three of them bus drivers subcontracted by the city's factories—who, he said, had played a role in a number of the recent killings. The four were subsequently rounded up and charged with murdering seven women between June of 1998 and March of 1999.

Nancy's story provided Ponce, the special prosecutor, with yet another avenue of suspects. In a bizarre twist, Ponce tied the bus drivers to the jailed Sharif Sharif. She announced that the four men, who were being called "Los Toltecas" after Guardado's nickname, had confessed to taking money from Sharif Sharif in exchange for the murders.

"Sharif paid to have the murders committed," Ponce told members of the press. She claimed "el monstruo" had again masterminded an elaborate plot—this time involving an El Paso resident and convicted drug dealer named Víctor Moreno Rivera, who went by the nickname "El Narco." Moreno allegedly made the initial contact with Sharif while visiting a friend who was also incarcerated at the hilltop jail.

Silvia Elena dressed in a long white gown typical of the quinceañera dresses girls wear in Mexico and other Latin American countries to mark their fifteenth birthday.

Teresa Rodriguez (LEFT) and Ramona Morales (RIGHT)

Olga Alicia

Irma Pérez (Olga Alicia's mother) cooking at her burger stand. This is the job that sustains her.

Sharif being interviewed by Teresa Rodriguez in a conference room at the El Cereso jail. During the interview he insisted he was not guilty of murdering Elizabeth Castro.

Sergio Armendáriz, aka El Diablo, also being interviewed by the author at El Cereso jail. He too denied any involvement in the murders.

Oscar Maynez

Esther Chávez

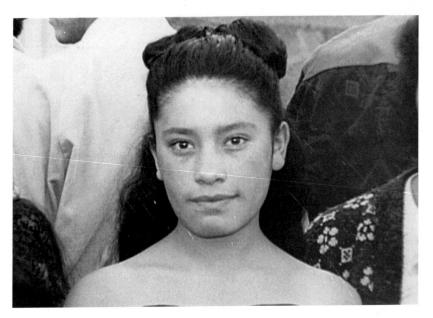

Sagrario González

Paula González kneels before her daughter Sagrario's tomb. Plastic flowers adorn the plot otherwise covered by dirt and rocks.

Sagrario González's neighborhood

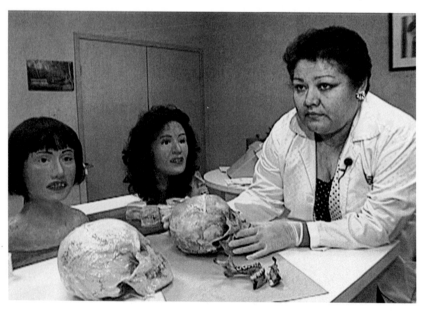

Dr. Irma Rodríguez displays how, from recovered remains, her office was able to re-create a face.

The Brick Jail

wooden cross stands
front of the offices
the Procuraduría as
eminder of the
ctims.

Gustavo González
Meza, aka La Foca,
one of the bus
drivers accused of
murdering eight
victims found at the
cotton field.

The cotton field where the bodies of eight victims were discovered in November 2001, which has since become a type of holy ground to the fallen women of Juárez.

From the Ciudad Juárez side of the Puente Internacional, Paso del Norte (one of the bridges connecting to El Paso), a cross symbolically reminds visitors that Juárez is a dangerous place where more than 400 women have met their death since 1993.

Sharif offered to pay him $1,200 a month if he agreed to kill four women every thirty days, according to Moreno's police statement. After some negotiation, Moreno said he agreed to take the money in exchange for two murders a month. He next enlisted the three shuttle bus drivers, Agustín Toribio Castillo, José Gaspar Ceballos Chávez, and Bernardo Hernández Fernández, to carry out the murders.

According to Ponce, there was just one hitch. In order to pay off, Sharif insisted on being shown a garment that had belonged the victim—preferably panties, along with a newspaper clipping detailing the crime. It was the Egyptian's way of ensuring that the murders had actually taken place.

"The Narco made the payments," the special DA explained to members of the press corps gathered outside her office that March. "But let's back up, let's start with Sharif, the intellectual author who paid them to commit these crimes. His contact was the Narco . . . and El Tolteca [Manuel Guardado], who received the money, and he divided it among his accomplices."

Critics were quick to point out the eerie similarities between Ponce's allegations against Los Rebeldes back in April of 1996 and these new charges being brought against Moreno and the four bus drivers.

"It's the same story invented about the Rebels," Sharif's poised and well-spoken criminal lawyer, Irene Blanco, told an American TV producer. "*¡Idéntico! ¡Idéntico!* [Identical! Identical!] He allegedly paid the Rebels one thousand pesos, and with the bus drivers it was twelve hundred dollars."

Not long after Los Toltecas were taken into custody, the

warden at El Cereso, Abelardo González, announced plans to resign from his position as director of the facility. The news was met with surprise. The prison warden was known for his dedication to his job and to the inmates at El Cereso.

Abelardo González believed it important to recognize the prisoners on an individual basis. Without prompting, he could recall their dates of incarceration and other, more intimate details. Mostly he prided himself on the rehabilitation programs he had implemented during his tenure.

González, who held a degree in social work, viewed his role at the "adult rehabilitation center" as one of educator and rehabilitator. To his credit, he had implemented several programs aimed at providing inmates with the skills to become productive members of society upon their release. Prison violence had actually dropped under his watch, and he proudly called attention to the fact that there had been no stabbings or violent deaths during his tenure, apparently a grand accomplishment considering the overcrowded conditions under which he had been asked to work.

Yet, in the days after the men's arrest, he was suddenly stepping down, reportedly to pursue other career avenues. In fact, one law enforcement official close to the investigation disclosed that González had been asked to falsify evidence in the case against the Toltecas. His refusal had prompted authorities to pressure him to resign from his post at the jail. Officials had reportedly called upon González to alter prison logs to reflect that members of the Toltecas had visited with Sharif Sharif at the jail. His refusal had cost him his job. But his integrity remained intact.

Like Oscar Maynez, the prison director would not participate in perjury.

The arrest of Los Toltecas provoked state officials to clamp
down on federal labor regulations, setting in motion a state-
involved investigation into underage employment at the city's
maquiladoras.

Routine state inspections of 500 businesses in Ciudad
Juárez in the spring of 1999 uncovered more than 550 illegal
workers. Companies in violation were given three months to
comply with the law or face hefty fines. In Mexico, minors can
work legally with special authorization that restricts the number of hours and shifts they can undertake. A labor registry was
also set up to ensure compliance.

In July of 1999, Motores Eléctricos agreed to pay 250,000
pesos, the equivalent of $25,000 U.S., in punitive damages to
Nancy resulting from the March 18 assault, according to a
report that appeared in *Frontera NorteSur,* a monthly online
report covering the borderlands of North Central Mexico.

The report also quoted former attorney general Arturo
González Rascón as saying that the state of Chihuahua had
added to the settlement, giving Nancy "land with municipal
services" so that she and her family could build a new house.
Rascón explained that the settlement was reached as a result of
the mediation of the local labor department, yet no details of
the actual settlement were released.

"This is a very responsible attitude on the part of both authorities and the maquiladora because we have always sought
to protect her [Nancy's] situation," Rascón told *Frontera
NorteSur.*

Meanwhile, Nancy's alleged attacker, Jesús Manuel Guardado, El Tolteca, remained in custody at the municipal prison, awaiting trial on charges stemming from the brutal assault. Guardado was claiming that he was held by police for nineteen days, during which time he was repeatedly tortured until he confessed to the rape and attempted murder of his teenage passenger.

Five days after the bus drivers were taken into custody, newspapers reported that the defendants told authorities of at least twenty more bodies they had buried in the desert.

Women's rights activist Esther Chávez demanded answers. "How in the world could they have hired such people to drive buses . . . with no background checks, with no controls?" Guardado had a criminal record, yet he had somehow managed to obtain a license to operate a bus—even though it was illegal to issue such a permit to persons with a criminal past.

Chávez was even more outraged to learn that Motores Eléctricos, the maquiladora that employed Nancy, was filing charges against Nancy—claiming that the young girl had "falsified documents" to gain employment.

"How horribly insensitive!" Chávez complained. "This girl lives in a shack with a dirt floor. She has six brothers and sisters to feed. She needs the work."

Since 1993, Esther Chávez had been leading the fight for justice for the city's women from a small office in the house she custom-built in the middle-class Juárez neighborhood of Colonia Nogales and she was still at the forefront. Hers was one of the first homes to be constructed on the quiet cul-desac, not far from the downtown and the bridges that linked Mexico to the United States.

It had taken Esther several years to build the white stucco house exactly as she had envisioned, with an open floor plan and multiple levels, and it was from her small home office that she had been advocating for change. While she was not a painter, Esther collected the works of painters and sculptors who shared her kinship with the women of the world; she displayed the artworks throughout the house, which she decorated in rustic Mexican style with brown terra-cotta tiles and area rugs.

Like all the houses in Juárez, Esther's home had security bars on its doors and windows. A stately palm tree provided shade for the no-frills Chevy Cavalier she parked in the driveway inside the chain-link fence that surrounded the residence.

She was always on call, ready to run on a moment's notice to help a woman in need. Esther thought nothing of jumping in her car late at night to rescue a desperate victim, or clearing her calendar so that she could accompany a child to police headquarters to report an incident of incest.

A mosaic-tile plaque next to the front door welcomed visitors: "My house is your house." The sentiment could not have been truer. While the house was not particularly large, it was inviting, with shiny wood floors and lofty ceilings. Esther spent most of her days in the converted bedroom on the first floor that served as her office. The room was just big enough to fit a computer desk and a small love seat.

For five years, Esther had devoted herself to the murdered women of Juárez, first on her own, and then as part of a coalition of women's groups lobbying on behalf of the victims and their families. Her efforts had been successful enough to prompt authorities to open the special unit dedicated to solving women's homicides. But the response didn't seem enough. Women were still dying in the border city, and sexual abuse and domestic violence were rampant. When television correspondent Brian Barger of CNN en Español asked Chávez in 1998 what she was doing to prevent these crimes, Esther realized she could step up her efforts. Still, Esther had been most outspoken, and while she had a way of irritating people with her frankness, her diligence and the advancements she was continuing to make for her cause could not be denied by politicians and police officials.

Her accomplishments in the area of women's rights were being lauded. She had been the first to call for equal treatment for women and was an outspoken critic of the state's investigation into the homicides, uniting with other local activists in demanding answers from public officials. Her persistence won her meetings with the state's governor and attorney general. She had even persuaded a federal congresswoman to join her efforts. With Esther at the helm, the city's women banded together, marching in protest, and even winning the attention of state officials, who responded with the creation of the special investigative unit now headed by Suly Ponce. Yet even that didn't seem enough.

Barger's question had struck a nerve, and his suggestion that Esther open the city's first rape crisis center in Juárez moved her to act. In early 1999, with help and support from

Barger, she founded Casa Amiga Centro de Crisis. The new shelter would operate from a modest canary yellow house in the working-class neighborhood of Colonia Hidalgo. It would be manned by a staff of two, and provide psychological, medical, and legal support to the victims of sexual violence and their families. Juárez's mayor, Gustavo Elizondo, promised that the city would pay 30,000 pesos per month, about U.S. $3,200, enough to pay the rent on the building and the salaries of Chávez and two assistants. In addition, the Mexican Federation of Private Health and Community Development Associations put up $25,000 in grant money, and the Texas attorney general's office offered to finance the training of rape crisis volunteers.

At the time, there were only six such crisis centers operating in Mexico.

Casa Amiga would soon become the sole refuge for the relatives of many of the murdered girls. Esther, it seemed, was the one ray of hope for these families.

One of Esther's first accomplishments as the center's executive director was to convince state authorities to create a dedicated area in the state attorney general's office where a woman or young girl could go to privately report a rape or incident of domestic violence.

Until then, domestic crimes had been lumped in with other offenses such as burglary and theft, and women were made to wait in a communal area at the state police headquarters until their names were called. Oftentimes, the officer manning the window would seek to intimidate the reporting party by yelling out the reason why she was there. "The woman is here to report a rape!" he would bellow, prompting all heads in the reception area to turn and stare at the alleged victim.

This was often enough to send the young woman fleeing or prevent her from getting up the courage to report the crime. Esther learned it was virtually impossible for a woman to report such crimes: those who tried were humiliated by police, who insisted they recount their ordeal in front of male officers, lawyers, and even their alleged abuser. In a number of cases, the victims were simply dismissed by officers who deemed it a waste of time to take a report when the woman would most likely go back to her abuser.

Mexico had no civil or criminal code to bring penalties for crimes related to family violence and rape. In fact, charges could only be brought if the woman could show bruises fifteen days after the alleged attack had occurred.

Esther's suggestion to put the unit in a separate part of the building was initially met with skepticism from the men in authority, who failed to see how providing a safe haven to report a domestic crime would make a difference. But much to their surprise, once a place was provided, women began to show up in numbers too large to ignore. That there was no glaring sign to direct the victims to the special domestic crimes division, but rather a series of arrows taped to the floor of the lobby to indicate where they needed to go, allowed them to retain some privacy as they arrived to report the violations.

Having a separate area in the rear of the building also meant that women were no longer required to report their abuse in a room full of male police officers taking reports from victims of petty crimes such as robberies and thefts.

Still, the families coming to headquarters to report their daughters missing were being directed to the window in the main lobby of the Procuraduría General.

Those cases were still not deemed personal—or pressing.

In fact, authorities were still mocking the efforts of local activists such as Chávez, and others who had followed her lead, organizing in protest against the way government officials were handling the investigation into the homicides. It had been Esther's early criticisms that triggered others such as Vicky Caraveo Vallina to join the fight.

In time, hundreds of the city's women would stage silent vigils at police headquarters and band together for monthly searches of the desert to look for the bodies of the missing girls.

One of the first searches took place just one month after Guillermina González's group, Voices Without Echo, was formed.

Coordinating the monthly search efforts was complicated, as many of the participants did not own cars, and needed to arrange carpools and other transportation. To avoid the heat, volunteers met at sunrise to begin trolling the empty lands on the outskirts of Juárez. By 9:30 a.m., it was already too hot to conduct the two- and three-hour expeditions.

Volunteers paired off to comb the barren lands encircling the city. Using long wooden sticks, they picked through heaps of trash and turned over the sand, hoping to find a single clue or piece of potential evidence. To cool the searchers off, the González family brought a cooler of cold drinks packed in the rear of their van.

In August of 1999, members of the state law enforcement agency agreed to join the volunteers on a desert search. Guillermina González and the others were excited that officials from the attorney general's office (formally known as the Procuraduría General de Justicia del Estado de Chihuahua, PGJE) were finally taking their cause seriously. But the group was quickly disappointed when it became clear that no one from the government agency intended to participate in the search. Instead, as the members of Voices Without Echo and the other searchers stood waiting, a handful of local law enforcement agents suddenly appeared. They were reportedly drunk and began harassing Guillermina and the other volunteers, demanding to know why the group was hanging around in the middle of nowhere.

Using her cell phone, Guillermina promptly dialed 060, the city's emergency line, and reported a DWI in progress. But no action was taken against the officers.

Dr. Eduardo Muriel, a well-respected criminologist from Mexico City, was invited to Ciudad Juárez in the winter of 1999 by State of Chihuahua Attorney General Arturo González Rascón. Dr. Muriel was one of three experts who volunteered to work in tandem with González Rascón to pursue other leads such as the possibility that the crimes were related to a religious sect or the increasingly lucrative industry of organ trafficking.

Unlike the FBI investigators, much fanfare surrounded the arrival of Dr. Muriel and his team.

The veteran scientist arrived in Juárez during the time that María Talamantes was first stepping before TV cameras to tell her story of alleged gang rape by police. Muriel told reporters he believed that Talamantes was most likely telling the truth. He said he too had had several disturbing interactions with authorities during his brief time in the city. The criminologist recalled a famous, and similar, case that had occurred several years earlier in El Pedregal, in San Ángel, a very exclusive section of Mexico City.

Dr. Muriel said the raping of women by police is not uncommon, but rarely happens to the women of the country's elite class. In that incident, police officers had reportedly raped two women from a very high class of Mexican society. "This sort of thing happens and is kept under wraps because they shush the girls by virtue of their uniforms," Dr. Muriel said.

Attorney General González Rascón publicly introduced Muriel and his team before the media, a gesture he hoped would ensure cooperation from journalists and local authorities. But right from the start, Dr. Muriel claims he was met with resistance. He charged that members of the district attorney's office continually denied him access to their files and that Special Prosecutor Suly Ponce provided no help.

In fact, just one week after he agreed to work on the case, the veteran criminologist handed in his resignation. He cited inappropriate behavior on the part of the district attorney's office and his contempt for local authorities who had allegedly placed hidden cameras in the offices he and his colleagues had been using.

"We had absolutely no support from the DA, and further-more, they were acting very inappropriately towards our team," Dr. Muriel told Univision in an interview days after his resignation. "They began to film us and tape-record our conversations inside their government office."

Ponce's office "didn't want us to go to the forensics lab, and didn't want to give us any leads or point us to any other witnesses or give us any additional information," Dr. Muriel said.

"They [the DA's office] should have left their more problematic cases to us and offered us those files. First of all, to see if they contained all the proper information, as is customary with criminal files. But not only that, there were a lot of women who were yet to be identified. We could have at least tried, or started to try, to put together a lot of the information."

Dr. Muriel claimed that during his short stint in Juárez, he had not been permitted to go anywhere near any of the crime scenes—with one exception. The criminologist explained that an opportunity finally arose one afternoon when he was in Ponce's office and overheard a phone call summoning her to a crime scene. Aware that she did not have transportation that day, he offered to drive her to the location.

"When we got there, the murder scene was already fenced in, for the purposes of preserving the scene," Dr. Muriel recalled.

"They mark off the scene to keep people from walking through, yet everyone from the DA's office comes and goes," Dr. Muriel said. "And I ask myself, 'What do they think their shoes are made of? Do they walk on air?' Even if only one person is walking through the crime scene, that's enough to contaminate it.

"Now, what if you have ten people walking through it?" he continued. "If you want to preserve a crime scene, it has to be done right from the beginning; from the very second the body is found. But they wait until they've been notified by police, after they've stepped all over everything."

Dr. Muriel charged that his team was refused access to the crime scene, forensics lab results, and the witnesses questioned in the case.

Muriel said he and his team subsequently commenced their own investigation. He noted that the case was very unusual because the woman had been murdered in a different fashion than in previous cases.

The investigative team learned that the victim, a young female factory worker, had arrived for work at the same time as a man considered to be a suspect in the case. The two worked the same shift, and on the same assembly line. The day the woman disappeared, the victim and the suspect had left the factory at the same time.

Through interviews, Dr. Muriel learned that the male employee phoned his sister-in-law, falsely telling her that he had been fired from his factory job—a lie he concocted to provide himself an alibi for his "early" departure. In fact, he did not leave the building that day but instead joined the woman on the assembly line and arranged to leave work at the same time she did. The girl was later found murdered.

"So we arrive at the *procuraduría*, the DA's office, with this accumulation of material, and when we get there, they have already arrested the man, and another friend of his. They already had them there. So I told them, 'Good work! You've already got him!' And the DA [Suly Ponce] looks at me utterly surprised and says, 'Who?' "

Dr. Muriel said he was stunned by the lack of communication between police and the prosecutor's office.

"To tell you the truth, the people who work in the DA's office, unfortunately, have a very limited knowledge of criminology," Muriel calmly observed. "So when someone comes along who knows a bit more than they do, I think they feel pressured."

He noted that as many as fifteen officers routinely respond to a crime scene, when the number should be just two—a lab tech and a crime scene photographer. Remarkably, key players such as Irma Rodríguez, the medical examiner, are denied access until members of the district attorney's office give them permission to begin their investigations.

"They are not limited by knowledge," Dr. Muriel said. "They are limited by the DA."

In response to questions, Dr. Muriel said he had come to believe that there might be some sort of cover-up going on in Juárez. "We have come to suspect that there could be people involved even from the ranks of the maquilas themselves, but it would be too presumptuous on my part to make a definitive statement at this point when everything is circumstantial."

He also expressed outrage that members of the prosecutor's office would surreptitiously set up a camera to videotape his work. "To tape us, everything we were doing, without our permission and then against our will," he said disgustedly. "And to record what we were saying. I find this offensive, and I find that it constitutes an enormous lack of professional ethics.

"But it didn't stop there. We moved to another office, not only to try to evade the invasion of privacy but to avoid any sort of confrontation, and they did it again! That was the final offense," he said.

Dr. Muriel said he was convinced that officials from the district attorney's office wanted his team to abandon its investigation. He also said he believed that Sharif Sharif and Sergio Armendáriz were merely scapegoats for the murders.

"I think they were [scapegoats] from the very beginning, from the moment they were arrested," he said. "I intended to go and speak with them and I tried to get the authorization to do so, but the police were the first ones who opposed it."

Countless letters and repeated phone calls to the district attorney for the state of Chihuahua asking for comment on Dr. Muriel's access to information and his allegations that members of the state district attorney's office had secretly videotaped the team's investigation were ignored. It was not until the Mexican consul in Miami was contacted and warned that Univision intended to air the story with or without a response that any action was taken. When officials from the Miami consulate found someone who would agree to an interview with the network, it was too late to include in time for the broadcast. Instead, a written statement was faxed to the network, and edited into the story.

It read, in part: "During the course of our investigation we have not found any police involvement in the cases of the crimes against women in Ciudad Juárez. We also wish to state that the independent investigators, headed by Dr. Eduardo Muriel, abandoned the investigation and resigned because they weren't able to obtain the desired results."

It made little sense that Dr. Muriel, who had been invited by the attorney general of Chihuahua to help investigate the murders, had been provided only limited access to the case files, when the team of FBI profilers from the bureau's Behavorial Analysis Unit at Quantico, Virginia, claimed to have been given broad access during their five-day visit to the border city that past spring. In an interview with a local Juárez reporter, Suly Ponce responded to Dr. Muriel's criticism of her office: "These criminologists had been in Ciudad Juárez since January 23, with all expenses paid by the state, and had made no effort whatsoever to open investigations as they publicly promised they would."

What was going on behind the scenes? Was there a cover-up or just complete incompetence? Or was it both?

CHAPTER EIGHT

A Ray of Hope

If you do not tell the truth about yourself you cannot tell it about other people.

—VIRGINIA WOOLF,
BRITISH NOVELIST AND FEMINIST

THE PEOPLE OF MEXICO elected a new president in the summer of 2000, defeating the ruling party's Francisco Labastida by a wide margin and ousting the political party that had ruled the country for seventy years. With the installation of Vicente Fox Quesada of the PAN party came the hope that government corruption would finally come to an end.

Fox's sweeping victory, which occurred on his fifty-eighth birthday, with 44 percent of the popular vote, was hailed as a triumph for democracy. His campaign promises were grand, calling for sweeping changes at all levels of government and economic improvement for the people of Mexico. He vowed to rid corruption, grant more power to state and local governments, and restructure Mexico's federal law enforcement system. He also proposed a number of solutions to the country's economic stagnation and ineffective judicial system, as well as a more progressive immigration policy with the United States.

He even promised to continue to wear jeans once in the presidential palace.

His assurances had wide appeal. But even more attractive was Fox's charismatic personality. Born in Mexico City to wealthy parents, and raised on a sprawling ranch in central Mexico's state of Guanajuato, Fox was a magnetic right-of-center populist who painted himself as an "honest" entrepreneur and "man of the people." Of mixed European roots—his father was Irish, his mother Spanish—he was at once continental and cavalier, with dark, chiseled features and a massive frame, towering over his countrymen at a lofty six feet five inches.

The former ranchero turned politician rarely wore suits, hitting the campaign trail in casual button-downs, faded jeans, and a flashy cowboy belt with an oversized buckle that bore his name. His down-home cowboy image and recent entry into politics were viewed as an attractive alternative to the long-standing and corrupt political machine of the incumbent PRI party. And many viewed his victory as a turning point for Mexico.

In Juárez, the women's groups were rallying to bring their cause to the attention of the new president. His election to office brought hope to the city's women, who believed that as "an outsider" his administration would bring about change. The situation had grown so critical in Ciudad Juárez that even officials on the U.S. side of the border were calling for a review of the homicide investigations.

Texas State Representative Norma Chávez, a Democrat

from El Paso, along with Senators Eliot Shapleigh of Texas and Mary Jane García of New Mexico, was among the U.S. officials now rallying for a binational investigation into the killings. The politicians suspected a cover-up and wanted authorities to solve the case. With Fox now in office, perhaps their appeals would finally be addressed.

Yet not long into his term, Fox's popularity was hurt when he became embroiled in a scandal that resulted in the resignation of one of his key aides over the purchase of expensive towels—$400 U.S.—for the presidential palace. But he quickly rebounded by shining the national spotlight on immigration reforms such as the Guest Worker Program and amnesty for undocumented immigrants in the United States.

During several very highly publicized meetings with U.S. President George W. Bush, Fox pledged to tighten security at the Mexican border in exchange for more inclusive immigration policies that would allow Mexican citizens to work legally in the United States and help millions of undocumented Mexican workers already living north of the border gain access to green cards and possibly even legal citizenship. But security concerns after the events of September 11, 2001, would all but close the door to any possible advances in that arena.

On the home front, Fox was meeting with staunch opposition to his attempts to clean house and stamp out corruption and would ultimately be criticized for his administration's failure to actively investigate and prosecute corrupt officials for illegal past acts.

Then, just two months into Fox's term, a seventeen-year-old named Lilia Alejandra García Andrade disappeared in Ciudad Juárez without a trace. The young mother was last seen leaving the factory where she worked assembling parts for water massage equipment. It was Valentine's Day 2001, and García had intended to catch the factory-sponsored shuttle bus for home that evening.

The missing girl's mother, Norma Andrade, posted flyers around the city, asking for information that could uncover her daughter's whereabouts. Her postings prompted threats of intimidation from anonymous callers—but no news about Lilia.

In theory at least, Lilia should have been safe. Sharif Sharif, members of Los Rebeldes, and the bus drivers and their alleged leader, Víctor Moreno, were all behind bars. Yet young women were continuing to disappear.

Norma told police that the last time she saw her daughter was at 6:00 a.m. on February 14, when the girl was leaving the house for work. For more than one year, the teen had been assembling parts at the downtown factory. Her shift usually ended at 6:00 p.m., and Norma liked to pick her up in the evenings. But the mother had to work late that night at the primary school where she was a teacher; there was a mandatory sexual education course she needed to attend.

Lilia would have to catch the bus. She was still nursing her infant son and needed to get home for his feeding. But she had no money that day and borrowed bus fare from a fellow worker.

Coworkers at Servicios Plásticos y Ensambles, the factory where García was employed, said they last saw the young mother walking in the direction of an abandoned lot near the factory just after dark to get to the bus stop on the other side.

This was the route she often walked to catch the bus for home. Many of the factory's employees used the shortcut, even though there were no streetlights illuminating the way.

Lilia's mother said she was instantly alarmed when she learned her daughter had not made it home that night. In addition to her work on the assembly line, Lilia was also a student at a local prep school, where she was in her fourth semester. She was studying to gain entry to a university in hopes of becoming a journalist. She loved to read poetry and play basketball when she had a free moment. But of late her hours were full, caring for her two young children, studying, and working at the factory.

Norma was certain her daughter had met with foul play. Lilia would never dream of going out on the town with so many responsibilities. Frantic, Norma dialed the Unidad de Atención a Víctimas de Delitos Sexuales y Contra la Familia (Unit for the Care of Victims of Sexual Offenses and Offenses Against the Family) to report her daughter missing. But her plea for help received little attention.

Just days earlier, Suly Ponce had publicly assured the city's residents that with Sharif Sharif and several of his alleged associates in jail, the main perpetrators of the serial crimes were off the streets. She boasted that thirty of the fifty-two sexually motivated femicides that had occurred in Juárez since 1998 had been solved under her watch. She also noted that the murder rate of the city's women had declined from March 1999 to February 2001, with just four cases in which the victims fit the earlier profile.

"We're conscious that copycats are going to imitate the

same [murder] patterns and we're going to be ready," she insisted. "In very little time, I'll have the pleasure of openly saying that in Ciudad Juárez there is not one sex crime." But just days after Ponce delivered her remarks, Lilia García was missing.

It was only after the young woman's ravaged, tortured, and mutilated body was found wrapped in a blanket on February 21, in the empty lot three hundred yards from the factory, that the story got any real attention. An autopsy revealed she had been dead for about a day and a half and that she had spent at least five days in captivity before her death.

The location of the young woman's body marked a change in the killer's signature. This was the first corpse to be found within the Juárez city limits. Up to this point, all the victims had been recovered from the outlying desert areas.

Criminologist Oscar Maynez saw the shift as significant. It was as if those responsible felt above detection, confident enough to dump the body in a well-traveled part of the city.

According to authorities, Lilia García had been savagely beaten, raped, strangled, and set on fire. The cause of death was determined to be asphyxia by strangulation. Oscar Maynez noted the MO was identical to that of several of the earlier killings. News reports indicated that Garcia's breasts had been mutilated.

Police were alluding to a "copycat" killer on the loose. "The most recent killings of women in Ciudad Juárez are related to a pattern of imitation of criminal conduct," said Chihuahua State Attorney General Arturo González Rascón at a press conference that March.

Suly Ponce, meanwhile, was working to minimize the outcry. She insisted that Lilia García was the first woman to be raped and murdered in that quarter of the city that year. Her claim was not accurate. In fact, the naked body of an unidentified female had been recovered just one week before near where García's body had just been found. Surely Ponce must have been aware of the earlier discovery.

Ponce's offhand response to the latest killing served to further fuel already flared tempers, with local activists again taking to the streets in protest. It was widely believed among them and nongovernmental organizations that Ponce and her special task force were nothing but "a sham," created to give the illusion that state officials were doing something about the murders—a place to point to when questions arose from members of the foreign media.

"I believe that a grave danger awaits every woman at every moment and every point of this city," Guillermina González told local journalists in the days after García's body was found. Though she had the stature of a little girl, Guillermina's eyes wore the pain of someone much older. She was a defiant young woman who had stared death in the face at far too young an age. By now her grassroots organization, Voices Without Echo, had its own Web site, which was designed and written by González. The group was also receiving letters of support from around the world.

The discovery of García's body and the fury that followed prompted high-ranking executives in the maquiladora industry to offer a reward of fifteen thousand pesos for information leading to the capture of the killer or killers of the teenage maquila worker. The announcement resulted in a flood of calls to the DA's office—mostly false leads from people anxious to collect the reward money.

Irritated by the burden the calls were placing on municipal employees, government officials lashed out at executives of Servicios Plásticos y Ensámbles, García's employer, labeling their decision to publicize a reward as "irresponsible."

One unnamed official even stepped before the cameras to accuse maquiladora executives of using the reward to gain positive publicity for the factory and not as a gesture of goodwill.

The situation hit a crescendo when an already enraged public learned that municipal police had failed to respond to an emergency call to 060 reporting "a rape in progress" in the exact location where Lilia García was last seen, and where her body was later found.

According to the official police log, it was 10:15 p.m. on February 19 when the emergency call came in, exactly five days after García was last seen alive. The caller reported that the rape was being perpetrated by two men in a car. The female victim, the caller said, was naked and crying out for help. Odd as it sounds, it appears that the rapists had taken García back to the same lot from which they'd abducted her five days earlier on February 14, and she was now fighting for her life.

Remarkably, police failed to dispatch a patrol car to the scene. It was not until a second call came into the station that night that a marked unit was finally sent to investigate. But the patrol car did not arrive on the scene until 11:25 p.m., more than one hour after the alert first was phoned in. By then, the location was quiet and the officers simply returned to head-quarters.

The emergency switchboard logs at 11:05 p.m. on February 19, the night the call to 060 was placed, simply stated "nothing to report," *"reporte sin novedad,"* according to Amnesty International USA, the not-for-profit organization that monitors the state of human rights in more than 150 countries. In addition, there is no indication that responding officers ever got out of the patrol car to check the location for any signs of foul play. If they had, they might have found Lilia García's personal belongings.

García's mother, Norma, was outraged when, shortly after her daughter's body was found in February, she learned that the owner of the vacant lot, Chihuahua's ex-governor, had ordered bulldozers to level the property—even though clearing the land could destroy potential evidence in her daughter's case.

Critics were livid that authorities had not commenced an investigation into the failure of the 060 emergency switchboard to respond to the initial call for police intervention, and over their inability to explain why it had taken seventy minutes for a patrol car to show up to investigate.

In addition, Amnesty International USA noted that Mexican officials neglected to review the mistakes made in García's case and subsequently denied any link between the emergency call and the abduction and murder of Lilia García—even though her body was found in the exact location described in the emergency call. Even with evidence to show that the two incidents were linked, authorities continued to maintain there had been no negligence in the municipal officers' response to the emergency call.

But new information would soon surface, pointing the finger directly at police once again.

García's murder, and the botched investigation that followed, led to demands for Suly Ponce's resignation. The tough-talking prosecutor proved no match for the women of Juárez. They had finally had enough, and on March 8, 2001, International Women's Day, they organized once again to storm the *procuraduría*. Many of the relatives and friends of the slain women were again charging that officials were not doing enough to quell the serial killings in Ciudad Juárez. The number of homicides against women had now topped three hundred.

Scores of demonstrators from Juárez and El Paso took to the streets that day, clutching wooden crosses and waving life-size photos of their lost loved ones. Others carried banners that read, "Not another one!" "Enough!" "No more corruption, no more ineptness!" "Out with Suly!" For nearly two years, the mothers of the victims had waited for justice from the brash woman appointed to head the investigation and prosecute those responsible for the crimes. But Ponce had failed to fulfill their hopes, and now they were insisting she be ousted.

En masse the protestors descended on Ponce's office, where they called for her resignation. "There were two crosses, one that the families carried, and one that we had ourselves," Esther Chávez wrote in an e-mail to Univision. "One we planted right in front of the *procuraduría*, where Suly Ponce was, and the other . . . the families took to the place where they found Lilia Alejandra García. . . . We also had other placards that read: "*If Suly is the best of the procuraduría, we don't want to see the worst.*"

Esther described how Ponce finally stepped out of the building, howling at the gathered crowd, "*¡No me griten!*" "Stop shouting at me!"

"Just a day earlier, the Chihuahua DA had stated that Suly Ponce was 'unmovable.' On this day, at least, we moved and shook her *tapete* [security blanket]," Chávez wrote.

Ponce had drawn a lot of criticism after attempting to tie Abdel Latif Sharif Sharif to all the crimes, alleging that while in prison the foreign-born scientist had paid, first, members of Los Rebeldes, and then several *ruteros*, or bus drivers, to kill the women in copycat fashion to exonerate himself.

"Perhaps the bad fortune that we had in Juárez was to attract an individual who never deserved to step on Mexican soil," Ponce insisted.

But her office had never been able to produce any proof that the Egyptian had been working from inside the jail since his arrest in 1995, or that he had paid members of either group to commit the murders.

Prosecutor Ponce tried to ally herself to the women of Juárez, telling them, "I'm a woman like you!"

She insisted that great strides had been made during her tenure, referring to the addition of new computers and state-of-the-art DNA testing equipment for the state's forensic specialist, Irma Rodríguez.

While the special prosecutor appeared anxious to tout her accomplishments, the angry women standing outside of her office that day dismissed her declarations; they were now convinced that she was a puppet who had been sent to patronize them. The protestors believed that Suly Ponce had no real intention of helping them in their calls to stop the violence.

In a bizarre twist, Esther Chávez came under verbal attack herself that morning from Guillermina González and members of Voices Without Echo. "They said vile things about me to the press, and they rejected my presence," Esther noted. González and members of her group were charging that journalists and nongovernmental organizations such as Casa Amiga, under the direction of Esther Chávez, were profiting from the murders. Now it seemed as if, aside from the crimes and the apparent cover-ups and botched investigations, the seed of discord had been planted in Ciudad Juárez, causing dissension in the already bleeding and broken heart of the city.

Chávez's Casa Amiga had been receiving donations from the community and using them to run the shelter. Now some members of other nongovernmental organizations, as well as employees of the attorney general's office, were charging that the donations had been intended for the victims' families and not for Chávez. Esther contended that she had used the funds properly.

Bereaved mothers including Irma Pérez and Paula Flores joined Guillermina González in accusing Esther of exploiting the deaths of their loved ones, charging that she was using the tragedies as a way to gain media attention and raise funds for her abuse and rape crisis center. Guillermina also complained that Esther was giving out private phone numbers of members of Voices Without Echo without permission.

Chávez maintained that she was helping the cause. She contended that she had only given out the group's main number.

The activist said the attack by Guillermina's group hurt. "It's something that affects me deeply, because they're people I tried to protect and help. . . . I love them a lot, their suffering has touched me . . . I've helped them and I'm ready to help them again, whenever they need me. I won't attack them. I respect them, and all society should respect them. . . . I'm not spiteful because they're victims and they feel pain."

It is not clear what finally prompted government officials to remove Suly Ponce from her role as special prosecutor, or whether the mounting protests by the women of Juárez played any role. Whatever the reason, word came in April of 2001 that she had been promoted to the role of regional coordinator of the North Zone and a new Juárez-based special prosecutor had been named—Zulema Bolívar, a former sex-crimes special investigator for the Chihuahua state attorney general's office.

In an article that appeared in the city's *El Norte* newspaper, Attorney General Arturo González Rascón acknowledged that Ponce had come under harsh attack from the families of the victims and many of the women's organizations. Still, he had nothing but praise for the auburn-haired lawyer and said that she had completed "very successful and very special investigations." Ponce was transferred to a position with the Chihuahua state governor's office in Juárez in which she was to oversee the investigations of the state police, and while not in the public eye, she was still reportedly keeping tabs on the investigation into the city's murdered women as part of her new, elevated post.

In the days and months ahead, an FBI leak had linked drug dealers to Lilia García's death. Ponce dismissed the notion that drug dealers had anything to do with the teen's murder and labeled the report as misinformation. Instead according to an article published in Salon.com, a respected online magazine, Ponce hinted that circus workers performing across the street from García's place of employment may have been to blame. But when a circus manager came forward alleging that she had "tried to bribe" them to finger coworkers as the perpetrators, the article reported that Ponce backed off.

Ponce vehemently denied the allegations of the circus manager, and the claims were never substantiated.

Former FBI agent Robert Ressler expressed disappointment in the turn of events in Juárez. In a telephone interview in September of 2001, the profiler, who had been so optimistic about the work of police and prosecutors in the border city, sounded weary and disgusted.

"I got caught up in the politics of the place," he said. "Everything that I did during one party was sort of scrapped completely by the next. I did one week of training, set up a task force with the El Paso police, and the new party disrupted everything we did."

In the late summer of 2001, an article appeared in *El Diario de Juárez* in which Norma Andrade de García expressed outrage that after nine months, police still had no leads in her daughter's rape and murder.

"We're talking about nine months during which they cannot give me a single answer. They tell me they're closing lines of investigation, that they're working, but they have nothing, there is nothing," Andrade told the newspaper. She went on to denounce authorities for their derogatory comments and the utter lack of respect shown by one municipal police officer.

"They told me that for the time being they were bogged down in the investigation, and when my eldest daughter got angry and told them not to throw away my daughter's file, the agent said to her in a very mocking manner as he threw it away, '*Mira, mira, mira, mira* . . . ,' " Andrade recounted. "These expressions are inappropriate. We deserve at least respect. Besides our being hurt and indignant, they have to be made to understand that sometimes we are very depressed, very sad, that we are filled with anger and that this anger may be against them, because they don't investigate properly."

According to the newspaper, Norma Andrade had found several irregularities in the investigation of her daughter's case—including an autopsy report that revealed a great quantity of semen present in the young woman's body. Despite the autopsy findings, authorities informed her that they didn't have the sperm that would help them find the perpetrator, or perpetrators, of Lilia's murder.

The bereaved mother was certain her daughter had been kept alive for several days while she was the victim of multiple rapes and tortured repeatedly until her death.

"According to the autopsy, my daughter passed away on February 19, which means she was held captive for five days," Norma said, weeping.

No one knows what horrors the seventeen-year-old suffered until she was, perhaps mercifully, killed. One state official who spoke to Univision on the condition of anonymity revealed that partially digested food had been found in the young woman's stomach. The autopsy suggested that Lilia García had eaten a meal approximately two hours before her murder, the official said.

What is significant about this finding is that it indicates that Lilia García did not feel threatened or afraid when she ate that meal, evidenced by the fact that her body was secreting stomach enzymes to digest the food. According to forensic experts, when a person is in fear or experiencing trauma, the body shuts down and will not produce these enzymes. This clue led some close to the investigation to theorize that García had felt safe with the person who had served her that last meal and had had no inkling she would soon be killed.

It also pointed to the possibility of a network of perpetrators and suggested that the person who was caring for Lilia while in captivity may not have been her killer.

Even more startling were the contents of a report written by the forensics experts who had examined García's body. In a lengthy article that appeared on Salon.com, freelance journalist Max Blumenthal reported that marks identical to those made by police handcuffs were found on García's wrists.

"Someone rich and powerful has to be involved in my daughter's murder," Norma told the *El Paso Times* in response to the finding. "I'm not an investigator, but only someone like that can keep getting away with this."

Three months after Suly Ponce's departure, Guillermina González announced the disbanding of her grassroots group Voices Without Echo. While many theorized that the rift between Guillermina's organization and the powerful activist Esther Chávez had prompted the young woman's decision to cease operations, others claimed the decision was totally unrelated to the angry disagreement. Guillermina was getting married to a man she'd met at a protest rally.

Her fiancé, Felipe Nava, had also lost a loved one to a violent death. His daughter by a previous marriage, seventeen-year-old María Isabel, had been abducted in January of 2000. Her ravaged and incinerated body was found three weeks later in a valley southeast of the city.

When María Isabel did not return home on January 4, her mother immediately reported her missing to municipal police. But like many of the relatives of the missing women, she was told her daughter had probably just run off with a boyfriend.

On January 28, more than three weeks after her disappearance, María's mother and father got the news that every parent dreads. Their daughter's charred remains had been located. An autopsy revealed that the teen had been held in captivity for two weeks before she was savagely killed and set ablaze.

The circumstances of her death seemed to mirror those of Lilia García, but officials failed to make the connection.

Guillermina had worked hard to keep the stories in the media. But in order to effectively run her small organization, she needed money. The mailings, the cell phone bills, and even the searches required some funding. In spite of promises of help from journalists and TV producers if she allowed them to tell her story, the much-needed funding never materialized and Guillermina finally decided to close down the organization.

At a news conference that summer, Guillermina's mother, Paula González, pointed to the strides her daughter's group had made during its brief undertaking.

"We lost our fear of authorities," she told members of the press on July 18, the day the group officially ceased operations. "We used to sit for three hours before they would talk to us. Now we walk into the investigators' office as if it were our home."

Even more significant, Paula noted, was that members of Voices Without Echo had won their fight allowing victims' families to view their daughters' bodies before an autopsy could be performed.

Still, with all their efforts, Paula and her family were no closer to finding out what had happened to their beloved Sagrario. Remarkably, Suly Ponce had ordered Sagrario's body exhumed and retested after an initial DNA test had returned negative results. Paula and her husband were devastated when they opened the official document stating that the body they had buried was likely not that of Sagrario. A second DNA test was quickly ordered and, as unbelievable as it sounds, it also returned negative results, prompting Guillermina González to take a closer look at the official paperwork. The young woman discovered that authorities had exhumed the wrong body.

They had mistakenly taken the corpse that lay next to Sagrario in an apparent mix-up over the grave numbers.

In an interview with Univision in early 2001, Suly Ponce insisted that her office would get to the bottom of the situation, and soon after, the correct corpse was exhumed for retesting. Those results were positive, confirming that it was, in fact, Sagrario González buried in that hilltop cemetery.

But the circumstances surrounding Sagrario's death would remain a mystery. One of the few facts the family knew for certain was that Sagrario, like so many of the murdered girls, had been killed soon after her hours at the factory were changed. That similarity raised questions as to whether certain employees at the city's maquiladoras were behind the murders.

Maquila worker Claudia Ivette González might still be alive if her employers at the Lear Corporation, the Michigan-based auto-interior supplier that operated a plant in Juárez, hadn't turned her away for being four minutes late to work in October 2001. When management refused to let her into the factory, the twenty-year-old assembly-line worker probably started for home on foot. Since she had lost a day's pay, she presumably wouldn't want to waste any of her hard-earned money on bus fare.

A month later her corpse was discovered buried in a field near a busy Juárez intersection. Next to her lay the bodies of seven other young women.

CHAPTER NINE

Killing Fields

When public pressure begins to grow, the scapegoat materializes.

—CRIMINOLOGIST OSCAR MAYNEZ

TENSIONS WERE ALREADY HIGH in Ciudad Juárez in November 2001 when police uncovered the eight decomposing corpses that had been tossed into a weed-infested former cotton field in the heart of the city, not far from the lot in which Lilia García's body was found. The makeshift gravesite was located just a few yards from the intersection of Paseo de la Victoria and Ejército Nacional, across from the headquarters of the offices of the Association of the Maquiladoras, the group that represented many of the city's U.S.-owned export assembly plants.

The horrific discoveries were made over two days, with law enforcement officials recovering three bodies on November 6, and five more, just skeletal remains, the following day.

A construction worker had stumbled upon the first victim, a slender, raven-haired teen whose body had been tossed in a ditch in the barren field, located between two heavily trafficked roadways. Investigators searching the trench for evidence that afternoon were stunned when they came upon the remains of two more young women within feet of the first corpse.

The next morning, a bulldozer was brought in to check the site, and five more bodies were unearthed.

The discoveries marked a turning point in the stream of rapes and murders that had plagued Juárez since 1993. The killers were now dumping bodies in the heart of the busy city, rather than in the desolate desert areas that ringed Juárez. It appeared that the perpetrators no longer feared the police.

Indeed, the placement of the bodies lent even more credence to theories that it was the police themselves who were committing the murders. The choice of location led many to believe that the killer was conveying a message. A majority of the murdered women were factory workers and their bodies had come to rest in a field facing the association of the maquilas that employed them.

Maquiladora worker Claudia Ivette González was among the victims police claimed to have found buried in the sandy field. Newspapers reported that it was still dark when Claudia had left her home early in the morning on October 10. But as fate would have it, she missed the bus that would have gotten her to her job on time. When Claudia reached the factory that morning, the doors to the plant were locked. There is no information on what Claudia did next, only that her corpse was among those dug up in the lonely cotton field.

Lear's director of communications, Andrea Puchalsky, told the online news magazine Salon.com: "We have a policy for tardiness, and she had been tardy many times. . . . She was not there in time to work her shift." When asked if the company adhered to that same policy with employees in the United States, Puchalsky insisted there was no official policy on the books at any of its facilities. She also declined to comment on whether González was locked out or turned away due to tardiness.

Mexican authorities later determined that Claudia Ivette González was killed in the same fashion as the seven other young women buried near her. Even more startling was that the modus operandi was similar to that in the case of Lilia García, whose mutilated body was found that past February.

Protestors from the city's various nongovernmental agencies descended on the office of the special prosecutor the day after the eight bodies were recovered. Attired all in black, the demonstrators carried a large pink cross they posted on the outside of the government building.

Pausing for a moment, the group lit candles to memorialize the latest victims before proceeding to the office of the new special prosecutor in charge of the investigation of murdered women. Zulema Bolívar was at her desk when demonstrators arrived and hung a poster on her door that read: "Closed for Incompetence."

Hearing the commotion, Bolívar stepped out into the hallway to invite several of the demonstrators inside to talk. But the group refused to single out representatives. They all wanted an opportunity to confront Bolívar.

Bolívar agreed, and found a suitable location to accommodate the crowd. The special prosecutor heard their concerns and expressed sympathy for their losses—but shed no light on the status of the investigation. The demonstrators ultimately left the building knowing no more than they did when they arrived.

In the days after the bodies were pulled from the abandoned field, authorities announced that forensic examinations were able to determine that some of the murders were recent. It was established that one murder had occurred just ten to fifteen days earlier, while two others had taken place at least six months before. The bodies were discovered just three meters from each other, and police believed that many of the women were killed in the location where their bodies were recovered. One of the victims was found with her hands tied behind her back.

A pair of shoes belonging to one of the girls was found beneath a bush at the entrance to the field, indicating that the woman had either been forced to remove them before walking to the site of her murder, or had voluntarily taken them off so as not to get them dirty, believing she would live to retrieve them and wear them home.

Authorities claimed that among the dead bodies exhumed from the abandoned field was a nineteen-year-old college student named Guadalupe Luna de la Rosa. Like Ramona Morales's slain neighbor, thirteen-year-old Celia Guadalupe, this girl also went by the nickname "Lupita." Many women in Mexico are named Guadalupe in honor of that country's patron saint, Our Lady of Guadalupe.

A stir had been made when the young girl first went missing the previous year. Unlike many of the victims, Guadalupe was a full-time student, attending the Instituto Tecnológico (Technological Institute) de Ciudad Juárez, and the daughter of a middle-class family that hailed from the border city. She had last been seen on September 30, 2000. She had left home that morning to catch a bus for town, where she intended to meet some friends for an afternoon of shopping. She was then supposed to go to one of the teens' homes to celebrate a friend's birthday.

Word of Lupita's disappearance had sparked fellow students, family, and friends into action. They formed search parties to look for the missing girl and, in the biggest mass public outcry to date, staged a two-thousand-strong demonstration through the streets of Juárez, demanding justice from authorities. Protestors distributed flyers with a photo of the stunningly beautiful young woman and even secured the services of a cadaver dog to aid in a search for her body.

Yet even in such mass numbers, the efforts of the protestors and volunteers had yielded few positive results. A threatening phone call was made to the parents of the missing girl, Epitasio and Celia Luna. The anonymous caller demanded ten thousand dollars from the Luna family to prevent the kidnapping of another of the Lunas' daughters.

Activists claimed that this kind of threat had become a common tool used by law enforcement officers to ward off questioning by family members. Many of the relatives of the missing young girls had reported these kinds of warnings, disguised as words of comfort, from the officers they had gone to for help.

"We didn't have money, we didn't have enemies," a disconsolate Celia Luna told the newspapers. "I never thought this could happen in the middle of the day, on a Saturday."

Guadalupe "Lupita" Luna had lived with her family just fifteen minutes from the office of the *procuraduría* in a cluster of concrete dwellings, where pristine white sheets waved from clotheslines. Hers was a working-class neighborhood with houses that had addresses and plumbing. The homes, for the most part, were neatly kept. Women spent their mornings outside washing clothes or doing chores like sweeping the entrances to the houses. Young children played with each other and the neighborhood dogs in the narrow alleyways that separated the rows of cookie-cutter dwellings.

Lupita Luna had been abducted, apparently, in broad daylight on a Saturday afternoon on her way to a friend's house.

Hers was a close-knit community. So when word circulated that the young woman had gone missing, everyone in the neighborhood had joined in the search.

In an interview with Univision, Lupita's mother recalled that her daughter left home at about noon. Her friends waited for her until two p.m. When she didn't arrive, the young girls figured Lupita had changed her mind, so they went shopping without her. Once they returned, they called Lupita's home to see why she had not come over. "I didn't know why," Celia Luna recounted.

Lupita was to take two buses to get to her destination that day—the one she normally took to get to school each morning, and a second bus to get to her friend's house. According to police, Lupita did board the first bus. But it was unclear if she had made the connection to the second one.

When Lupita didn't return home by eight o'clock that evening, her mother began to visit the local hospitals to see if maybe the teen had been in an accident. "We went over the entire route she would have followed to get to her friend's house. We went to the department stores, and then we went to the police stations."

Officers told the family that they didn't have any reports of an accident or a kidnapping. It was 3 a.m. when Celia called 060, the police emergency line. She tried to provide officers with a description of her daughter but was told that she would need to come to the police station in person to file a report. When she arrived at the downtown offices of the *procuraduría* the following morning, she was told to come back on Monday at 10 a.m., at which time police would assign two agents to her daughter's case. Celia did as she was told, returning the following day to make the report. It seemed remarkable that with all of the murders, families were still required to wait to file a report.

The heartsick mother carried on for more than one year with no news of her eldest child. She was a working mother, supporting Lupita's thirteen-year-old sister and an elderly mother as well as her young son. Still, she clung to the hope that the young college student would return home at any moment. Even though space was tight, Celia hadn't moved a single item of her daughter's belongings from the bedroom the missing teen had shared with her younger sister, Rosaura. On the dresser were framed pictures of Lupita embracing her baby brother, at her first communion, and posing in the cap and gown she wore to her high school graduation. Celia had made it a point to keep everything as it was when her eldest daughter left home that Saturday, from the stuffed animals lining her bureau to the school notebooks filled with homework assignments for which she had earned A's. Posters of the American pop band Hanson and album covers of well-known Mexican musicians filled the room that looked much like that of any typical teenager in the United States.

A young woman had lived, laughed, studied and dreamed about her future there. Now her family was wondering if she would ever return.

To keep her daughter's story alive, Celia had erected a miniature chapel with Lupita's photo in the front yard of the two-bedroom house. Beside the picture she had placed a statue of the Virgin of Guadalupe, the saint she prayed to each day in hopes of a miracle.

When she heard the radio reports of the bodies being ex-humed from the cotton field that November 2001, she immediately dialed police to learn if her daughter had been found among the dead. While she was initially told her daughter was not among the dead, that information would later change. Lupita's remains would indeed be identified as those pulled from the vast open field. Officials said that what remained was little more than bleached bones. But still Celia was not completely convinced. The clothing authorities told her they found on the body didn't match what her daughter was wearing the day she disappeared.

Celia could never have imagined that her eldest child would become one of the city's homicide victims.

"Lupita was mature for her age, yet innocent," the distraught mother told Univision. "She was always happy and loving. She didn't have a mean bone in her."

On November 21, less than three weeks after the latest grisly discoveries, investigators announced the arrests of two more bus drivers. According to authorities, Javier "Víctor" García Uribe and Gustavo González Meza, both twenty-eight, had confessed to kidnapping, raping, and killing the eight women.

García had been among those rounded up in the fall of 1999 during the initial arrest of the city's bus drivers, after members of the Tolteca group implicated him—claiming García knew one of the young women they had "sacrificed." He was subsequently released for lack of evidence, but police kept him on the radar and had immediately grabbed him when the eight bodies were discovered.

González, meanwhile, had never been implicated in any of the crimes. Only later would it be revealed that his name came up during the police interrogation of fellow bus driver Víctor García.

In an attempt to link the new suspects to the group already in custody, Fernando Medina, spokesman for the state attorney general's office, told members of the media that the bus drivers did, in fact, have ties to the Toltecas, the first group of bus drivers arrested in connection with the homicides.

Attorney General Rascón claimed García and González had "snorted cocaine, smoked marijuana, and drunk liquor" before setting out in search of their victims. When they spotted a vulnerable woman, they forced her into their van, where they raped and killed her, before dumping her body in the cotton field, he said.

At the time, officials positively identified the murdered young women as Guadalupe Luna de la Rosa, nineteen, a student; Verónica Martínez Hernández, nineteen, a maquiladora worker and student; Bárbara Araceli Martínez Ramos, twenty-one, a maid; María de los Angeles Acosta Ramírez, nineteen, a maquiladora worker and student; María Juliana Reyes Solís, seventeen; Claudia Ivette González Banda, twenty, a maquiladora worker; Esmeralda Herrera Monreal, fifteen, a domestic servant; and Laura Berenice Ramos Monárrez, seventeen, a student.

News reports stated that police got the break in the case that led them to García and González after a witness came forward claiming to have seen one of the suspects dumping a body into the grassy field. The woman, a nurse, reportedly told authorities that the man she saw dumping the body was driving a blue van that night.

Not surprisingly, the *ruteros*, bus drivers, alleged police violence and torture were used to extract their "bogus" confessions.

On the day that police came for bus driver Víctor García Uribe, known as "the Match," there was a party going on for García's wife, Miriam. It was November 9, 2001, the day after Miriam's actual birthday. But Víctor and his father and sister had pooled their money to throw Miriam a special barbecue at his father's home that day. The family feasted on "good" meat to celebrate the occasion.

After the festivities, Miriam and her husband boarded the bus her husband used to transport the maquila workers to and from their factory jobs and returned to their simple, neatly kept house. Theirs was a modest existence, a home with running water, electricity, and enough money to buy diapers for their new baby.

Miriam had come to Juárez fifteen years before and considered the city her home.

As they pulled up in front of the small, two-bedroom dwelling, Miriam's father appeared from his house next door. Eager to hear about the barbecue, he invited the family over for a snack. Miriam smiled, explaining that they would come another time. They were full from the barbecue and ready to retire for the afternoon.

In an interview, Miriam recalled how, cradling her infant daughter, she had started down the walkway after her husband, when suddenly he turned and asked that she retrieve the diapers and carriage he'd left in the bus.

Within seconds, Miriam said, she heard strange noises coming from inside the house, as if someone was being punched repeatedly. Frantic, she climbed from the bus, falling onto the street with the baby still in her arms. As she struggled to get up, she said, she saw through the front window that at least a dozen men were in her living room viciously beating her husband. He was fighting to place his hands over his face to deflect their repeated blows.

Miriam said the men were laughing as they struck him over and over, threatening to kill Víctor.

Clutching her baby, Miriam started toward the house when suddenly she saw the front door fly open and several men pushed past her, dragging Víctor in their arms. She recalled that they were dressed all in black and wore masks, some ghoulish Halloween-type masks, grotesque with exaggerated features and pretend blood; others had ski masks pulled tightly over their faces to conceal their identities.

Several were clutching long-barreled guns as they dragged Víctor down the walkway to a gold Chevy Suburban waiting at the curb, where a dozen similar vehicles were lined up behind it, sleek and glossy as if they had just been washed and buffed, she said. None of the vehicles had license plates or any identifying tags.

With the baby still in her arms, Miriam said, she raced after the group, demanding that they free her husband at once. She even grabbed at one of the men, pulling back his mask enough to reveal a face scarred by acne. That's when one of the men, she recalled, grabbed onto strands of her hair and began pulling her away from Víctor. She claimed that she was yanked from the vehicle, as she tried to get in next to her husband, and thrown to the ground with the baby still in her arms.

Unable to stop them, Miriam said, she raced to her father's house just next door for help. He was already standing on the sidewalk when, she claimed, gunshots rang out. According to Miriam, the men fired at her father from their vehicles.

Miriam claimed that several neighbors had witnessed

the event and, as she did, believed her husband had been abducted.

Unsure what to do, Miriam by her own account commenced a search for her husband, first checking the local police headquarters to see if he had been brought there. She recalled seeing a police shield while struggling with one of the men; it was on his shirt, concealed beneath a black jacket. But members of the municipal police told her that they were not holding Víctor.

Miriam said that when her visit to the local hospitals turned up no clues, she dialed Sergio Dante Almaraz, the criminal attorney whom she and Víctor had retained when her husband was temporarily taken into custody eighteen months earlier with the other shuttle bus drivers. While García was subsequently released for lack of evidence, his name was entered into the district attorney's computerized database of sexual offenders. Since then, police had been pulling him in for questioning every time the body of a dead woman turned up in the city.

Now it appeared they were looking at him once again, the lawyer later said in an interview. Ciudad Juárez was currently in the hands of the PRI party under the direct control of the governor. Local elections were around the corner, and it seemed authorities were anxious to make an arrest in the case. Almaraz said it was only after a tip from an employee at the Department of Investigations that he learned where his client was being held.

Miriam said she was furious with authorities for misleading her about Víctor's whereabouts. She had gone to the *procu-*

raduría those first days in search of information and had been turned away—even as her husband was being held in another part of the same complex. Authorities later claimed that Miriam was not deliberately misled. The *procuraduría* is a large building, and officers in one area are often unaware of what is going on in other parts of the sprawling headquarters, they said.

The response seemed absurd. But there was little that Miriam could do, she recalled. When she was finally permitted to see her husband on November 12, she said, he was ill. He couldn't stand up or walk. He was just lying in agony on a stone bed, running a high fever.

Before she could say anything, Víctor García told of his hours of torture, she recalled. He said police beat and burned him until he could no longer endure the pain and, along with the other bus driver, had confessed to the murders of the eight women found in the cotton field.

Miriam said she later learned that Víctor had been beaten and burned on the anus, testicles, stomach, hand, and face. One of his hands was immobile from having been bound for so long.

"I couldn't take the torture" is what her husband allegedly told her that day.

At a press conference at the jail soon after their arrest that November, the two bus drivers spoke out about their days-long interrogation. Just like Sharif Sharif, these men had been permitted by the facility's director to come before the press with their story. El Cereso was a city-run facility; members of the state attorney general's office had no jurisdiction over its staff.

Gustavo González, a paunchy twenty-eight-year-old with thick, dark, curly hair and round, full cheeks, looked edgy, slumped in a chair behind the same wooden conference table at which Sharif Sharif had spoken out in the past. He had been limping when he first entered the room, as if he had suffered a painful leg injury. Because of his fleshy build, he had been given the nickname "the Seal."

As he faced reporters, González claimed that police had pointed guns at members of his family when they came to arrest him, an account that sounded a lot like that of the Rebels' alleged leader, Sergio Armendáriz.

During his brief remarks, González claimed he had been taken to a private home after his arrest, where he was beaten and tortured and threatened with the assassination of his mother and his wife if he didn't confess into a tape recorder to the murders of the eight women. He said police also forced him and García to sign some photographs, presumably of the eight young women.

"They told me they were going to kill my entire family if I didn't come out of my house with them," González said, his voice barely audible. "They took down my pants and wet my parts and gave me electrical discharges there with a prod.

"They beat me, burned me with cigarettes, and told me I wasn't going to get out of there, and that they had my dad and my wife." González lifted his shirt to display the wounds, and news photographers snapped the photos, which appeared on the front pages of the city's newspapers the following day.

Suddenly, a flood of tears poured from the man's eyes, accompanied by loud, uncontrollable sobs. Trembling as he faced the cameras, González said, "My wife is pregnant, and they said they were going to take our baby out of her!"

Víctor García, a seemingly stronger, sturdier man, told a similar story. In a quiet voice, he too alleged that he had been beaten repeatedly about the face and body before he was made to pull down his pants. As with González, police allegedly poured water on García's penis and testicles and then prodded them with electrical discharges.

"They held me by the arms and legs and they kept prodding me, down there, in my parts . . . and I heard people telling me to 'tell the truth.' I asked, 'What truth? What do you want to know?' And they told me to tell them about the women I had killed. I had no knowledge of these women, but they kept on doing it, giving me the electric shocks and beating me. Then they would stop and ask me again."

The painful recollection also brought García to tears. "And finally I couldn't stand it. I wanted them to leave me in peace. They were doing this to me since the Friday afternoon when they picked me up, until the next day, Saturday morning."

The alleged torture had produced the desired effect. The two bus drivers had now become the most recent scapegoats in a rash of arrests that had become known to many in the border city as the proverbial Band-aid for the epidemic.

Yet this time, the citizens of Juárez were asking questions. Few believed the two bus drivers arrested for the murders of the eight young women had committed the crimes. Even members of the victims' families were calling for the men's release. This would mark the first time that the victims and the alleged perpetrators were on the same side against the police.

For one, the families noted that several of the victims had disappeared more than thirteen or fourteen months earlier. Yet within two days of finding their bodies, authorities had the presumed suspects in custody with a mountain of accumulated evidence against them.

Chihuahua State Attorney General Arturo González Rascón and Chihuahua State Deputy Attorney General José Manuel Ortega were in office and overseeing the investigation at the time of the men's arrests. When questioned about how their officers had obtained such evidence, the men divulged that their investigators had been secretly surveilling one of the men for some time.

In other words, they claimed that police had been monitoring Javier "Víctor" García and were hot on his trail, even as he was allegedly murdering the women. The explanation was mind-boggling. How had authorities stood by and allowed the crimes to continue? It made no sense.

Ortega argued that García had opportunities to rape and murder even while under surveillance because police had only been watching García on a part-time basis, not on a twenty-four-hour schedule. Police didn't have the funding to conduct around-the-clock surveillance. Ortega added that they feared if García knew he was being watched, he would change his modus operandi and stop the murders.

The response was startling, and yet officials seemed perfectly comfortable making the ludicrous statement. They even trotted out a videotape of the men's alleged confessions while in police custody. However, later, when reporters wanted to view it first-hand, authorities couldn't produce the videotape. The video had aired on local Juárez television. It showed the two men reciting the details of each of the eight abductions, including the first and last names of their victims, the exact locations where the women were picked up, and descriptions of the garments the women had been wearing, right down to the color of their bras and underwear.

Many questioned how the men, who were supposedly high on drugs and alcohol at the time of the killings, could recall such particulars with unerring accuracy. Authorities responded by claiming that some people get high to stay more alert.

Even more troubling was that the director of El Cereso resigned just one month after the bus drivers' arrests. His resignation happened after he reportedly signed off on the release of a medical report that documented specific injuries consistent with police torture found on the men's bodies when they first arrived at the facility that November.

When Ortega was asked about the director's departure, he said it was not linked to the release of the medical findings. He pointed out that the prison director had not conducted the examination of the alleged killers, the prison doctor had, and the physician was still employed at the facility.

Interestingly, news reports claimed that the prison doctor had observed burns and bruises on the men's bodies that were consistent with the marks left by a cattle prod—a finding that was vehemently denied by state officials.

In response to questions about the men's injuries, Attorney General González Rascón insisted they had burned themselves in order to claim that they had been tortured while in police custody. How the bus drivers were able to get a hold of matches or a lighter to inflict the burns while under lock and key made little sense. González Rascón also claimed that injuries that had been photographed on Gustavo González's leg were the result of varicose veins that had become severely inflamed—not the result of beatings, as he was claiming.

In the days following her husband's arrest, Miriam García began receiving death threats. People were calling her home and taunting her in public. She grew afraid for her life, and for the life of her baby and the young attorney Sergio Dante Almaraz, who had agreed to represent her husband pro bono.

Miriam García insisted that her husband was innocent. She claimed that she worked alongside him on bus 77, collecting fares from passengers using route 1-A. Her normal work schedule was Monday through Saturday. Sunday was a day of rest for the family. Since she was constantly by his side, she questioned how and when he would have had the opportunity to commit these eight murders without her knowledge.

"My husband has always been very serious in his work, very discreet," she declared in an interview soon after García's arrest. "With some men, you know, something gives them away even if they're discreet. As a woman you perceive those things. And my husband, from the time that I met him, has been very respectful, very sweet. A walking tenderness."

CHAPTER TEN

Labyrinths

*People are scared. People are whispering . . . when
you instill fear, when you divide, you conquer.*

VICKY CARAVEO,
WOMEN'S ACTIVIST AND FOUNDER,
MUJERES POR JUÁREZ

WHILE SULY PONCE PRIETO was no longer the special prosecutor in charge of the investigation of women's homicides, she
was still active in the state's ongoing investigation into the
murders. As regional coordinator of the North Zone for the
state prosecutor general's office, she was now at the head of
the justice system in Chihuahua.

In November 2001, Ponce found herself in a quandary
when members of her own staff, including the state's head of
forensics, Oscar Maynez, told her that the two bus drivers she
had locked up might not be responsible for the deaths of the
eight young women found in the middle of the city. She could
ignore the issue and hope the media didn't pick up on it, or she

could buttress her case that it was, indeed, the bus drivers who were responsible for the killings.

Ponce opted to go after the bus drivers once again.

In November, Ponce held a press conference to present to the media a thirty-seven-year-old woman who claimed to have been raped by one of the suspects in July of 1996. Ponce identified the woman she was putting forth as "Luz" and claimed that the witness had come forward after recognizing Víctor García from TV news accounts as the same man who had raped her five years earlier.

The woman was heavyset and did not fit the profile of the murdered girls, yet she stood before Chihuahua state police and members of the press and tearfully recounted how García had forced her into a car, beat her, and then raped her at gunpoint. When questioned about her appearance, she claimed that she had been thinner back then. Luz explained that her vehicle had broken down and she was waiting on the side of the road for a taxi when García drove past, stopped as if he intended to help, and then pulled her inside his vehicle. During the attack, she managed to break free, exiting the vehicle and crawling under a nearby car to hide. She said her eyes were bloodied and she could barely see, but she could hear García's footsteps coming closer when the headlights of an oncoming car startled him back to his own vehicle.

When asked why she had waited so long to come forward, the woman explained that García had driven off with her purse and house keys that night. He knew where she lived and she feared retaliation.

Luz's horrific account resulted in the filing of additional

criminal charges against García. But the case was ultimately dismissed when she declined to testify at trial.

Univision later learned that the woman was not, in fact, a rape victim at all. Rather she was the girlfriend of a taxi driver who was in jail and facing charges at the same time the two bus drivers were arrested. Sources close to the investigation claimed that Luz was promised a plea deal for her boyfriend in exchange for her bogus rape story before the media.

Raising further questions about the men's guilt was lead criminologist Oscar Maynez. He claimed that an order to plant evidence in their case had come down from state officials at the top. The allegation was stunning, and yet many in Juárez were not surprised.

Maynez alleged that after an inspection of the men's brown van had yielded no evidence linking the two bus drivers to the murders, he was instructed to "plant" hairs and fibers from the dead women in the vehicle to incriminate them in the killings.

When he refused, Maynez said he began receiving threats. The threats were so serious that even Maynez's enemies at the attorney general's office were warning him to be careful.

At one point, he said, Suly Ponce took him out to lunch, and during the meal, she stressed the importance of "protecting the institution." While Maynez interpreted the statement as a cryptic message from a person with a "bureaucratic mindset," urging him to be a team player, there is no evidence to support his belief.

Maynez opposed the theory that officials were trying to float with regard to the men's participation in the crimes.

Maynez had repeatedly warned authorities that the hypothesis they had chosen to adopt in this case was flawed and would not stand up to scrutiny. If they continued, it would come back to haunt them, he insisted. Maynez's warnings were ignored, and he could do little more than stand by as authorities pressed forward with their theory of the murders.

Maynez linked the rush to solve the case to the upcoming political elections. "This investigation ought to have been worked scientifically and not politically to stifle social pressure," he said during an interview with Univision.

In spite of his frustration, Maynez was determined to ensure that the evidence and reports he had compiled were not tampered with. He decided to stay on as head of the Department of Forensics and Legal Medicine until the bus drivers' case went to court. For nearly two months, he anxiously kept the files in his possession. Finally, in January of 2002, he passed them along to a judge.

Oscar Maynez was also keeping a close eye on the case against Sharif Sharif. He was dismayed to learn that the accused killer's repeated requests to review the state's DNA evidence against him had been denied.

Maynez was also aware that Sharif had contacted his attorney, Irene Blanco, after his transfer to the maximum-security facility outside Chihuahua City, claiming that officials were deliberately trying to kill him by forcing him to take pills. When he refused to go along with his jailers' demand to swallow the drugs, Sharif said they ground them up and shoved them down his throat.

Maynez was troubled by Sharif's claims and feared that the

Egyptian might wind up dead. He was also disturbed by the fact that Sharif's file contained just one highly doubtful murder charge. Now authorities were looking to pin the latest murders on two bus drivers—men who could not be tied to the crimes through any forensic evidence. It was clear to the criminologist that every time public pressure rose to find Juárez's killers, police suddenly fingered a suspect. In the case of the cotton field killings, it appeared that García and González were the chosen scapegoats.

Maynez was certain that—if given the opportunity—he could solve the eight murders. An initial investigation had revealed that at least three of the girls had been killed and maimed in the exact same fashion as young Lilia García, whose mutilated corpse had turned up in the field across from the factory where she worked earlier that same year. The site of García's murder was less than one hundred yards from the field where the eight bodies were found, and Maynez was convinced the cases were linked.

On January 2, 2002, the embattled criminologist submitted his resignation under pressure from his superiors. Oscar Maynez, who later admitted that he would have been fired if he had not agreed to leave, said he was "disgusted and ashamed" over what had transpired in the investigation.

"We were asked to help plant evidence against two bus drivers who were charged with the murders," he later told members of the media. "A couple of police officers brought items for us to put in the van they said was used to abduct the women. We had already checked the van and another vehicle belonging to the suspects for such things as human hairs, fibers, and blood, anything that could link the two suspects to the victims. . . . We even conducted a luminol test for traces of blood that might have been wiped off. We found nothing; the van was clean."

While Maynez declined to name the officers involved in the alleged cover-up, he assured the public that he had turned over the information to his supervisors. Unbeknownst to his superiors, he had also delivered a copy of the DNA profile conducted on semen collected from Lilia Garcia's body to a friend in Juárez in case something should happen to the original report.

Chihuahua state deputy attorney general Ortega publicly refuted the claims of the state's former chief forensics officer. "As far as I know, no one asked [Maynez] to plant evidence," Ortega declared. "The suspects confessed to the murders and that is an important part of the investigation."

In a subsequent interview with Oscar Maynez in February of 2002, he offered his views about the case that had come to be known as "the cotton field murders."

"It was like a scene from a horror movie, finding the bodies of eight women in such a relatively small area," Maynez recalled of the crime scene. "The bodies were already in a very advanced state of decomposition, which makes it extremely difficult to determine the cause of death, because they were mostly skeletons."

Photographs and footage of the excavated field looked more like a macabre anthropological dig than a homicide scene. Maynez admitted that the magnitude of the discovery had overwhelmed him. "Ciudad Juárez is a very violent city, and homicides are the order of the day, but a situation like this . . . the bodies of eight women found in the same area, it was not what I had expected."

Maynez had resigned from his post just shy of two months before he sat down for his interview with Univision, and it was clear he was choosing his words carefully. Still, he was unable to conceal his disbelief when asked to respond to an official government statement concluding that the deaths of the eight women found in the cotton field were not related.

"It's an enormous coincidence finding eight bodies all so close to one another," he said. "It's undeniable that the entire scene looks highly organized. They could hardly not be related, these eight homicides."

While the decomposed state of some of the bodies had made it nearly impossible to determine a cause of death, Maynez believed that the women had most likely fallen victim to the same killer or killers. "I insist that it would be too much of a coincidence that eight different perpetrators or groups of perpetrators, acting on their own, would have disposed of bodies in the same area, especially when there was the same pattern," he concluded.

The criminologist said he could not discount the possibility that drug traffickers or members of the state police force were involved in the killings. He said he was quite certain the murders had been committed by a highly organized group of people with resources—and not by the two poor and uneducated bus drivers now in custody. Maynez pointed to a series of different factors. For one, the location of the crime scene in the heart of Juárez suggested that the perpetrators had access to multiple vehicles. Authorities had claimed that the two bus drivers had used a beat-up brown van to transport the bodies to the former cotton field. But Maynez argued that it would have been virtually impossible for someone to escape detection using the same vehicle to transport all eight bodies to the same location over a period of time. He believed that more than one car or truck must have been used to keep people in the neighborhood from becoming suspicious.

In addition, the criminologist said he was highly skeptical of an eyewitness account from a local nurse who claimed to have seen one of the suspects driving a blue car or truck into the vast open field and dumping a body there. The witness, whose story seemed to change over time, would ultimately recant what she'd told authorities.

But Chihuahua state deputy attorney general Manuel Ortega later claimed that the woman had seen "a person bearing a great physical likeness" to Víctor García at the location of the "event" and "disposing of something heavy . . . a pig, the person thought." Yet García remained behind bars.

In addition, the witness had described the vehicle used by this man as a blue sedan. Police had claimed the two bus drivers had been using a brown van.

Some journalists were wondering how the bus drivers, who worked long hours and had wives and children at home, were able to concoct and carry out such an elaborate murder

scheme—one that required extensive planning and ma-
neuvering.

None of it made much sense to Maynez. Until authorities
were ready to order a proper investigation, the crimes would
go unsolved and the real culprits would remain at large, he
said.

"I think that based on the irregularities in this case, the way
in which these two men were arrested, the possibility that torture may have been used in order to obtain their confessions—
everything leads me to think that the person or persons who
are committing these homicides have yet to be detained,"
Maynez told Univision.

The criminologist also noted that several of the bodies
found in the old cotton field had been dumped where they
were only partially hidden by bushes and could have been spotted by passersby. The others had been purposely buried beneath some rubble, indicating that some care had been taken in
trying to conceal them from discovery. In Maynez's view, it was
just one more indication of two different modi operandi being
used by the killers of Juárez that was being ignored by authorities.

Maynez said he'd believed since the first bodies were found
in 1993 that there was at least one serial killer on the loose in
Juárez, and he recounted that he had made his suspicions clear
to his superiors and others. But he argued that, for whatever
reason, authorities refused to pursue that line of investigation.

"In 1993 . . . a very evident pattern was beginning to
emerge, not just around the killings, but through the meander-

ing, crooked trail of failed investigations, firings, lack of physical evidence, false accusations, forced confessions, evasions,
and obfuscations," he noted. "The problem is that when you
have a disease, you have to diagnose it correctly before you can
give it adequate treatment, the right medicine.

"A lot of these murders are linked," he continued. "But
which ones, I don't know because there has never been a serious investigation."

At the time of the interview, Maynez clearly had his own
theory about who committed the murders. But he was hesitant
to divulge too much.

"The killers couldn't be the bus drivers, who have a two-
bedroom bungalow in a lower-middle-class section of Juárez
and don't even own a car. It's a well-organized group with resources and a clear hierarchy," he said, suggesting that drug
traffickers, politicians, or even members of the police department may be to blame.

"The government can be bought," he said. "It has to be
people with power and money because they view poor girls as
disposable.

"Unfortunately, if in the case of the bus drivers, it is proven
that there was indeed kidnapping and torture, we are taking a
most serious step backward in our execution of justice. Because
imagine doubting your own police force, your own officers. It's
terrible. Who's going to protect you?"

It was a sentiment that the women of Juárez had suspected
long before. But unlike Maynez's, their opinions carried little
weight and they had no alternative but to continue working for

a meager salary, relying on public transportation to get them around, all the while knowing that they were targets.

Three months after the eight bodies were pulled from the cotton field, police reopened the location to the public. Quickly, members of Juárez amateur search groups descended on the property to conduct their own investigation. Armed with long sticks and other primitive search tools, teams of searchers arrived early one frigid day in February 2002 and went to work.

Volunteers broke off into small groups and began to scour the overgrown field. During their search, the volunteers found some items they believed might be potential evidence: torn panties, a pretty dress, several pairs of women's shoes, strands of human hair, and a pair of tan overalls. The overalls had belonged to Claudia Ivette González.

González's mother, who was among those searching the field that day, broke into tears when she was shown the garment, which was stained with grass and dirt.

Remarkably, municipal police had conducted their own sweep of the site just after the women's corpses had been discovered there some three months earlier. Somehow they had missed this garment and other evidence found by the ill-equipped volunteers.

When a state investigator was later notified of the group's findings, he faulted the volunteers for contaminating "possible evidence" by touching it with their bare hands.

"It's incredible that the authorities would leave behind so many items at the site, like women's underwear, shoes, and clumps of human hair," Victor Muñoz of the Coalition on Violence Against Women and Families on the Border told the *El Paso Times*. Muñoz, a resident of El Paso, was among the volunteers who took part in the February 24 search. "They [the police] did not do a good job."

It wouldn't be long before police incompetence would be in the headlines once again.

CHAPTER ELEVEN

"A National Shame"

*The government of the state is supporting criminal
elements, and unfortunately, we are going to continue seeing more missing and murdered women
in Juárez.*

EXCERPT FROM LAST INTERVIEW
GIVEN TO THE PRESS BY MARIO ESCOBEDO,
MURDERED ATTORNEY REPRESENTING
ACCUSED BUS DRIVER GUSTAVO GONZÁLEZ MEZA

IN LATE 2001, President Vicente Fox announced his intention
to involve federal authorities in the investigation being conducted by state officials in Ciudad Juárez. Calling the murders
"a national shame," Fox promised federal help in solving the
ongoing killings of the city's young women.

Despite the efforts by Ponce and the others to convince
residents that authorities had locked up those responsible, the
killings continued to draw coverage in Juárez newspapers. Perhaps that was why local officials opted not to criticize the PAN
president for trying to wrest control of the matter away from

the state's governor, Patricio Martínez García, who was a member of the opposition PRI party.

In December, Fox ordered the federal attorney general's office to commence its own investigation into the murders, directing that seventy-six of the city's files be transferred by January 7, 2002.

Yet, only ten of those cases files arrived by the president's deadline, according to news accounts. State officials promised the remainder of the documents would be on their way within several days.

Soon after the transfer of the case files, Suly Ponce Prieto handed in her resignation as the state's regional coordinator, under pressure from the public, but was quickly transferred to a new post as minister of the interior. Ponce's superior, Chihuahua attorney general Arturo González Rascón, also left his position that January amid ongoing criticism of the way the investigations had been handled under his direction. *El Diario de Juárez* reported that González Rascón had wanted to resign for some time, but was forced to stay on by Governor Martínez, who had reportedly refused to accept the attorney general's resignation. Like Ponce, González Rascón was also assigned a promotion to the role of head of the state council for public safety, and Martínez appointed Jesús José Solís Silva to the role of attorney general.

One local business leader, Maurilio Fuentes Estrada, head of a statewide business group called Canacintra, voiced outrage over Martínez's decision to reward government officials who underperformed with promotions.

Despite changes in the governor's office, officials were still pressing ahead with the case against the bus drivers accused of murdering the eight women found in the former cotton field. Javier "Víctor" García and Gustavo González were now isolated in a state penitentiary that was some two hundred miles away from their families and their attorneys.

Within days after the installation of the new governor, the bus drivers were transferred from El Cereso to the penitentiary in distant Chihuahua City, the state capital. It is believed that members of the state police had orchestrated the move, which also happened to coincide with the resignation of forensics chief Oscar Maynez.

Sergio Dante Almaraz, the lawyer for bus driver Víctor García, was furious over the transfer of his client and called the move illegal. In an interview in the spring of 2002, Almaraz spelled out his concern that the transfer would negatively impact his ability to mount a solid defense on his client's behalf. He pointed to the Mexican constitution, which states that a trial must take place where the presumed crime was committed because that is where the witnesses are and that is where the evidence is found. The state-run facility was a five-hour drive from Juárez through rough terrain.

Almaraz had already asked the court for a change of venue back to Ciudad Juárez. But he had little faith his request would be granted.

"The hair samples found in the vehicles didn't correspond to any of the victims, the luminol testing didn't find any blood samples, and there was absolutely no evidence to prove that there were any crimes committed," the attorney said. "That exasperated the DA's office, and as a result, the state police gave orders to take, forcibly, abruptly, and illegitimately, the two detainees to the jail in Chihuahua."

There was another problem with the state's case against the bus drivers too: tests performed on the men by the Department of Public Transportation found no evidence to suggest that they had used marijuana or cocaine, undermining the state's hypothesis that the bus drivers were addicts who ingested the substances, got excited, and went out to torture and kill young women.

The state's secretary of transportation was subsequently fired. Some observers suggested that the firing may have been linked to the negative test results. They wondered if, like Oscar Maynez, the secretary had been asked to falsify findings and refused. When asked, Juárez District Attorney Manuel Ortega was unable to explain why the state official had been let go. "That decision was not up to me. That fell under someone else, just like the ousting of the director of the penitentiary," he said in an interview with Univision that spring.

Ortega also dismissed the defense lawyer's assertion that the bus drivers had been transferred to the state penitentiary in a deliberate effort to prevent them from mounting a solid defense by putting 230 miles between lawyer and defendant, thus limiting the time that Almaraz could spend with his client. The district attorney insisted that, no matter where the men were incarcerated—Juárez or Chihuahua City—they would be given a fair trial on the eight homicide charges.

Authorities had claimed that the bus drivers' transfer was made for security reasons. Ortega argued that their high-profile status made them potential targets of aggression from inmates at El Cereso, whose staff was already overtaxed by the overcrowded conditions. The state facility could offer the men better protection, he said.

The defense attorneys for the bus drivers did not accept the argument about the men's safety. Sergio Dante Almaraz and Mario Escobedo Jr., the lawyer for bus driver Gustavo González Meza, had agreed to seek a change of venue back to Juárez.

From the moment they agreed to represent the suspects, both lawyers had received repeated death threats. While fearful, both men were determined to forge ahead. In court, they entered more than forty pieces of evidence into the record, including declarations from the director of El Cereso documenting the men's torture, photos of the wounds on the men's bodies, and testimony from witnesses placing the men in other locations at the times the crimes were allegedly committed. Neither attorney was willing to discuss the details of their submissions with the media. However, Almaraz said he was confident that they had provided sufficient material to demonstrate that their clients had been framed for the eight murders.

Soon after the defense evidence had been filed, a judge ruled that no more evidence could be submitted. Some observers wondered if the court was growing uncomfortable with the evidence that was being entered by the defense. Perhaps the judge felt that the defense was well on its way to building a successful case.

Mario Escobedo Jr. was undaunted. In early February 2002, he made public his intent to file a criminal complaint against state police officials for allegedly kidnapping and torturing his client, Gustavo González Meza. The lawyer took what he perceived as a calculated risk in opting to challenge the state police directly. His decision would ultimately prove fatal.

On February 5, Escobedo spoke to his colleague, Sergio Dante Almaraz, by phone. During the call, he confided that an anonymous caller had been making threats on his cell phone and his office line. Escobedo said he didn't recognize the voice but suspected it was someone from the state police. Officers had been after him to abandon the criminal complaint, but that day he made it clear that he intended to go forward nonetheless.

That evening, the young lawyer, a father of two daughters ages seven and ten, was on his way home from work when he noticed that he was being followed by a sport utility vehicle. Worried, Escobedo immediately dialed his father on his cell phone for help.

"Dad, I'm being tailed," the lawyer told Mario César Escobedo Sr. The elder Escobedo, also an attorney who had been assisting his son in his defense of González, would later reveal that he too had been the target of death threats.

In fact, the father and son had been tossing about the idea of abandoning the high-profile case altogether. The threats were escalating and it was becoming clear that they were serious in nature. While the elder Escobedo favored bowing out, his son had been on the fence. Convinced of his client's innocence, the young Escobedo was torn over the prospect of allowing an injustice to occur. Still, he had his family to consider.

"It's a coincidence," the senior Escobedo assured his son during the phone call that night. "Not to worry."

"No, Papá, don't hang up! I'm being followed. Papá, they're following me!"

Panicked, the elder Escobedo held the cell phone to his ear as he raced toward his truck. "I'm coming, I'll be right there with you," he assured his son. "Describe the vehicles to me."

"It's a Grand Cherokee, Papá, covered in mud. Hurry!"

"I'm on my way, son. Stay calm. Keep your wits about you!"

"Papá, hurry, they're pulling out their weapons."

At that moment, Mario Escobedo Sr. heard gunshots, the screeching of tires, and a crash. "Son, answer me. Answer me!" he yelled into the phone. There was no response.

In an interview with Univision, the elder Escobedo re-called how he cried as he raced to the local hospital, only to learn that his son was dead.

"I still didn't know then that my son's own executioners were the agents and comandante of the judicial police of the state," he said. "I thought it was a group of thugs, of assassins who had already made death threats against us for undertaking the defense of Gustavo González Meza."

The following morning, Escobedo learned that members of the state police had indeed shot his son. They claimed that it was a case of mistaken identity and that they never intended to do the lawyer any harm. Officials explained that the officers thought they were chasing an alleged drug dealer who went by the nickname "El Venado," the deer.

An official for the state police told the local Ciudad Juárez newspaper, *El Diario de Juárez*, that his officers had opened fire on Escobedo after he failed to pull over. He then added that the attorney began firing at officers as they approached his vehicle. Crime scene photographs showed that there were at least ten bullet holes in Escobedo's Chevy pickup. It was later reported that the officers who fired at the attorney that night were allegedly under the direction of the commander who had supervised the detention of the two bus drivers then in custody.

The official, Chihuahua district attorney Manuel Ortega, insisted that Escobedo Jr. was in the wrong and that it was the attorney who had opened fire on the agents when they told him to get out of his vehicle.

"Instead of doing as he's told, the driver pulls out a firearm, one which his father had previously given to him, and he fires against the police officers," Ortega said in an interview with Univision. "He fires, the police officers fire back . . . after that, he drives away and fires again, and the police officers return fire."

The dead lawyer's father quickly pointed out that the officers had been driving an unmarked vehicle, did not identify themselves as state police, and were chasing his son at ten o'clock at night. In addition, the Jeep they were in was not an official state police vehicle but a private vehicle registered to one of the department's commanders, Roberto Alejandro Castro Valles.

Castro was later cleared by a judge of any wrongdoing and, according to news accounts, left the state police for a position with the federal government as a security officer in their anti-corruption ministry in Mexico City.

"There are many inconsistencies to this story," the elder Escobedo said. "The agents were pursuing the attorney's vehicle in a high-speed chase, and the attorney was also talking to his father on his cell phone at the same time. Now, how is it possible for someone to be *driving* at a high speed, *talking* on his cell phone, and *shooting* a gun at the same time? With what hands? With which hand is he firing? At what point?"

In an interview with Univision, District Attorney Ortega demonstrated how he believed the slain lawyer had managed to drive his Jeep with one hand on the wheel, holding a cell phone to his face with his shoulder as he fired on officers with his free hand. Yet his explanation and the accompanying on-camera demonstration were hardly convincing.

Photographs taken for the city's *El Norte* newspaper suggested that members of the state police department may have tampered with evidence after the accident in order to substantiate that they had fired in self-defense.

There were no bullet holes in the unmarked Jeep Grand Cherokee that the officers were driving when the photographer from *El Norte* snapped images of the vehicle at the crime scene. But when the same photographer snapped more pictures of the Jeep as it was parked outside the attorney general's office, there was a bullet hole in a front fender and fresh mud on the tires. *El Norte* contended that someone from the state police department had taken the Jeep to another location and then fired a shot into the fender to make it appear that Escobedo Jr. had been firing at police.

"Their vehicle had fresh mud on its tires, and it had an impact, an orifice from a firearm on its front left fender," the senior Escobedo said upon producing the two sets of photos for Univision. "The mud had dried by then, except on that side where the hole was. There was even water leaking out on that side of the headlight."

The following day, the Chihuahua state attorney general's office issued a press release citing Escobedo's cause of death as a brain injury suffered as a result of an auto accident that occured while the lawyer was fleeing state police officers. Another city newspaper, *El Diario de Juárez*, however, reported a different outcome. Citing the official autopsy report, the paper described the lawyer's death as the result of "a gunshot wound to the head."

There were other inconsistencies in the incident as well. In the days following the lawyer's death, authorities claimed a gunshot residue test performed at the scene was consistent with Escobedo having fired a gun. Those test results would appear to support the police claim that the attorney had fired on the officers that night. But in an interview with Univision conducted that February, the senior Escobedo produced official state documents showing that the gunshot residue test had, in fact, come back with negative results for gunpowder residue— meaning that his son hadn't fired a gun that night.

The grieving father said he had also located a witness who was willing to testify that one of the police officers involved in the high-speed chase had gotten out of the Grand Cherokee that night and fired on his son as he sat in the pickup truck— after it had already crashed.

To confirm the witness's account, the elder attorney hired a crash reconstruction expert to inspect his son's Chevy pickup. The consultant and several other attorneys examined the vehicle on February 19. According to news accounts, the team concluded that several of the gunshots had struck areas of

Escobedo's truck that had been exposed only after it had crashed that night. The finding would suggest that police had fired additional rounds at the vehicle after it had crashed.

Two weeks before the attorney's death, the father-and-son law team had been sitting together in their law offices, relaxing. With his feet propped up on his desk, the younger Escobedo asked his dad, "*Compa*, what do you think about La Foca's defense?" referring to his client, the bus driver, Gustavo González Meza, by his nickname "the Seal."

Recalling the chat, the senior Escobedo said that he told his son, "*Mijo*, to tell you the truth I don't want the case. I have a feeling something bad is going to happen to us."

But the son wanted to go ahead. "Don't be afraid, *jefe* [boss]," he told his father. "But I'll tell you something. If you don't want to continue, I will."

Dozens of community activists and others attended the press conference held by the senior Escobedo after his son's death to denounce police claims about the events surrounding the shooting. Community members screamed, "*¡Asesinos! ¡Asesinos!*" and "*¡Justicia! ¡Justicia!*" Others carried huge placards that read, "*No hay justicia en Ciudad Juárez.*" "There is no justice in Ciudad Juárez."

Many of the city's residents found it difficult to believe that state agents had actually fired at, and killed, an attorney in a case of mistaken identity. Yet the young Escobedo was no stranger to these men. In fact he regularly visited the *procuraduría* and the court and knew many of the officers by name. It was hard to believe they could mistake him for a criminal. Had the attorney been deliberately silenced by police? Some of the people attending the elder attorney's press conference knew of others in the case who had reportedly been silenced as well.

In fact, members of the Univision crew insist they were being followed while in Juárez and claim to have received suspicious phone calls late one evening to one of their Juárez hotel rooms from a person who failed to identify himself. The caller did not speak, but was breathing heavily into the receiver. After checking with front desk personnel, they learned that the hotel phones were routinely shut off from outside callers promptly at 11 p.m., indicating that the late-night caller was phoning from inside the hotel. Even more frightening was that this person had somehow obtained information about the crew's hotel arrangements, and might have even been eavesdropping on interviews the crew had conducted with lawyer Sergio Dante Almaraz and Miriam García earlier that day.

Amid cries for a full investigation of the attorney's death, authorities announced the suspension of several of the police agents involved in the pursuit—albeit with pay. But no charges would ever be filed against any of the police who had been involved. A judge would rule in June 2002 that the officers had killed the attorney in "self-defense."

Escobedo's death had rattled his colleague, Sergio Dante Almaraz, the attorney defending bus driver Víctor García. Dante Almaraz's decision to remain on the case created a rift within his family; his two young sons, both attorneys, questioned their father's decision to intentionally place himself in harm's way.

"My sons asked me to reflect on what I am doing," Dante Almaraz said in an interview with Univision that February.

"They say to me, 'Papa, you are risking your life, and by our being with you, you are risking our lives as well.' That does cause me to reflect, but then my sense of ethics and my personal dignity get the best of me. I think to myself, 'Why the hell did I study law?' I wanted to remedy the injustice; I wanted to fight with all my might against the injustice. That's when I stay firm and stay the course.

"I recognize that Mexico is a leading violator of human rights," the lawyer continued. "We in Mexico haven't succeeded in establishing some sort of criteria that will protect the dignity of people who are detained by the authorities. We haven't established a set of rules to protect the human rights of detainees.

"Even delinquents have a right to a fair trial. And fairness dictates that there be an arrest warrant issued by a competent judge and that their families be notified that they are being arrested and informed as to their whereabouts. Otherwise, it is the equivalent of kidnapping, isn't it?

"It's not enough to grab a couple of guys and take them forcibly from their home, beat them for five or six hours, burn their genitals with an electric prod, and make them confess even to the murders of [Mexican war hero Emiliano] Zapata or Pancho Villa. You have to have proof!" the lawyer demanded. "You have to have evidence!"

It seemed that whoever tried to get to the bottom of the crimes was either threatened, fired, forced to resign, or killed. The murdered attorney was not the only one to run afoul of authorities. A popular radio talk show host was also fired in February

2002—the same month Escobedo died. The talk show host, Samira Izaguirre of Radio Cañón, was luckier; she survived.

The incident occurred after Izaguirre and several members of her station angered officials with their public criticisms of the investigation into the cotton field murders. The host had provided an "open forum" to the families of the bus drivers charged with the murders, as well as to other women in the community who spoke out against the arrests.

Almost immediately after the radio show aired, advertisements began appearing in the local newspapers suggesting Izaguirre was a bar owner and a regular at the city's strip clubs; one ad even linked her romantically to one of the bus drivers in custody. News outlets in both Ciudad Juárez and El Paso followed up with stories accusing the government of placing the advertisements, citing as evidence paid receipts that had been signed by a government staffer.

It was not long before the radio host joined the growing list of people receiving death threats from anonymous callers. In an interview, Izaguirre said the situation grew so terrifying that she was forced to relocate across the border to El Paso. Though frightened, she was also furious over what she labeled "the worst case ever of political harassment against journalists in Ciudad Juárez." The talk show host contended that local and state officials had pressured advertisers to pull their ads from her show. Citing a decline in revenue, the radio station subsequently canceled the program.

"The pressure was such that they succeeded in driving us out," she said in an interview with Univision that spring. "I felt such impotence; not only was my freedom of expression curtailed and finally silenced, but at the national level we proclaim that Mexico has a real lack of freedom of expression, and as a result of allowing people to express themselves, I am now out of a job.

"My family was afraid for my life," Izaguirre continued. "And I was afraid myself, for my life and my personal safety. Look what happened to Defense Attorney Escobedo. He got killed by the state police, and after they killed him, they made the statement, 'Yes, we killed him, but we killed him because he was disguised as a killer!' "

In addition to going on a hunger strike herself, Samira Izaguirre had been instrumental in organizing a candlelight vigil held in early December to memorialize the eight victims found in the cotton field. During her radio show, *Calibre 800*, she had asked for donations of 10,000 candles for the event. Remarkably, her request had yielded nearly triple that number: 27,000 candles illuminated the otherwise sterile field like a warm carpet of lights. Eight tall pink crosses were erected that night, bearing the names of the eight young women whose bodies had been found there.

Mourners stood by in silence as the mothers of the dead girls placed bouquets of plastic flowers at the foot of the crosses, which were inscribed in bold black script. One family had carefully formed the shape of a human body with the artificial floral arrangements to memorialize their dead child.

"It was a way of showing the mothers and the families of the victims that the community feels their loss," Izaguirre said of the candlelight vigil. "It was a way of telling them, 'We are with you.' "

The event, which had garnered enormous local and national media attention, culminated with demonstrators, including Izaguirre, carrying an enormous steel cross from the cotton field to the downtown building housing the offices of the state attorney general and state police. There the mourners planted the giant symbol for all to view, a poignant message to state officials not to forget the victims.

Once in El Paso, Izaguirre joined demonstrators and Texas state legislators on March 9, 2002, in a binational protest to demand justice for the slain women of their sister city, Juárez.

Eyebrows were raised that afternoon when one federal official from Mexico City, Deputy Attorney General Jorge Campos Murillo, stood before reporters and charged that some of the murders were the work of a group called Juniors, sons of wealthy Mexican families whose influence and clout were such that authorities were turning a blind eye to their culpability in the killings.

Campos's accusation was stunning. But like so many other possible leads in the case, it went nowhere. In a daring move, Campos contacted officials at the Mexican consulate in El Paso to ask for assistance from the FBI. Soon afterward, he was transferred to another department. After the transfer, Campos refused to answer questions from the press.

Campos was not the only federal official to make allegations. Other federal law enforcement officials said that six people, all prominent men from the Juárez–El Paso region and the Mexican border city of Tijuana, had arranged abductions of Mexican women, who were forced to participate in orgies and then murdered, according to a story that appeared in the *El*

Paso Times. The newspaper alleged the suspects were "men who cross the border regularly, are involved in major businesses, are associates of drug cartels and have ties to politicians in President Vicente Fox's administration."

In response to the accusations, a spokesperson for the federal attorney general's office, Gabriela López, told the newspaper, "These cases do not fall under [federal] jurisdiction . . . the Chihuahua state attorney general's office is handling the cases."

Chihuahua state officials in 2002 acknowledged they were investigating "a high-profile suspect" whom they would not identify because the information was part of "a pending investigation."

That September, members of the Juárez business community were up in arms over the erection of a giant wooden cross calling attention to the unsolved murders, that had been placed in the downtown area, on the Mexican side of the border, just over the Santa Fe Bridge. In a letter to Major Jesús Delgado of the Juárez Police Department, members of the Association of Business Owners and Professionals of Juárez Avenue, a main shopping street, expressed their displeasure with the message the large symbol was sending, calling it "a horrible image for tourism."

While officials were responding to the complaint, residents learned that two more bodies had been found. Initial reports claimed that one of the victims, Erica Pérez, a twenty-six-year-old mother of two, whose partially clad body was discovered in a vacant field on September 23, had been raped and strangled. Family members of the unemployed maquila worker said Pérez had vanished on the day she went out in search of a job.

The second victim, officials claimed, was an unidentified female whose skeletal remains were found behind a maquiladora plant that same day.

In a bizarre twist, then Attorney General Jesús José Solís Silva quickly revised information released about the circumstances of Pérez's death, insisting that the young woman had died of a drug overdose, not strangulation as had first been reported. The new finding was questioned by a special investigator. Still, it allowed officials to remove Pérez's name from the official femicide roster.

State lawmakers would later come under fire for "downplaying" the murder rate in Ciudad Juárez by omitting the cause of death from official reports and fabricating information to close the cases. In addition, for the first time in the city's memory, the families of victims and the families of the supposed killers were joining to demand an official inquiry into the handling of the investigation into the cotton field murders. Neither party believed the bus drivers were behind the killings, and they were rallying against the authorities.

By the fall of 2002, even activist Esther Chávez was growing weary. By then, she had changed her focus and was no longer leading protest marches and fighting so aggressively for the dead women of Juárez. Instead, she was struggling to keep Casa Amiga, her center for poor and abused women, open and afloat. Like many other nonprofit organizations, Casa Amiga was running out of government funds and was facing the possibility of having to close its doors. In late 2001, the center's funding had been halted after Juárez mayor Gustavo Elizondo's PAN party lost control of the city. The local election had resulted in an annulment, and state officials had appointed a PRI interim mayor. Chávez was on pins and needles waiting and wondering if Casa Amiga would be able to continue on donations only.

In February 2002, two local politicians agreed to postpone any decision on funding for the crisis center, and a subsequent review by members of two local agencies determined that Casa Amiga was receiving too much money from the municipality.

While one PAN city counselor spoke out in favor of Chávez and her important work for the city's women, others were expressing a desire to cut back on the financing.

Still, Chávez remained active, continuing to collect and record data on the murdered girls and advocating for justice for the families. Her latest fight was over a proposed state law in Chihuahua that would reduce the sentence for rape from four years to one year if a man could prove that a woman had provoked him.

The proposed law, Chávez argued, "shows the root problem behind the Ciudad Juárez murders—that in a society where men cannot be charged with raping their wives and domestic abuse is rarely prosecuted, authorities simply do not take violence against women seriously enough."

Several politicians in Juárez renewed their calls for the resignation of Chihuahua attorney general Jesús José Solís Silva after he sought to minimize the significance of the crimes against women there, insisting that local activists and others who had come to Mexico from the United States to advocate for the victims and their families were "blowing the crimes out of proportion."

The political climate grew even worse when authorities announced that DNA results on the eight bodies found in the cotton field that past November did not match seven of the supposed victims. The findings raised new questions about the identities of the women dumped or buried in the overgrown field. The revelation sent shock waves through the city, also raising questions about the case against the two bus drivers being held for the murders.

According to the test results, released by the federal attorney general's office in late October, only the DNA from the family of Verónica Martínez Hernández matched the DNA of the body found in the abandoned field.

In addition to creating uncertainty for the relatives of the other seven women—whose families had already buried the bodies given to them by state authorities—the negative test results also contradicted the state's case against Gustavo González Meza and Víctor García Uribe, who had supposedly named the women during their confessions. The new development bolstered the men's claims that they had been tortured into admitting to the killings.

Even more troubling was that authorities were now asking members of two families, those of Esmeralda Herrera Monreal and Claudia Ivette González, for additional "data" for more forensic studies in light of "inconclusive" findings in their cases. In an interview with a local Juárez newspaper, Mayela

González, the sister of Claudia Ivette, said that while "disturbed" over the recent developments, the family still believed the body they had been presented was, in fact, Claudia Ivette. Mayela noted that dental work, and other physical characteristics, including hair color, ponytail holders, and a curve in the bone of one of the fingers, led them to believe that the body they had buried that past November was, indeed, her sister.

But others remained in doubt and were calling on federal authorities to get to the bottom of what many viewed as ongoing cover-ups and conspiracies at work in the border city.

Officials offered no explanation for the DNA debacle or any justification for their continuing to hold the two men who had allegedly confessed to killing women whose bodies were not even among those recovered from the crime scene. What was clear was that the early warning issued by Oscar Maynez was now coming to fruition: the authorities' case against the bus drivers was not holding up. Nevertheless, they continued to stand behind the flawed theory.

CHAPTER TWELVE

Impunity Reigns

"I realize that Mexico is a leading violator of human rights."

SERGIO DANTE ALMARAZ,
ATTORNEY REPRESENTING ACCUSED BUS DRIVER
VÍCTOR GARCÍA

TWO SIGNIFICANT MILESTONES in the history of these cases occurred in February 2003 when the attorney for Sharif Sharif appealed his conviction in the Elizabeth Castro case and one of the accused bus drivers linked to the cottonfield eight, Gustavo González Meza, was found dead in his prison cell.

Sharif Sharif's attorney, Irene Blanco, had won the right to appeal citing problems with the evidence used in the lower-court conviction. But the Egyptian's appeal failed and the convicted murderer was sent back to prison. "I am innocent!" Sharif had shouted when the judge upheld the sentence. "I'm afraid. I don't know what's going to become of me." Sharif Sharif did win a small victory, though, when the judge presiding over his appeal agreed to shave ten years off his sentence, reducing it from thirty years to twenty years for the single murder charge. Both the defense and the prosecution promised to appeal the judge's ruling. Furthermore, prosecutors suggested that additional murder charges against Sharif were pending.

Meanwhile, González was discovered dead in his cell at the maximum-security facility in Chihuahua City on February 8, leaving behind a wife, three young children, and the infant girl who was born after his arrest. While authorities listed the official cause of death to be "disseminated vascular coagulation," or cardiac arrest as a result of a blood clot following a hernia operation, news outlets called his death "suspicious."

The attorney Dante Almaraz and members of the González family, including the bus driver's twenty-three-year-old widow, Blanca Guadalupe López de González, raised questions as to who had ordered the surgery be performed. Relatives claimed that no one was contacted prior to the operation, nor had they granted permission for González to be transferred from the prison to the hospital where the operation was allegedly performed. In addition, it seemed irregular that the bus driver would have been left alone in his cell following major surgery, although in an interview with Univision, the twenty-three-year-old Blanca González said she had spoken with her husband after the surgery and he told her, "They've operated on me. I'm out. I'm fine."

Blanca vowed to move "sea and land" to get a second autopsy performed on her husband's body and clear his name. "This is cruel," she told the Juárez newspaper *El Norte*. "We don't believe the official version of events. It was bad enough that they kidnapped him from his home, arbitrarily jailed him and continued torturing him until they injured him and then the authorities still decided to end his life." Still, authorities were standing by the official determination of the state's medical examiner, ruling the death to have been from natural causes.

In an interview following La Foca's death, Sergio Dante Almaraz, the attorney representing the surviving bus driver, contended that state officials "are eliminating us one by one." He pointed to the suspicious shooting death of his colleague, criminal lawyer Mario Escobedo Jr., by members of the state police that previous February.

One administrator with intimate knowledge of the post-mortem examination disclosed that authorities had changed the "official" cause of death listed on the death certificate of Gustavo González three times before finally agreeing on a determination. The official also maintained that authorities were struggling to find someone in the department willing to sign the document: at one point, it looked as though it would be released without an official signature.

Miriam García, the wife of bus driver Víctor García, the dead man's supposed accomplice, was meanwhile insisting that González's death was no accident. García claimed that two state police officers had broken into her home several days before González's death and threatened her life. She said the men told her they would track her down and kill her if she attended a demonstration scheduled for that Friday at which Eve Ensler, author of *The Vagina Monologues*, was to address protestors rallying against the ongoing violence directed at the city's women. During the men's visit, García contended, they warned that they would kill her, her jailed husband, and Gustavo González if she dared to show up to the demonstration.

It wasn't the first time that members of the bus driver's family were targeted. Ever since police had detained the two drivers, members of both their families claimed they had been harassed and threatened. Miriam maintained that on the day that the attorney Mario Escobedo Jr. was gunned down by officers of the state police, she had received a threatening phone call from someone claiming that she too would die if she continued to speak out.

Amnesty International confirmed that it had received several reports of unknown persons surveiling the residences of the relatives of the detainees, even after the Inter-American Commission on Human Rights (IACHR), the human rights arm of the Organization of American States based in Washington, D.C., issued protection measures in 2002 on behalf of Miriam García and Blanca Guadalupe López (the wives of the accused bus drivers) and the lawyer Sergio Dante Almaraz. In addition, the commission had also granted "precautionary measures . . . in favor of Esther Chávez, a human rights defender who has been deeply involved in pursuing justice for these crimes, who had received a series of threats in evident connection with that work." Following the death of Gustavo González in his cell on February 8, 2003, "under circumstances that remain under investigation," the IACHR extended the protection to include Víctor García, who was still incarcerated at the state-run prison.

The IACHR had received a formal request in late 2001 signed by hundreds of organizations and individuals, asking that the commission's special rapporteur visit Mexico to examine the situation. Noting that more than two hundred women had been murdered in the state of Chihuahua since 1993, the signers suggested that inefficacy on the part of law enforcement was responsible for the ongoing murders.

The three-day visit commenced in Ciudad Juárez on February 11, continued with meetings in Mexico City on February 12, and concluded with a press conference on February 13, 2002. During her visit, the special rapporteur, Dr. Marta Altolaguirre, met with nearly two dozen prominent federal authorities and conducted interviews with officials of the state of Chihuahua and of Ciudad Juárez, who presented information about the killing of 268 women and girls since 1993.

Among those interviewed were Suly Ponce, now the regional coordinator of the North Zone, and Zulema Bolívar, special prosecutor for the investigation of the women's murders. Information and testimony from victims' relatives and from representatives of nongovernmental human rights organizations and other representatives at the local and national level were also solicited. Pioneer activist Esther Chávez was among those who spoke.

In her 24-page report, Dr. Altolaguirre noted that the homicide rates for women had "experienced an unusually sharp rise in Ciudad Juárez in 1993" and had remained elevated since that time. It also suggested that the rate of homicide for women compared to that of men "was significantly higher than other similarly situated cities" and that the "brutal circumstances" of the murders and the "possible character as serial killings" had focused attention on the ongoing situation.

The report noted that based on the information provided by those interviewed, the root of the violence was "integrally related to a larger situation of gender-based violence that includes disappearances, other sexual crimes and domestic violence."

Among the deficiencies noted was an inability on the part of the victims or their families to obtain "prompt access to effective judicial protection and guarantees," and a common denominator in a majority of the cases was identified as a pattern of "historical gender-based discrimination.

"The denial of an effective response both springs from and feeds back into the perception that violence against women—most illustratively domestic violence—is not a serious crime," Dr. Altolaguirre wrote. "The lack of an effective official response is part and parcel of the larger context of discrimination."

Dr. Altolaguirre suggested "the lack of basic information" from authorities had led to "a profound lack of confidence" on the part of family members of the missing and murdered girls, as well as the community as a whole.

"Family members in these and other cases reported having received conflicting or confusing information from the authorities, and having been treated dismissively or even disrespectfully or aggressively when they sought information about the investigations."

The report cited one instance in which a family member

had reportedly been denied the possibility to see the remains "for her own protection," and other cases in which the remains "had not yet been returned to the presumed families."

In addition, it noted that certain families "expressed grave doubts as to whether the body of their loved one had really been found, or whether they might keep hoping that the person reported missing was still alive."

In the case of the cotton field killings, the report explained that while DNA tests had been ordered, months had passed with "no answers." "As of October of 2002, authorities of the PGJE [state prosecutor's office] indicated to the Commission that the results of these tests had not yet been received."

While authorities pointed to the detention of bus drivers Gustavo González Meza and Javier "Víctor" García Uribe in connection with these crimes as evidence of its "prompt response," the report noted that "numerous individuals, including some Mexican state officials," had voiced concerns about allegations "that these detainees had been tortured to coerce confessions."

In fact, Dr. Altolaguirre had received "two distinct sets of medical certificates" during her visit documenting the suspects' injuries once in custody.

"The set provided by the PGJE [the state's prosecutor's office] was prepared by the Department of Legal Medicine on November 11, 2001, at 02:40 and 02:45 hours, respectively," the report stated. "The certificate relative to González indicates no external signs of violence, while that relative to García refers to a small zone of equimosis [bruise] on his right arm that would heal in less than 15 days.

"The other set of certificates, prepared by the Medical Unit of the detention center at 21:00 hours on November 11, 2001, attested in the case of González to 'multiple quemaduras en genitales' [multiples burns to the genitals] and areas of equimosis in the area of the thorax and edema.

"In the case of García, it refers to 'multiples quemaduras de 1er grado en genitales' [multiple first-degree burns to the genitals] and . . . marks on his right arm."

Despite public allegations of torture and complaints to state officials that the confessions were coerced, "the judiciary rejected the claims with respect to coercion as unsubstantiated," the report stated.

It was further noted that information obtained during the visit suggested that "only a small number of files (fewer than 10) were transferred from the prosecutor in charge of missing persons to the prosecutor for homicides" and "a delay on the part of authorities in initiating investigations. . . .

"On the one hand . . . family members who went to police to report a missing person might be told to return in 48 hours, with the explanation that the missing woman or girl must have gone off with a boyfriend and would soon return. On the other hand, they indicated that even with a missing person's report, the response was neither rapid nor comprehensive."

Authorities acknowledged that, in the past, the police tended to require such a lapse of time before taking a missing persons report, but claimed "this had been remedied through changes in policy."

Still, Dr. Altolaguirre found that "while there have been some important advances, the response of the Mexican State to the killings and other forms of violence against women has been, and remains, seriously deficient."

Remarkably, even after the visit by the special rapporteur for the IAHRC and the release of her highly critical report, similar accusations of police brutality and torture continued coming out of the state capital.

In 1999, authorities in Chihuahua City began noticing the bodies of young women turning up murdered in the state's capital city, just as in Ciudad Juárez. The numbers had risen even higher by March 2003. One case in particular was drawing international attention, first because the sixteen-year-old victim was the daughter of a powerful Chihuahua family, and also because authorities had arrested an American woman and her Mexican-born husband for the murder. The couple was alleging tortured at the hands of police officers who forced them to sign confessions to the murder of the sixteen-year-old, Viviana Rayas. Their accounts of torture while in police custody were eerily similar to those of bus drivers Gustavo González and Víctor García.

While the story of what happened to Viviana Rayas is long and convoluted, her case gained international attention after it was learned that police had allegedly used underhanded tactics to make an arrest in the young girl's homicide. According to authorities, the teen disappeared on March 16. She was last seen at a city park, where her father had dropped her to do homework with some schoolmates.

It was nearing four o'clock when José Rayas, a powerful union leader, let the child out of the car that afternoon, with the understanding that he would see her at home later that evening. The slender teen with the flowing hair and cocoa brown eyes had spent nearly an hour and a half studying with her peers before waving good-bye at a nearby bus stop, from which Viviana would make her way back to her upper-class enclave.

It was after 8 p.m. when her parents arrived home that night to find that their daughter was not there.

Frantic, José Rayas grabbed the phone and mobilized his entire union chapter to search for his daughter. For months, police followed every lead the powerful union leader brought to their attention. While officers appeared to be doing little investigating of their own, they continued to diligently research the countless tips being delivered by Rayas—all of which led nowhere.

Viviana Rayas was the eighth young woman to disappear in the city of Chihuahua since December 2002. The first victim, Paloma Angélica Escobar Ledezma, had turned up dead nearly a month after she vanished. Her raped and tortured body had been tossed near the main road to Ciudad Juárez.

Word of Rayas's disappearance prompted members of Amnesty International to call for an immediate investigation, with full cooperation from state and federal authorities. Yet only after the child's father threatened to shut down the city's transportation system by calling for a strike did a lead surface in the case.

The angry ultimatum came on May 26, when José Rayas led demonstrators to the private home of then Attorney General Jesús Solís Silva. A megaphone in hand, he shouted his message directly into the politician's window: "Either my daughter is found and those responsible for her fate are arrested, or I will see to it that all the road workers in the state walk off the job, including the toll takers."

Not surprisingly, two days later there was movement in the case. The head of the attorney general's office telephoned Rayas on May 28, alerting him to a body that had been recovered about five kilometers off a desert highway. Two women en route to a pilgrimage site had reportedly spotted the decomposing corpse and run to alert police.

The following evening, police detained American Cynthia Kiecker and her Mexican husband, Ulises Perzábal. The couple's arrest and subsequent interrogation came after a tipster contacted the victim's father from a public phone booth and urged Rayas to check out the owners of a local jewelry shop—Kiecker and Perzábal. The caller claimed the couple were odd, with long hair and tattoos, and that strange things took place at their boutique, which stayed open late into the evening. One of the allegations was that the male owner liked to photograph young girls who frequented his shop, an accusation that has never been substantiated. Another was that the couple hosted parties where sex and drugs were free-flowing.

Rayas passed the tip to authorities, and the couple were immediately hauled in for questioning and transported to the former police academy in Chihuahua City, where they later claimed to have been tortured by members of the state police for two straight days before finally signing false confessions. Soon afterward, on May 31, the husband and wife were paraded before the press as the guilty parties in the Viviana Rayas murder.

In an account that echoes those of Juárez bus drivers Gustavo González and Víctor García, the couple said officers kicked and beat them, and burned them with electrical prods. Cynthia Kiecker later told how police had drenched her shirt with water and then applied electrical shocks to her back and legs. At one point, she said, they even stretched her out on a cot and threatened to rape her if she didn't sign a confession.

Their signed documents told an unbelievable and dramatic tale of the young girl's murder—admissions that, critics would later point out, differed from each other in critical ways.

According to their declarations of guilt, it was Cynthia's husband, Ulises, who had first befriended Viviana. The wife's jealousy over his affection for the young girl was what ultimately led to her death.

On the night of March 16, according to their admissions, Viviana was to come to the store for an Aztec ritual. Ulises had prepared a pot of special peyote tea for the young girl to drink. But when Viviana grew ill from the concoction, Ulises became alarmed. His concern for the teen incited jealousy in Cynthia, and in a wild rage, she attacked the young girl, first with a baseball bat and then with a piece of steel reinforcing bar, or rebar, the confessions read.

Cynthia then turned her rage on her husband, who confessed to having grown emotionally charged by his wife's anger. In the throes of excitement, Ulises said, he struck Viviana himself, hitting her so hard in the head that she fell to the ground dead.

While the autopsy made no mention of blunt force trauma to the head, the admissions pointed to a violent blow as the cause of death. The couple wrote in their purported confessions that when they realized Viviana was dead, they set about to cover up the crime, transporting her body to the desert, where they hid it beneath a sheet of metal roofing. The chilling account was bolstered by accounts from several supposed witnesses to the young girl's murder—all friends of the couple who claim to have been detained by police and also tortured into signing confessions.

Authorities held a press conference at the state prison just outside Chihuahua City to announce the arrests of Cynthia and Ulises. The couple had been transferred there for the event. Authorities labeled the couple *"narco-satánicos"* and claimed the murder was committed as part of a satanic ritual under the influence of illicit drugs.

Cynthia later told a reporter that she was initially relieved to be in prison, in a place where the *judiciales* (members of the state police) could no longer get to her. But her relief quickly turned to fear as she realized she was being charged with murder, a state crime in Mexico for which she could spend up to thirty years in prison.

The couple's story made national news and caught the attention of a Juárez resident who immediately contacted the United States Consulate to alert them to the arrest of one of their citizens. In response to the call, a representative from the consulate went to see Cynthia at the prison and allowed her to use his cell phone to contact her mother. Unlike in the United States, the two detainees had not been permitted to make a single phone call. It was unclear if they would have ever been allowed to alert family members to their plight.

Many observers were skeptical of the investigation, and of the guilt of the couple charged with the crime. After a time, even the victim's father, José Rayas, began to question their involvement in Viviana's murder. That past May, another family in Chihuahua City had come forward, accusing police of official misconduct in the murder investigation of Neyra Cervantes. The eighteen-year-old had disappeared from a computer training school. Her skeletal remains, which had been sawed into three pieces, were found in a shallow grave on July 14, just yards from the state police academy.

Neyra's mother, Patricia, had been vigilant in her attempts to get police to help in locating her missing daughter. But when her efforts failed to rally their support, she contacted a family member in Chiapas to assist in the search for his missing relative.

Distraught over learning that his cousin was in trouble, David Meza traveled two hundred miles to Chihuahua City to help his aunt, boldly confronting police about their unwillingness to get involved. His outspokenness landed him in jail, charged with his cousin's murder. News accounts reported that state police arrested Meza based on his "odd" behavior, denied him a lawyer, and then tortured him over six hours, until he finally confessed to killing the computer student—even though he wasn't even in the city at the time his cousin disappeared. Meza claimed that more than a dozen officers participated in the torture: ordering him to strip, they wrapped him like a mummy in twelve-inch-wide bandages, leaving barely enough space for him to breathe, before dousing him in water and shocking him with a cattle prod. They also kicked him, forced spicy water up his nose, and held a plastic bag over his head until he nearly suffocated. The allegations were horrific, and they mirrored those being lodged against state police officers in Ciudad Juárez.

Like the Juárez bus drivers, Meza alleged that police officers had dictated his confession to him and then forced him to sign it. Meza insisted that police first discussed possible scenarios in front of him before settling on a confession: that Meza was sexually excited and that he paid two men seven hundred dollars apiece to kidnap his cousin and bring her to a house outside the capital, where he met the men, purchased a gun, and borrowed their car. From there, he allegedly drove the teen to the desert, where he sexually assaulted her and then shot her, execution-style, in the head.

Officials later acknowleged they had no evidence linking Meza to the crime. They were unable to locate the two men he had allegedly hired to abduct his cousin or the gun he supposedly used to kill her. Neyra's body had been too decomposed to determine if a sexual assault had occurred. Nevertheless, Meza was charged in the homicide.

In a surprising turn of events, Cynthia Kiecker and Ulises Perzábal were finally released from prison in December 2004 after a judge found the couple innocent of the murder of Viviana Rayas. Their release came under intense pressure from U.S. politicians in Kiecker's home state of Minnesota.

In an unusual and controversial move, President Fox had even visited Minnesota that past June, assuring then U.S. Senator Norm Coleman and Cynthia's mother, Carol Kiecker, that the young woman would soon be released.

In September, however, Fox was forced to publicly announce that he had misspoken, after his demand that Kiecker be freed was ignored by state officials—who claimed that Fox had misunderstood their intentions. According to members of the Mexican Consulate, authorities had advised the president that the charges against the police officers accused of torturing the couple would be dropped—not the murder charges against Kiecker and her husband. Even after the parents of Viviana Rayas stepped forward to criticize the investigation and call for the couple's release, authorities maintained the couple's guilt.

That December, just minutes after the Chihuahua state judge delivered the "not guilty" verdict in the cases against Kiecker and Perzábal, the couple and members of their family were quickly loaded into a car with bulletproof windows and escorted to El Paso by officials from the U.S. Consulate. Surrounding the vehicle to provide additional protection was an entourage of law enforcement officials from both the Mexican federal police and the FBI.

Chihuahua state prosecutors later filed an appeal, maintaining that the couple were guilty as charged. Activists worried that the pending appeal served to guarantee that authorities would not pursue other avenues of investigation in the case.

Meanwhile in Ciudad Juárez, the discoveries of six more bodies in a mass gravesite on a deserted stretch of land at the base of Cristo Negro mountain in northeast Juárez had residents again looking into the possibility of a satanic motive behind the killings.

Teenagers had stumbled upon three of the corpses in October 2002 beneath the giant black cross that marks the site while searching the land owned by a sand and gravel company for recyclables to sell for cash. Then on February 17, 2003, family members of several missing girls found three more bodies in the exact location after a sandstorm exposed some hair on the side of the sandstone hill. News accounts stated that the second group of women had been placed about ten feet apart from each other. Their wrists had been tied with rope and their dresses were pushed up above their waists. Cement covered parts of their bodies. Several items pointing to a satanic cult were reportedly found nearby, including symbols such as a star in a circle, and drawings depicting devil worship were carved into the hillside. Some in the city believed the clues had been left to throw investigators off the trail of the real killers.

Authorities later identified the dead women as Juana Sandoval Reyna, Violeta Mabel Alvídrez Barrios, Esmeralda Juárez Alarcón, Teresa López, Gloria Rivas Martínez, and an unidentified woman believed to be Mayra Yesenia Nájera Larragoitia. There was speculation that victims had been abducted from the downtown area, but not on the same dates.

Soon additional theories began circulating the city. One tied some of the murders to several national computer schools with branches in Ciudad Juárez and Chihuahua City. At least seven of the murdered girls, including slain maquila worker Elizabeth Castro, whom the jailed Egyptian scientist, Sharif Sharif, had supposedly murdered, and Violeta Alvídrez, whose decomposing body had been found at the base of Cristo Negro mountain that past February, were students of a downtown computer school.

There was also speculation that the computer schools were somehow linked to several shoe stores in the city center. One news article pointed out that a number of the computer schools were located within close proximity to busy shoe stores, such as Tres Hermanos, the boutique where Silvia Morales had been employed in the days before she disappeared and where Elizabeth Castro had been seen just before her murder.

Another of the earlier victims, Olga Alicia Pérez, had also worked a shift at a downtown shoe boutique on the day she went missing.

A spokesman for the state attorney general declined to comment on the cases or possible links to the computer schools. State officials were also mum about the discovery of yet another body along the highway Eje Vial Juan Gabriel that medical examiners identified as Verónica Martínez, the missing woman whose family had been told that their daughter was among those found in the abandoned cotton field and whose murder had been linked to bus drivers Víctor García and Gustavo González. In fact, state officials had assured the family that DNA tests performed on one of the bodies recovered from the cotton field confirmed it was their daughter.

It would later be alleged in an article in *El Diario de Juárez* that authorities had participated in a cover-up to avoid fouling up the case against bus driver Víctor García. That allegation would be bolstered by a team of Argentine forensic scientists who traveled to Juárez in early 2005 at the request of federal authorities. Among the team's findings was that DNA studies performed on the body presumed to be Verónica Martínez did not match the remains found in the cotton field.

In its noteworthy report, *Intolerable Killings*, released in August 2003, Amnesty International faulted state law enforcement officials for their handling of the investigation into the femicides that had been occurring in the state of Chihuahua since 1993. The report criticized Mexican authorities for regularly ignoring the murders occurring in Ciudad Juárez, and for the fabrication of confessions from scapegoats under torture.

The organization noted that the motives behind the killings in the border city varied from domestic violence, suspected drug-related executions, gang shootings, and sexual assaults. But the report highlighted that a number of the killings had followed a pattern in which young women disappeared and were later found raped and murdered. Chihuahua State Governor Patricio Martínez had all but ignored Irene Khan, the organization's international secretary general and her group, when they came to Juárez from Mexico City earlier that year to look into what was being done to stop the decade-long killing spree.

In fact, his administration had been accused of downplaying the city's femicides; it had even claimed that NGOs inflated the homicide numbers to create a stir and win funding for their organizations. In a public statement that year, Martínez told reporters that his office had been researching the killings and had concluded that there was no evidence of a serial killer on the prowl in Ciudad Juárez.

His viewpoint was shared by many of the city's politicians,

and even many of its residents. When asked, local citizens still pointed a finger at the victims for bringing on the attacks. Both men and women on the streets of the city said they believed the girls were to blame, for being out alone after dark and for dressing provocatively. It appeared the government's campaign to undermine the reputation of the victims had been extremely effective in swaying public opinion—especially in light of the fact that many of the dead women had been abducted in broad daylight and were clothed in slacks or blue jeans and tennis shoes when they were plucked from the streets.

Yet it was just that kind of attitude that had earned state officials a black mark in the Amnesty International report. The lengthy document chastised early investigators for displaying "open discrimination towards the women and their families in their public statements." "On more than one occasion the women themselves were blamed for their own abduction or murder because of the way they dressed or because they worked in bars at night," the report stated.

It also found that the creation in 1998 of the Special Prosecutor's Office for the Investigation of Murders of Women had "failed to live up to the expectation that there would be a radical change in the actions of the state authorities to stamp out such crimes."

The report pointed out that the institution has had seven different directors, and yet "there has been no significant improvement in the coordination and systematizing of investigations in order to put an end to the abductions and murders."

Arturo González Rascón was criticized in the report for his public comments about the victims. "In February 1999, the former State Public Prosecutor . . . was still maintaining that 'women with a nightlife who go out very late and come into contact with drinkers are at risk.' "

"It's hard to go out on the street when it's raining and not get wet," Rascón was quoted as saying.

The report also charged that "the failure, time and again, to keep the families informed of developments" had caused "deep distrust of the judicial apparatus and politicians."

"Impunity reigns" was the subhead to the organization's finding with regard to the handling of the investigation by Chihuahua state authorities. "As far as the state authorities are concerned, most of the murders—including cases of domestic violence or other types of violence—have been 'solved.' However, although, according to their figures, 79 people have been convicted, in the vast majority of cases, justice has not been done. Impunity is most evident in the case of the so-called 'serial murders' that have been recognized as such by the state but in which there has been only one conviction for the kidnapping and murder of a young woman and eighteen detainees awaiting the outcome of the judicial process, in some cases for several years."

The organization was referring to, among others, Sharif Sharif, who had been labeled the serial killer of Juárez but had been charged and convicted of only one crime, and the six members of the Rebels, who were still in custody after seven years awaiting an outcome on their cases.

Furthermore, the quality of the investigations and the alleged failure to provide adequate guarantees during the trials cast doubt on the integrity of the criminal proceedings brought against several of those arrested in connection with these crimes. Meanwhile, year after year, the crimes continued.

The discovery of the body of Viviana Rayas in May 2003 in the city of Chihuahua and allegations that those arrested in connection with the case were tortured demonstrate yet again that the abductions and murders in question are far from being solved.

The fact that the state authorities have not managed to clear up or eradicate these crimes has led to much speculation about who might be behind the murders. There is talk of involvement of drug traffickers, organized crime, or people living in the United States, as well as rumors that those responsible are being protected. There are also theories about the motives being connected to Satanism, the illegal trade in pornographic films, and the alleged trafficking of organs. However, at the moment, since the investigations have so far not been able to confirm any of them, such hypotheses are simply helping to fuel even greater fear among Chihuahuan society.

Finally, the report faulted federal authorities for "overtly" staying out of the investigations on the grounds that "unlike organized crime, the murders of women in Chihuahua State did not come under their jurisdiction as they were not federal crimes.

"Amnesty International believes that, in order to prevent, punish, and stop the abduction and murder of the women in Ciudad Juárez . . . as well as the abuses of power which have hindered the earlier investigations, it is essential for mechanisms to be set up to ensure proper coordination between all authorities at the municipal, state and federal level."

The report recognized that some progress had been made under the country's new president, Vicente Fox, citing the creation in February 2003 of the Commission for the Prevention and Elimination of Violence Against Women in Ciudad Juárez. At a press conference held earlier in the year, President Fox had announced the formation of the new federal commission, which would consist of eight members of the *procuraduría* and two local citizens appointed by the president.

Fox named María Guadalupe Morfín Otero, a human rights lawyer and the former director of the Jalisco State Human Rights Commission, to head the new commission, which, Fox said, would oversee state police investigations and "clarify what has happened over the past ten years and to work so that this painful experience doesn't repeat itself."

Guadalupe Morfín immediately announced her intent to implement a federal "Forty Point Plan," although the particulars of that plan were never fully detailed. Still, her enthusiasm brought a renewed hope to families of Juárez's murdered and missing young women. Morfín had a good track record as an advocate of human rights, although critics feared that her loyalties lay with the PAN party.

The president next appointed María López Urbina, former head of the Coahuila Justice Department, to the newly created role of special federal prosecutor to review the investigations into the Juárez murders. In a press release, López Urbina vowed to investigate the cases "where there is evidence of inefficiency, negligence or tolerance on the part of public servants so there is no more impunity for those who failed to fulfill their duty." She maintained that her first task would be to establish a DNA bank to store evidence. The idea was one that criminologist Oscar Maynez had suggested years earlier. Investigators in the border city had first resisted the use of DNA testing in their investigations, citing a lack of funding.

But the excitement surrounding the new appointments was soon forgotten as police announced the arrest of thirteen members of the state police on suspicion of drug trafficking and murder that January. The stunning declaration was made on Thursday, January 29, 2004, six days after authorities unearthed the bodies of twelve people in the backyard of a Juárez home that was linked to a member of the state police department.

The house, located at 3633 Parsioneros, near the major intersection of Avenida Tecnológico and Bulevar Teófilo Borunda, was occupied by a man named Alejandro García, who, once in police custody, allegedly confessed to taking part in the killings on orders from members of the state police and the Vicente Carrillo Fuentes drug cartel. Under Vicente, who had succeeded his brother Amado, the Juárez Cartel was still considered the most powerful drug organization in Mexico for moving marijuana and cocaine.

Officials learned that García was not the house's owner but was renting it from an unnamed party. Police believed the residence, later dubbed "the house of death," actually belonged to Umberto Santillán Tabares, an underling of Umberto Portillo, a fugitive smuggler facing drug charges. A search of the home had been done after authorities arrested Santillán in El Paso, Texas, earlier that month. Law enforcement officials suspected members of Santillán's gang were using the Juárez residence as a safe house.

An initial search of the house by authorities yielded four bodies. Eight more were found during subsequent searches of the home's backyard. Authorities reported that all of the bodies exhibited signs of torture, and an autopsy later determined that at least three of the men had died as a result of strangulation. A fourth man was suffocated by tape that had been placed over his mouth and nose, officials said. Others had been suffocated with plastic bags.

It was later reported that a group of heavily armed men were behind the abduction of at least three of the victims, although it is not known how long the men were held at the residence, or what had actually transpired there.

The thirteen officers were taken into custody on Wednesday, January 27, when they arrived at headquarters for the night shift. Four others, including the department's commander, Miguel Angel Loya, failed to report to work that evening and warrants were issued for their arrests. Five more commanders were later fired in connection with the torture and killing of the twelve men whose bodies were unearthed at the Juárez property. News accounts claimed the officers belonged to a corrupt gang of drug traffickers called La Línea, a group so feared that it is reportedly forbidden to say their name aloud.

An article in the *Dallas Morning News* quoted a former drug dealer who claimed to be a member of the organized drug gang that counted, among its members, officers from both the state and municipal Juárez police departments. The informant, who declined to reveal his identity, maintained that some of the rape-murders occurring in Ciudad Juárez were in celebration of successful drug runs across the U.S. border.

"Sometimes, when you cross a shipment of drugs to the United States, adrenaline is so high that you want to celebrate by killing women," the newspaper quoted the unidentified man as saying.

It was a horrific admission, and one that was substantiated by another former drug dealer during an interview with documentarian Lourdes Portillo for her film *Señorita Extraviada*. This man also maintained that some of the gang members liked to wear the victims' nipples like trophies on chains around their necks.

In the days after the arrests, *El Diario de Juárez* stated that several of the bodies exhumed from the Juárez backyard had been buried at depths between three and four feet. There were also reports that plaster had been found on some of the corpses, all of which had been doused in lime to conceal the stench of rotting flesh.

Search warrants were secured for six other houses in the border city, and a full-blown investigation into all state police officers assigned to the night shift was ordered. It is not known what, if any, evidence was found during the execution of those additional searches.

Still, the arrests of the thirteen state police officers once again brought to the forefront what many in the city had believed all along; that members of the police were somehow linked to the ongoing femicides. The officers in custody were immediately flown to Mexico City, where they were questioned by federal agents about their alleged role in the killings of the twelve as-yet-unidentified men.

The unfolding police scandal eventually led to the resignation of Chihuahua State attorney general Jesús José Solís Silva that March, after he'd served little more than one year in the top law enforcement spot. His resignation came amid allegations that officials in his office had ties to drug trafficking.

Allegations of corruption were also lodged against former state police commander Francisco Minjares and Antonio Navarrete, who led the investigations into Sharif Sharif and Los Rebeldes. According to U.S. anti-narcotics agents in El Paso, Minjares was one of the most corrupt police officers and had provided protection to narcotraffickers. Minjares was gunned down in early 2003 in Chihuahua City in what authorities called a "gangland-style" killing.

Lawyers for Sharif Sharif alleged that Navarrete pointed a gun to the head of a witness while he was being videotaped giving testimony against Sharif. While this allegation was never substantiated, and there is no evidence that this actually occurred, one news account described how the judge threw out the tape after attorneys were able to show that the tape had been edited.

Navarrete, who was never charged with a crime, denied any wrongdoing in the case, telling one reporter that the allegations "were not true."

Ironically, the fallout from the state police scandal came on the heels of what many viewed as promising year-end crime statistics. According to data from the Chihuahua State Attorney General's Office, Ciudad Juárez had experienced a 27 percent decline in murders from 2002 to 2003, down more than fifty homicides from the previous year.

Instead of patting themselves on the back for the improved crime statistics, however, police officers were being ordered to submit to mandatory drug tests, with federal authorities warning that those who returned a positive result would be immediately terminated.

In early February 2004, *El Diario de Juárez* reported that two officers had tested positive for drugs and were immediately expelled from the department. One of the agents, the newspaper stated, was said to be part of the Special Prosecutor's Office for the Investigation of Murders of Women, an allegation that again opened the door to the probability that police had played a role in some of the killings.

Word, in February 2004, that yet another member of the state police had been arrested for "attempting" to form a prostitution ring of adolescent girls further fueled the controversy. Two young women had come forward to file a criminal complaint alleging that a senior law enforcement officer in Juárez, later identified as Héctor Lastra, was reportedly pressuring underage teens employed at the city's fast-food restaurants to engage in sex with wealthy businessmen.

News accounts maintained that Lastra, who was identified as a Juárez state police chief, had allegedly provided his clients with a catalog of photographs of the girls, all minors. According to prosecutors, the supposed photo album contained pictures of five underage girls, reportedly taken by Lastra.

Interestingly, Ramona Morales, the mother of one of the murdered girls, had spoken of a man in her neighborhood who had been seen driving around taking pictures of young girls. And Sagrario González's family had reported that their daughter's photo was taken by factory personnel just days before she disappeared. Also of note is the fact that in almost all the victims' homes, professional photographs of the slain young women adorned the walls. The portraits, taken to commemorate their fifteenth birthdays, were prominently displayed in ornate frames, capturing the teens in lacy quinceañera dresses with matching veils to mark the special coming-of-age celebrations. The photos, intended to capture a tender moment, were now serving as memorials for the families of the slain young women.

Could the local photographers be somehow involved in the murders? Perhaps they too were providing their negatives to these depraved killers? Anything seemed possible in this lawless border city.

Less than one month after Lastra was taken into custody for allegedly starting the underage prostitution ring, he was released on bail. Lastra vehemently denied the allegations and won his release based on the argument that "he had only kidnapped two young girls, but didn't do anything to them," Adriana Carmona, a lawyer for the Mexican Commission for the Defense and Promotion of Human Rights, told CNN.

In an article that appeared in the *Albion Monitor* in January 2005, freelance journalist Kent Paterson reported shocking allegations lodged against the former state police official. According to Paterson, a reporter who had been covering the Juárez murders for some time, the attorney representing the two young women who filed the criminal complaint against Lastra alleged that the police official had been taking minors from Ciudad Juárez to the Chihuahua City campaign headquarters of the PRI. Lawyer Lucha Castro made the allegations at a meeting with the Mexican Chamber of Deputies femicide commission held in December 2004, the article claimed.

The allegations have never been substantiated.

The claims called to mind the eerie circumstances under which twenty-year-old Olga Alicia Pérez had disappeared some years earlier. According to her mother, Irma, the young woman had vanished after attending a political event at the local PAN headquarters in the summer of 1996. Her decomposed remains were later found in Lote Bravo.

CHAPTER THIRTEEN

Waiting for Justice

*Until there is a serious investigation, any hypothe-
sis is valid.*

OSCAR MAYNEZ, CRIMINOLOGIST

BIG-NAME STARS from Hollywood arrived in Ciudad Juárez
on Valentine's Day 2004 to join local demonstrators in their
demands for justice. Actors Jane Fonda, Sally Field, Salma
Hayek, and Christine Lahti, along with Eve Ensler, creator of
The Vagina Monologues, and U.S. Representatives Hilda Solis of
California and Janice Schakowsky of Illinois, united with thousands of protestors as they marched across the international
bridge linking Ciudad Juárez with El Paso.

The march was organized by a coalition of Mexican organizations; among them were Esther Chávez's Casa Amiga and
the Center for Labor Workshops and Studies. Present as well
were representatives from Amnesty International and the
V-Day Foundation. Since 1998, V-Day, on Valentine's Day,
had been a worldwide event staged in tumultuous countries,

including Afghanistan and Croatia, to call attention to violence against women.

Marchers also included two key figures in the investigation, Guadalupe Morfín and María López Urbina.

The fact that the two federal prosecutors were among the demonstrators that day, not only as representatives of the government but also as women taking a stand against violence toward women, was both groundbreaking and courageous. Their participation in the event seemed to signal a turning point in the relationship between government officials and the women they represented.

In the months prior, there had been marked criticism of the arrival of foreigners such as Fonda and other heavy hitters from the United States and other countries shining a spotlight on the plight of women in the city. State officials were charging that local activists, as well as these foreign protestors, were blowing the murders in Ciudad Juárez out of proportion.

The following month, those same two officials tried to put a positive spin on the discovery of yet another murdered woman, whose sexually abused and tortured remains were found on March 10, tossed amid trash on the outskirts of the city.

Soon after the body of Rebeca Contreras was identified, Guadalupe Morfín, the head of President Vicente Fox's new commission, touted the joint police investigation into the Contreras murder as significant because it marked the first time authorities had properly preserved the crime scene. "The difference from earlier cases is that local authorities, with the presence of federal authorities, took care from the first moment to preserve the scene and do a careful handling of the evidence," Morfín told a reporter for CourtTV.com, the Web site operated by the popular cable network, during a telephone interview that April.

That May, authorities tied a pair of narcotraffickers allegedly belonging to the Juárez Cartel to Contreras's death, charging them with the young woman's rape, torture, and murder. While optimistic about the breakthrough investigation, Morfín and other advocates noted that the root of the problem—the city's thriving drug trade and corrupt police officials in Ciudad Juárez—still needed to be confronted before authorities could appropriately move ahead with the murder investigations.

"There are serious institutional defects in the division of power in our state," Morfín said that spring. "The state government of Chihuahua lacks an ethical system of checks and balances. We need better coordination of federal authorities and to strengthen the lines of cooperation with the civilian society and local authority."

In April 2004, the United Nations released a scathing report, labeling the state's inquiry into the crimes as "tainted by corruption." Of particular concerns to the commission were the pace of the investigation, which was criticized as "slow," and the fabrication of evidence in a number of the homicide cases.

The United Nations committee also criticized Chihuahua officials for their improper handling of the inquiries and suggested that the Mexican government sign a protocol with the United States to conduct a joint investigation into the murders.

Still, the killings of women continued in Chihuahua State amid allegations of political and police corruption. By year's end, authorities were reporting twenty-four femicides in Ciudad Juárez and another eight in Chihuahua City. Of the twenty-four that had occurred in the border city, at least eight had conformed to the earlier profile, according to local activists.

Even more alarming was the fact that the number of femicides in Ciudad Juárez in 2004 was up 58 percent from the previous year. While many in the city hoped the new federal prosecutor would commence an investigation of her own, one year later, her record was no better than the state's.

As part of her role as federal special prosecutor, López Urbina was expected to file periodic reports on her findings. During her investigation, she identified more than 125 former and current state police officers who, she charged, were guilty of torture, abuse of power, and negligence in the investigation of women's murders.

López Urbina requested that authorities in Chihuahua State take immediate disciplinary action against the policemen: she turned over a list of names to state officials. Soon after, she was rotated back to Mexico City, and a replacement, Mireille Roccatti, the former president of Mexico's National Human Rights Commission, was sent to take her place in Ciudad Juárez. Roccatti arrived in Juárez on May 30 but, after only four months, handed in her resignation, taking a new post as a cabinet member for a recently elected public official. Still, Roccatti vowed that her work into the handling of the murder inquiries would be completed by year's end. It was never clear if she intended to finish the job or turn it over to other federal officials for completion. No one was sent to take her place. Instead, the office was dissolved and yet another commission formed.

During her one-year stint, López Urbina had released three separate reports covering a review of 205 of the city's homicide files, comprised of 233 femicides. It is important to note that as special federal prosecutor, López Urbina had no authority to commence an investigation, only to review cases and make recommendations. She found a variety of motives behind the killings, noting that of the 233 homicides she looked at, there was evidence that 84 of the victims had been raped prior to their deaths. In those cases, it was presumed that the crimes were "sexually motivated."

López Urbina noted that of the 205 files she reviewed, 101 had not advanced past the investigative stage. Of those cases, 61 were found not to have a sexual motive.

The remaining 104 had gone to trial, including five in the juvenile justice system.

The report cited that "notorious inactivity and negligence" had led to the "loss of evidence and the inadequate protection of crime scenes."

In her first progress report, López Urbina cited what she termed the most "blatant" failures in 29 cases that were still in the investigatory stages. None of the files showed that the investigators had sought fibers or other forensic clues about the perpetrators; prosecutors had failed to get testimony from key witnesses, such as those who had discovered the bodies; and in some cases, the procedures carried out by investigators were dated before the murders they were investigating had even occurred.

A later report pointed to forensic tests that had been "riddled with grave problems of validity and trustworthiness."

"As a result of these serious deficiencies," López Urbina's final report concluded, "some of the homicide investigations will be practically impossible to solve."

She claimed to have found evidence to presume that 130 Chihuahua justice officials had committed acts of "omission, negligence, malfeasance, or abuse" in their handling of the investigations, and urged state authorities to "prevent impunity for those who acted negligently or were remiss in their duties." She also noted that in a number of the cases, it would be nearly impossible to "capture the killers, given the loss of evidence and inadequate handling of the investigations and the crime scenes."

Surprisingly, López Urbina found no evidence of "irregularities or wrongdoing" in the handling of the 104 cases that had gone to trial—a finding that had some raising questions about her investigation.

Based on the findings, some twenty state officials were suspended. But those who lost their jobs were mainly low- to mid-level employees. Glaringly absent were the names of several high-ranking officials who had led the investigations.

López Urbina did, however, name one former state special prosecutor for women's homicides. Zulema Bolívar, who had served in Ciudad Juárez from July 2001 to March 2002, was cited for "negligence."

Bolívar, who was now the assistant director of the Juárez

city jail, fired back in November 2004, charging that her former superiors, state attorney general Arturo González and
Juárez district attorney José Manuel Ortega, had directed her
investigation into the highly controversial cotton field murder
case in 2001. During testimony before a federal investigation,
Bolívar alleged that, at one point, the two men had even pulled
her off the investigation.

It is widely believed that the police "framed" the two bus
drivers, Víctor García and Gustavo González Meza.

While Bolívar's allegations pointed to actions greater than
negligence on the part of Arturo González and of Ortega, who
was now the legal director of the state attorney general's office,
neither man was cited in López Urbina's report.

Members of the local press demanded to know if Bolívar's
allegations would be pursued. In response, the current attorney general, Patricia González, claimed that legal hurdles
barred her from taking any action. For one, she could not commence an investigation unless Bolívar agreed to testify to her
allegations at the state level. So far, that had not occurred.

More than twelve of those named by López Urbina in her
reports subsequently filed defamation charges against the special prosecutor. The outcome of those filings is not known, as
of this printing.

In mid-2005, the nonprofit Washington Office on Latin
America (WOLA), a human rights group based in the U.S.
capital, criticized López Urbina's report, suggesting that the
data she had used to identify alleged state law enforcement violations was "deficient" and in some cases had even been falsified. The agency pointed to the case of Erica Pérez, whose

death was initially ruled a homicide but later determined to be a drug overdose.

And while the special federal prosecutor had been the target of much criticism, she had made several positive contributions during her short time in Ciudad Juárez, founding a DNA bank and victims' registry that now contains the remains of more than one hundred women. An Amber Alert program was also implemented in the months after her departure.

Guadalupe Morfín, meanwhile, the head of Fox's new federal commission to look into the murder investigations in Ciudad Juárez, had won a small victory in early 2004, gaining the transfer of murder suspect Víctor García (the bus driver charged with the eight cotton field murders) from the state prison in Chihuahua City back to Juárez's El Cereso jail. But her subsequent efforts on García's behalf proved unsuccessful.

Morfín filed an application with the court to invoke the Istanbul Protocol. First adopted by the United Nations in 1999, the protocol outlined international guidelines for the assessment of persons who allege torture or maltreatment by members of law enforcement, the military, and others. Morfín arranged interviews with federal officials to verify the bus driver's claims of torture at the hands of members of the state police.

But her application to invoke the Istanbul Protocol in García's case, and a second filing, in which she called for the charges against the bus driver to be dropped for "lack of physical evidence," were ignored by Chihuahua State Justice Javier Pineda Arzola of the Seventh Criminal Court. Instead, on October 13, 2004, just ten days after a new governor took office,

Justice Pineda dismissed Morfín's calls for a review of the case. He convicted García of the eight killings and sentenced him to fifty years in prison for the crimes. Conspicuously absent that day was García's alleged accomplice, Gustavo González Meza, who had died in jail under mysterious circumstances the previous year, and González Meza's lawyer, Mario Escobedo Jr., who had been "mistakenly" shot by members of the state police just days before he was expected to file a criminal complaint against the state police department.

Even President Fox had been unsuccessful in his calls for García's release. Soon after the judge sentenced the bus driver for the murders, the Mexican president spoke out, insisting that the evidence against García did not appear to be enough to convict him of the homicides. Yet even Fox could do little to stop the corrupt justice system in Chihuahua State.

Interestingly, Justice Pineda, according to news reports, was married to Patricia González, the then newly installed attorney general of Chihuahua State. Growing discontent among Chihuahuans led to yet another shift in political power that October with voters choosing José Reyes Baeza of the PRI party as the state's new governor. Victims' families and human rights advocates again had hopes his victory would lead to a change in the handling of the murder investigations. Once in office, Baeza named Patricia González, a former judge, to serve under him as state attorney general.

While women's rights activists were, at first, pleased that a woman had been installed in the powerful law enforcement post, there was some concern that Patricia González might not be an independent thinker but rather "part of the system"—

someone who would have been called upon to overlook certain matters. Time would prove to be her best, or worst, ally.

In late August of 2004, federal officials announced an assistance program for the families of the murdered women in Ciudad Juárez. Authorities selected thirty mothers from a group of forty-seven families whose cases "fit the serial rape/murder profile" to be given houses the following month. The residences would be in a remote desert area on the outskirts of the city. The remaining seventeen families were told they would receive housing by the end of 2004.

In January of 2005, Justice Pineda returned guilty verdicts against six members of Los Rebeldes. The men had been in prison for eight years awaiting trials when the decision to convict was rendered on January 6, 2005. It was a clear violation of the Mexican justice system that the men were allowed to languish for such an extended period of time. A report by the United States Department of State that looked at human rights practices in Mexico in 2005 found gross violations of the Mexican constitution as it applied to the legal rights of detainees.

Under Mexican law a prosecutor may hold a person up to forty-eight hours (ninety-six hours in the case of organized crime) before presenting the suspect to a judge and announcing charges. "The law provides that authorities must sentence an accused person within four months of detention if the alleged crime carries a sentence of less than two years' imprisonment, or within one year if the crime carries a longer sentence; in practice, judicial and police authorities frequently ignored these time limits," the report charged.

The report also noted that Mexican law "prohibits arbitrary arrest and detention, as well as sponsoring or covering up an illegal detention; however, police routinely ignored these provisions.

"Judges continued to allow statements coerced through torture to be used as evidence against the accused, a practice particularly subject to abuse because confessions were primary evidence in nearly all criminal convictions. Members of the non-government agencies (NGOs) declared that judges often gave greater evidentiary value to the first declaration of a defendant, thus providing prosecutors an incentive to obtain an incriminating first confession and making it difficult for defendants to disavow such declarations."

At one time, the six members of Los Rebeldes had been implicated in seventeen of the city's homicides, but little by little, those charges had been scaled back to include just six homicides. The gang members received sentences ranging from twenty-four to forty years in prison for the crimes. Said to be among the cases for which the men were convicted was the murder of Olga Alicia Pérez, the young woman who was last seen attending a meeting of the PAN political party. Police had first attributed her murder to Sharif Sharif but later charged that members of the violent street gang were responsible for her death.

That it took so many years to finally convict these men of the charges against them raised suspicions among members of the city's women's rights groups. "If they were sure these men committed the crimes, why did it take eight years to find them guilty?" asked Esther Chávez. "What worries me is that the government may be trying to say the cases have been solved when there are still so many gaps in the investigations."

Ironically, on the same day the gang members were sentenced, a second judge, Héctor Javier Talamantes of Chihuahua's Fourth Criminal Court, rendered a guilty verdict against the four members of Los Toltecas, who were also facing six counts of murder. Like the Rebels, these men had sat idle in jail for five years before going to trial on the charges. Manuel Guardado, the alleged leader of Los Toltecas, received the stiffest sentence, of 113 years, for the crimes. The three other men received 40 years each for their roles in the slayings.

And still, the murders continued. The number of homicides against women rose from eighteen in 2004 to thirty-one in 2005, according to the special federal commission for the prevention of violence against women in Juárez. Eight of those murders were determined to have been sexually motivated.

At the request of Commissioner Morfín, a team of Argentine forensic scientists came to Juárez in January 2005 to help identify the remains of what were believed to be more than twenty people sharing a common grave in the city's graveyard. The team first gained recognition in the mid-1980s by implementing advanced DNA techniques to learn the identities of victims killed during Argentina's military coup, in which members of the country's armed forces overthrew the government, leading to allegations of human rights violations and war atrocities. The forensic scientists had also assisted U.S. officials to identify victims of the World Trade Center bombing that occurred on September 11, 2001. It was decided that the scientists would work in tandem with state forensic experts but would remain independent of the Chihuahua State Attorney General's Office to ensure their freedom from political pressure.

When the team offered its findings to State Attorney General Patricia González, however, she declined to review the documents. News reports indicated that González's office had stated that the report was not relevant to the state investigation.

In August, the team concluded that many of the bodies they studied had been misidentified, including at least some of the victims found in the abandoned cotton field. The forensic team determined that Guadalupe Luna de la Rosa, Verónica Hernández, and Bárbara Martínez were not among the bodies exhumed from the abandoned field, delivering an emotional blow to the young women's families, who had believed they had buried their murdered children. The questions remained, who were these girls and what would be done to rectify the botched investigation?

It is likely that many of the earlier cases of misidentification may never be sorted out, since it has been documented by federal officials in Mexico, as well as independent foreign organizations, that officials had either lost, mishandled, burned, or intentionally destroyed much of the evidence collected in those cases.

The *Dallas Morning News* reported one example of the gross neglect that has been occurring since the first bodies were plucked from the desert in 1993. Apparently, when one crime scene investigator could no longer endure the putrid smell of the blood-soaked clothing of a ten-year-old murder victim that was being stored in the warehouse where he was assigned, he ordered the garments washed and then deodorized with fabric softener. The officer's action, whether unwitting or intentional, destroyed any possible clues that might have helped authorities solve the crime.

An equally startling occurrence was related to members of Mexico's National Human Rights Commission during an investigation they carried out around that same time. Members of the commission learned that in the winter of 2003, some homeless men had taken shelter in one of the warehouses where a number of the state's case files were being stored. The men had allegedly used the documents to start a fire so they could stay warm. There were even allegations that some of the files had been sold to criminal suspects intent on clearing their names, according to the *Dallas Morning News*.

On March 9, 2005, the Seventh Judge of Juárez City indicted former state prosecutor Suly Ponce on charges of "authority abuse and negligence" during the investigation of 47 cases. That same year, a judge from the First Court found Ponce guilty as charged and ordered her to jail. But penal judge Juan Carlos Carrasco, who ruled to acquit Ponce of all charges, quickly threw out her sentence.

News accounts stated that in addition to Ponce, 150 other state officials cited for negligence by former federal prosecutor Maria López Urbina were later exonerated.

Bus driver Víctor García finally won his freedom in the summer of 2005. On July 14, Judge Rodolfo Acosta overturned

García's conviction on the eight cotton field killings, ruling that testimony from a key witness in the case was "unreliable."

Amid much fanfare, Víctor García walked out of the Chihuahua state prison just twenty minutes after the ruling was rendered. While the victory was sweet, it was dampened by the fact that the judge declined to rule on García's claims that he, and his alleged accomplice, Gustavo González Meza, had been tortured into making a videotaped confession of their complicity in the murders. Worse, during his more than three years in prison, García lost his business, his savings, and his wife to another man, according to a story that ran in the *New York Times*. "Imagine it," he told a reporter. "Everywhere she went, people looked at her like she was married to a terrible criminal, when the real criminals were outside. They still are."

In a poignant statement, García later apologized to his slain friend, Gustavo González, for falsely naming him under conditions of extreme torture. One news report contended that the reason García had implicated González was that the day before he was detained by state police, he had been a passenger on a bus driven by González.

Remarkably, it is still unclear whether the public prosecutor's office will appeal the overturned verdict in García's case. Statements by Governor Reyes Baeza suggested that García was still considered a suspect, in part because the federal government's application of the Istanbul Protocol had failed to find evidence that he was tortured.

The year 2006 brought more substantive developments, beginning in January with what can only be described as a gang hit on criminal defense lawyer Sergio Dante Almaraz. Dante Almaraz was the former defense attorney for now released bus driver Víctor García. According to news accounts, on the afternoon of January 25, Dante Almaraz was accompanied by a friend and driving a Chevy Suburban through downtown Juárez when a group of unidentified men fired on the lawyer's vehicle from a dark-colored Ford Expedition with New Mexico license plates. Almaraz's passenger survived the attack, but the lawyer was struck by a bullet and killed that afternoon. Police determined the bullet was fired from either an AK-47 or a nine millimeter weapon but made no arrests in the case.

In recent days, Almaraz, president of the Chihuahua State branch of the alternative Convergence for Democracy Party, or Convergencia, had been involved in an angry and highly publicized dispute with the Juárez district attorney over alleged links to stolen vehicles. Days before his murder, Almaraz announced that if anything should happen to him, members of the public prosecutor's office would be responsible. Others speculated that the lawyer's murder could be linked to his representation of Víctor García. In the days after the shooting, it was reported that three cameras set up on nearby intersections to monitor traffic had not captured any of the incident. Two were reported as being inoperable, and a third was facing the opposite direction at the time of the shooting.

Almaraz's murder prompted the lawyer's brother to call for a tourist boycott of the border city. He later confided that he and other relatives were too scared to cross the border from their home in El Paso to attend Dante's funeral.

Less than six months later, on June 1, news came that Sharif Sharif had died at a state hospital in Chihuahua after having served eleven years of his thirty-year sentence at Chihuahua's Aquiles Serdán prison for the murder of Elizabeth Castro. According to authorities, he had been transported there several days earlier for "digestive problems."

At the request of the New Mexico office of the state attorney general, Ross Reichard, an assistant medical investigator for the New Mexico office of the medical investigator, was immediately flown to Chihuahua City to conduct an autopsy.

Dr. Reichard concluded from his examination that Sharif had died of natural causes stemming from cirrhosis of the liver and hepatitis C, which can cause cirrhosis. In an official report, the U.S. forensic pathologist determined that an "upper gastrointestinal hemorrhage" had led to Sharif's death at the age of fifty-nine. He also noted that Sharif suffered from heart disease.

Dr. Reichard told authorities he found no indications of abuse or acute, traumatic injuries on the body. "There was no evidence . . . of foul play at the time of his death," he told local journalists.

Sharif's former attorney, Irene Blanco, now a federal congresswoman for the PAN party, had once overheard the Egyptian complaining to representatives from the National Human Rights Commission that prison personnel were "force-feeding" him unknown medications, yet no toxicology tests were performed upon his death.

Blanco had done what she could to bring his allegations to light, but after the near-fatal attack on her son, she moved out of the area to an undisclosed location. Still, she continued to speak out on Sharif's behalf. At the time of his death, a new lawyer had taken up the Egyptian's cause.

In an interview with the local Juárez media, Blanco recalled that in a conversation with Sharif about one month before his death he spoke of knee problems. News accounts portrayed the Egyptian as suffering from depression over his inability to prove his innocence. Ulises Perzábal, the Mexican national who, along with his wife Cynthia Kiecker of Minnesota, was arrested for the 2003 murder of Viviana Rayas, told a Mexican journalist of his encounters with Sharif in the prison infirmary during his eighteen-month incarceration at Aquiles Serdán. Perzábal described Sharif as "rebellious, isolated and incredulous," and recalled several instances in which prison staff had administered medication to his fellow inmate. "He couldn't believe what was happening to him," Perzábal recalled. "I think that was killing him little by little."

Sharif was laid to rest in a plot at the Panteón Municipal No. 1 of the city of Chihuahua. His grave was identified in case relatives wanted to claim his body and return it to his native Egypt for burial. To date, no one has come for him.

At one time, Sharif had been portrayed as the most feared person in Juárez, yet his passing came with little more than a mention on the evening news and a few lines in the local newspapers. The prison director at Aquiles Serdán told the local TV station that Sharif had spent his last years teaching English and Arabic to other inmates.

"The news hit me hard," said Esther Chávez Cano of Sharif's death. "I was driving when I heard the news and I said to myself, 'Has an innocent man died, or a guilty man?' The uncertainty will forever remain."

Irma García, the mother of Sharif's alleged victim Elizabeth Castro, told a local newspaper that she still had faith that authorities had detained the "right man who had killed her daughter."

Yet Ramona Morales expressed uncertainty of Sharif's guilt. Ramona said that when she first read about Sharif's passing in *El Diario de Juárez*, she reported a sense of relief that the man police had told her was responsible for her daughter's murder had finally died. Now Silvia could rest in peace, she thought.

At sixty-seven, Ramona was operating a small trinket shop out of her home. She had been inconsolable since Silvia's death; even visits from her grandchildren had failed to lift her spirits. Concerned for their mother, Ramona's sons had cleared out the furnishings in the family's small living room and set up a tiny shop with glass counters for their mother to display a hodgepodge of cake toppers and party favors. Ramona would also sell cold sodas and ice cream from a small freezer and other plastic toys and knickknacks to the neighborhood children. Tending a business from the house seemed to help pass the days without Silvia. Yet Ramona still broke into tears whenever she spoke about her daughter's murder.

In an interview in June of 2006, Ramona said that in the days after Sharif's passing, she went to the court in Juárez to find out more about the Egyptian's role in the killing. She had not heard anything about the investigation since police had informed her of Sharif's role in the murder back in 1995. But with his death, she believed that she was legally entitled to a copy of her daughter's homicide file. That day, the clerk at the Fifth Circuit court told her something unbelievable. "No, Sharif had nothing to do with your daughter's case."

Ramona was floored. "They say that a victim cannot be at peace until the killer passes away or pays for the crime," she explained. "I thought my daughter would finally rest in peace with Sharif's death. But now I find out he's not the killer."

That Ramona had had no idea that Sharif Sharif had not been implicated in her daughter's murder was nothing short of shocking. Even more astounding was that state authorities had allowed the relatives of the murdered girls, as well as the community of Juárez at large, to believe that Sharif Sharif had been responsible for many of the crimes against the city's women, when in fact he had been found guilty of just one murder.

Spurred into action once again, Ramona Morales reached out to several others whose daughters had also supposedly died at the hands of the Egyptian chemist. She had stayed in close contact with Irma Pérez, the mother of Olga Alicia, and several other families of murdered girls. During her phone call with Irma, the two women decided they would try to get a meeting with the new governor, José Reyes Baeza, who was coming to Juárez that month. They had heard that he was more humane than the past state governor and was also more sympathetic to the plight of the murdered women.

Irma had moved, but continued to flip hamburgers to make ends meet.

Suddenly Ramona found herself feeling sorry for Sharif. From the start, she had never really believed that he had been responsible for Silvia's murder. Her suspicions had grown even more as time passed and the scapegoats began to surface. It appeared that like Silvia, Sharif too had been a victim of the state's corrupt justice system.

In the end, Ramona and the other mothers never sat down with Baeza when he came to town. They had wanted to make sure their daughters had not died in vain and that something had come of their deaths. The statute of limitations of ten years was about to run out on many of the cases, and the mothers of the murdered girls wanted to ask for an extension in light of the recent government findings that corruption and negligence had pervaded the investigations.

In a telephone interview in the fall of 2006, Ramona explained that illness had prevented her from pursuing the meeting with the governor. Her blood sugar was high and she was suffering from severe leg pain. During the call, Ramona related news on some of the other families. The family of her slain thirteen-year-old neighbor, Lupita, had moved to Veracruz soon after the murder, vowing never to return to Juárez.

Jesus González, the father of murdered maquila worker Sagrario, had died just two months earlier. His eldest daughter, Guillermina, was now a mother of two and was living with her husband.

Meanwhile, Sagrario González's case would remain open—and see no police involvement until 2005. At the urging of family members, authorities finally arrested a local man, José Luis Hernández Flores, and charged him with the slaying of the seventeen-year-old factory worker. It took the family seven years to convince police that their Lomas de Poleo neighbor was responsible for the April 1998 murder of the young maquila worker.

The family had first became suspicious of Hernández after he suggested they look for Sagrario's remains in the Valley of Juárez, in the exact location where her body was later found. Guillermina González claimed that the family had alerted police to the eerie coincidence but officials had simply brushed the lead aside and done nothing.

For years, Sagrario's father unsuccessfully scoured the neighborhood looking for Hernández until one day in February 2005, when Jesús González spotted the slim, dark-haired man in a local store buying beer. González hid from sight until the man returned to his house, and then immediately called police. Once in custody, officers contended, Hernández confessed to Sagrario's murder and named two other men who had participated in the killing. It is unclear whether the police questioned the two other suspects for the crime. There are those in the community who have raised doubts about Hernández's confession and his culpability in the crime.

At last account, Guillermina González and her siblings were working together in the family's grocery store. Paula and Jesús constructed and opened the small bodega on their property in Lomas de Poleo to ensure that their remaining children would not have to leave home to earn a living.

Since early in the investigation, former Chihuahua State forensics chief Oscar Maynez had been urging officials to entertain the possibility that a serial killer was on the loose in the

city. He later theorized that an "organized group with resources" was behind the homicides.

Some of the recent government findings suggested that
Maynez was on target with his suspicions. The reports pointed
to a combination of corrupt police officers and local drug traffickers as collaborators in a number of the killings. But still,
there were no arrests.

Since resigning from the *procuraduría* under pressure to
plant evidence in January 2002, Maynez had found work with
another state agency. But he continued to closely monitor the
ongoing investigation into the city's murdered women. Maynez
maintained that the answer to many of the unsolved cases lay in
the abandoned cotton field where officials had exhumed the
eight bodies in November 2001. The two bus drivers had been
cleared of the eight murders, yet an investigation had never
been commenced to locate those responsible for the crimes.

While authorities were calling it a cold case, Maynez insisted there were a number of lines of investigation that had
never been followed up on. For one, there appeared to be
DNA evidence that could link a suspect to the murders. And
Maynez was certain the same people who had killed Lilia García several months earlier had committed the eight murders. In
that previous case, DNA had been collected but nothing had
come of the forensic sample, although Maynez had sent a copy
of the DNA profile to García's mother for safekeeping.

Former FBI profiler Robert Ressler had theorized that
several serial killers were crossing into Mexico from the
United States to commit the murders.

On August 15, 2006, his theory would also prove credible. That day, U.S. Immigration and Customs Enforcement arrested Edgar Alvarez Cruz in Denver, Colorado, on immigration violations and later announced that Cruz was a member of a gang of killers who had purportedly raped and killed at least ten women in Ciudad Juárez between 1993 and 2003.

The break in the case had come several months earlier on March 24, when a man named José Francisco Granados de la Paz, a relative of Alvarez Cruz by marriage, was questioned by a Texas Ranger about possible links to the crimes in Juárez. This occurred while Granados de la Paz was in U.S. custody in Sierra Blanca, Texas, on immigration charges.

Prosecutors said that during an interrogation, Granados admitted to participating in the murders of several women in Ciudad Juárez, and he implicated Alvarez Cruz in the killings. Among the murders for which the men were being investigated were the eight women found in the cotton field in November 2001.

Granados claimed he and Alvarez were responsible for those homicides. He also took responsibility for the murders of at least two women the duo allegedly killed in the rear seat of Alvarez's red Renault. Granados told law enforcement officials the two had wrapped one of the bodies in black plastic before disposing of it. During his alleged confession, Granados had even supplied authorities with a map of the locations where he said the bodies had been dumped or buried.

According to law enforcement officials, Granados claimed that beginning in 1993, when he was fifteen and Alvarez Cruz was seventeen, the two pals would drive around the city, sometimes accompanied by a third man, Alejandro "Cala" Delgado Valle, kidnapping women, raping and killing them in the back seat of Alvarez's car, and disposing of their remains throughout the city.

Granados blamed his role in the murders on Alvarez, who he claimed would supply him with drugs or pills and then threaten him into taking part in the crimes. "They never told me, 'Let's go kill women.' They didn't say that. They'd say, 'Let's go drinking, let's go crazy,'" Granados reportedly told investigators in a taped confession that March.

Sgt. Brooks Long of the Texas Rangers told reporters that he had no reason to doubt Granados's accounts during their fifty-minute interview—although Sergeant Long had been unable to get Granados to commit to specific dates as to when these crimes had occurred. He had also failed to provide physical descriptions of the supposed victims when interviewed by Long.

In one instance, when the sergeant asked him to describe one of the victims he claimed to have tossed into the desert in Lomas de Poleo in 1993, he simply said, "She was hot," according to the taped confession. Granados also described stabbing one victim "right there in the heart. Pow-pow."

Relatives of Granados painted a picture of a man who abused drugs, talked to the devil, broke beer bottles over his head, and set his mother's house ablaze. He had also been known to walk the streets naked, according to family members.

When asked why he had made the confessions now, after all these years, Granados pointed to his faith. He said that as a Christian, he wanted absolution for the crimes.

U.S. federal law enforcement agents were acting on information gleaned from the interview with Granados when they arrested Alvarez Cruz and charged him with the murder of seventeen-year-old Mayra Juliana Reyes Solís, whose body was found in the abandoned cotton field in 2001. Authorities had linked Alvarez Cruz to Reyes Solís's murder, in part because the young woman's body had been wrapped in black plastic when it was found that November, a detail provided by Granados's alleged confession. Alvarez was quickly transferred to a U.S. federal facility in El Paso to wait for a request for extradition to Mexico.

Encouraged by the news, Chihuahua Attorney General Patricia González traveled to El Paso in August to meet with Immigration and Customs Enforcement, the U.S. Marshals, and the Mexican consulate about the men's alleged connection to some of the crimes. Authorities were looking to connect Alvarez to fourteen of the murders.

Denver police officials confirmed that since 2002, Alvarez had been arrested three times in the Colorado capital on minor offenses. According to police, the first arrest was on January 15, 2002, for destruction of private property, disturbing the peace, and threat. He was arrested a second time that October for "threat to injure a person or property" and "disturbance by phone" and again in April 2006 for "destruction of private property." Authorities said they were holding the third man, Alejandro Delgado, who Granados claimed had accompanied the men on their killing spree in Juárez, as a "protected" witness.

But already there were inconsistencies in Granados's account of the crimes. While the twenty-eight-year-old Mexican national had described the murders as stabbing deaths, criminologist Oscar Maynez pointed out that most of the killings had been the result of strangulation. In fact, he said, an autopsy conducted on all of the bodies exhumed from the cotton field revealed that the women had died as a result of strangulation. Maynez insisted that even though many of the bodies were simply skeletal remains when they were recovered, there were no "telltale" nicks that would indicate a knife had been used in the slayings. And he and other forensic experts were convinced the young women had been strangled to death.

During an interview with one U.S. newspaper, Maynez likened Granados's confession to that of John Mark Karr, who in the summer of 2006, claimed to have killed Colorado pageant princess JonBenét Ramsey. Maynez pointed out that during the confession, Granados admitted to closely following the Juárez murder cases on TV.

Maynez also insisted that three men, acting on their own, could not have carried out the numerous murders and the dumping of the bodies without being detected.

Even Alvarez's former common-law wife, Beatrice Sánchez, who was a U.S. resident, told a reporter that she and Alvarez had purchased the red Renault that he had allegedly used to carry out the murders in 1993 and then quickly sold it the following year to cover the medical expenses of their disabled son. Sánchez claimed that when the car's new owner was involved in an accident, Alvarez bought the car back from him, hoping to repair it and get it back on the road. But he never realized that dream. The parts for the car proved too expensive, and the Renault sat on blocks until the couple finally sold it as junk in 1998. A lawyer for Alvarez claimed to be in possession of a receipt documenting that the sale had indeed taken place that year.

In addition, employment records on Alvarez from the Denver construction company Allphase Concrete, where he had worked from mid-July 2001 to November 2001, and again from April 2002 to April 2004, indicated that the alleged killer was not even in Mexico for any except five of the homicides, according to the *Denver Post*.

While residents of the border city expressed a certain amount of faith in the latest string of arrests, in part because they had been effected with assistance from U.S. law enforcement officials, the emerging inconsistencies were troubling and many feared that Alvarez and Granados would soon join the growing list of scapegoats who had been charged with the serial killings.

"I can't believe it would be only three people," Esther Chávez told the *El Paso Times* in response to word of the men's arrests in the United States. "I think you would need a much stronger network to do these killings."

U.S. Ambassador to Mexico Antonio Garza was more optimistic. In a written statement in late August 2006, he called the arrests "a major breakthrough" in the investigation into the killings.

Oscar Maynez, however, remained cautious in his reaction.

In an interview in 2006, he adopted a wait-and-see attitude. While he viewed the U.S. ambassor's statements about the men's culpability as positive, he noted that members of the suspects' families were insisting the three were not involved.

By November 2006, the cases against the men were already falling apart.

"We don't want scapegoats. We don't want torture . . . or lies," said Josefina González, whose daughter, Claudia Ivette, died after being locked out when she showed up three minutes late for her factory shift. "What I want is the truth."

It was a sentiment shared by all the families of the fallen daughters of Juárez.

"We don't have bodies, but we still have missing girls," Maynez said. "The fact that we don't have bodies is circumstantial. We just don't know where they are buried."

Epilogue

Since the year 2000, when President Vicente Fox took the helm, Mexico has received seven visits from human rights experts including representatives from the United Nations and Amnesty International.

In 2005, the U.S. Department of State issued a report on human rights practices in Mexico. The report, released by the Bureau of Democracy, Human Rights and Labor on March 8, 2006, cited that while the government "generally respected and promoted human rights at the national level," violations persisted at the state and local level.

"The government investigated, prosecuted, and sentenced several public officials and members of security forces involved in criminal acts; however, impunity and corruption remained a problem," the report noted. "Local police released suspects who claimed to have been tortured as part of investigations, and authorities investigated complaints of torture, but authorities rarely punished officials for torture.

"There were marked increases during the year in narcotics trafficking–related violence, especially in the northern border region. Violence against women continued to be a problem nationwide, particularly in Ciudad Juárez and the surrounding area.

"Government efforts to improve respect for human rights were offset by a deeply entrenched culture of impunity and corruption," the report maintained. Among the human rights violations cited were kidnappings, including by police; corruption, inefficiency, and lack of transparency in the judicial system; statements coerced through torture permitted as evidence in trials; corruption at all levels of government; domestic violence against women often perpetrated with impunity; and criminal violence, including killings, against women.

It is clear from the findings that more work needs to be done to stop the violence against the country's women.

Local activists continue to work for justice for the women of the state of Chihuahua and of Mexico. Their efforts have served to raise international awareness of the ongoing crisis. Even as these brave women risk their lives to publicize these great atrocities, impunity and corruption continue to thwart their efforts.

Another report by the Comisión Mexicana de Defensa y Promoción de los Derechos Humanos, entitled "Murders and Disappearances of the Women and Girls in Ciudad Juárez and the State of Chihuahua," presented to the special rapporteur of the Commission on Human Rights on the Independence of Judges and Magistrates in Mexico in March 2005, found that the situation in the state of Chihuahua "symbolizes the extreme vulnerability of women in the professional, social and private spheres.

"This stigmatization, within a context of economic liberalization and consequent deterioration of the social fabric, has been exacerbated by the prevalence of discrimination and indifference, in addition to the lack of effort and political will shown by the Federal, Chihuahua State and Municipal authorities in addressing the killings, investigating and prosecuting the perpetrators of the crimes against women, a situation corresponding to what is generally known as 'femicide.'"

In light of the "more than 430 women" murdered and hundreds more who have disappeared in the state of Chihuahua since 1993, the report blamed pervasive sexism in Chihuahua for hindering the adoption of public policies that would protect women.

At the time of this writing, the murder rate in Chihuahua continued to climb, with many of the city's women reporting that they felt no safer in 2006 than they did ten years ago when the serial killings first grabbed the headlines.

Despite the findings of several prominent organizations, the formation of numerous commissions, the appointment of federal special prosecutors, and the undying efforts of local women's rights activists to right the wrongs, the abuses against Juárez's young women continue seemingly unabated.

Happy endings in fairy tales are what everyone hopes for. Yet for the families who have lost a loved one, there remains no closure. For mothers like Ramona Morales, Irma Pérez, Paula Flores González, Celia de la Rosa, and Norma Andrade, there is no justice, only empty promises and nights filled with sorrow and tears.

And the list of grieving mothers continues to grow. Statistics from the Washington Office on Latin America and the Mexican press reflect a murder trend in Chihuahua State higher than the rates for either 2004 or 2005 with domestic violence, sexual attacks, and suspected narco-related crimes topping the list of motives.

The names and the faces have changed, but the stories are sadly the same. Although some say that the dead can speak, the families of the victims ask themselves if anyone is listening.

These daughters of Juárez never had the opportunity to speak out. Their cries were brutally silenced. Now those voices ring out from these pages. Perhaps this time someone will listen.

THERE ARE SEVERAL ORGANIZATIONS IN AND OUTSIDE
MEXICO CURRENTLY HELPING THE WOMEN OF
CIUDAD JUÁREZ, MEXICO, SOME OF THEM INCLUDE:

(IN ALPHABETICAL ORDER)

AMIGOS DE MUJERES (FRIENDS OF WOMEN)

AMNESTY INTERNATIONAL

CASA AMIGA CRISIS CENTER

JUSTICIA PARA NUESTRAS HIJAS
(JUSTICE FOR OUR DAUGHTERS)

MUJERES DE NEGRO (WOMEN IN BLACK)

MUJERES POR JUÁREZ (WOMEN OF JUÁREZ)

NUESTRAS HIJAS DE REGRESO A CASA
(SO THAT OUR DAUGHTERS MAY COME HOME)

Acknowledgments

THERE ARE COUNTLESS PEOPLE to thank for helping me make this book a reality. If I forget anyone, please forgive me. Because it is a story that I began covering almost twelve years ago, any omission is strictly accidental.

First of all, I wish to thank Diana Montané, a friend and talented writer who talked me into the idea of writing a book about these horrific crimes. It took several years for our manuscript to come together. It began as a first-person account of a journalist and her crew; then it became a fictional story, only to return to the first-person narrative. During the process, I witnessed the tragedies of September 11 and for the very first time felt as violated and helpless in my country as many of these victims must have felt in Mexico. Then on June 6, 2002, my husband Tony passed away of a sudden heart attack. His loss shook our family, but we were blessed with many special friends, relatives, and colleagues who became our pillars of strength. Shortly thereafter circumstances beyond our control made it impossible to publish our original manuscript.

Then, about two years ago, I received a phone call from Johanna Castillo, editor for Atria's Spanish-language division. She remembered reading that manuscript and wondered what had happened to it. "It's sitting on a shelf gathering dust," I replied. "Well, not anymore," she answered. To Johanna and Judith Curr, executive vice president and publisher of Atria Books, I would like to extend my heartfelt gratitude for believing in this story and considering it compelling enough to publish. Both of you and Wendy Walker, the remarkable editor, embraced this project from the beginning, knowing our journey would take us into unfamiliar territory. It was a harrowing tale of murder, corruption, and deceit in a foreign country where the rules of justice seem quite different from the ones we are accustomed to in the United States.

Wendy, I've witnessed your commitment, dedication, and belief in this manuscript. Your assurances that we would make this happen, despite the obstacles along the way, gave me strength to keep going.

And to Lisa Pulitzer, who has done such an outstanding job of transforming a first-person narrative into a true crime story, your professionalism, sensitivity, compassion, and sense of humor have made working with you a true pleasure. Last year, when we met at a fashionable bistro in New York, perhaps you never imagined that our work would take us to the shanty-towns of a Mexican desert plagued with poverty and crime. Our trip took us far away from the city that brought us together, but I commend you for agreeing it was necessary. I thank you for your willingness to immerse yourself in all that is Juárez, its smells, tastes, laughter, and pain. I will always appreciate how you stressed it was my book and my story. Today I am proud to say that *The Daughters of Juárez* is also your story. I know how touched you were by the stories of the victims and their families and the unending determination of advocates and experts to close this cycle of violence.

Johanna, Judith, Wendy, and Lisa, I know you share my desire for justice. Perhaps this book will become a catalyst for change in Ciudad Juárez, México.

To our production editor, Nancy Inglis, we couldn't have done it without you! Despite our last-minute additions and changes to the manuscript, you understood it was all in the interest of making *The Daughters of Juárez* the best it could be. Our gratitude to copyeditor Peg Haller, whose attention to detail made this manuscript shine, and to our dedicated and resourceful publicist, Melissa Quiñones, for her enthusiasm in marketing this book to the different media outlets in order to ensure its success.

To Jorge Ramos, a dear friend, respected journalist, and author, you paved the way for all of your colleagues at Univision in being the first to publish a book. I thank you for your guidance and pep talks throughout the entire process and for always having the time to help me (with a smile), despite your busy schedule. To my close friend, distinguished journalist and author Maria Elena Salinas, with whom I have shared so many different life experiences, thank you for your words of encouragement when I felt I couldn't handle the pressures of motherhood, my work for *Aquí y Ahora*, and finishing this project. To Coynthia Pérez Mon, my esteemed friend, meticulous producer, dedicated colleague, and perfectionist, whose colored pens are as etched in my mind as the many chocolates we consumed along the way. You have been and continue to be an example of strength, and perseverance. Yoly Zugasti, you may not have known it, but when the stories we heard in Juárez became too painful, your positive thoughts helped me refocus, reminding me that by broadcasting these appalling accounts, perhaps we could save a life. Roxana Soto, your enthusiasm in picking up the story and running with it during our 2002 trip to Juárez speaks volumes about your professionalism. Thank you for your camaraderie and your continued desire to be a part of the solution. To Univision president Ray Rodriguez, senior vice president Alina Falcon, and vice president, co–news director Sylvia Rosabal, my deepest gratitude for allowing us to continually update this ongoing saga. To my cameramen Angel Matos, Jerry Johnson, Martin Guzman, and Jorge Soliño, your talent, creativity, hard work, and friendship will always be appreciated. I also salute my outstanding editors, Maria Piñon, Rick Ramos, and Frank Linero, and the creative Univision promotions team past and present, from Mario Rodriguez to Otto Padron and Chela Mason—thanks for producing promos that were so compelling. To the extraordinarily helpful news team at our El Paso/Juárez Univision affiliate, KINT, Channel 26—Luis Escalera, Gustavo Barraza, Raul Morales, Germán Sáenz, and Roberto Delgado—there are not enough words to express how grateful I am for your generosity, references, and confirmation of information. I would also like to acknowledge Jorge Domínguez, Luz María Cárdenas, and Laz Hernández from the Univision and Galavision art departments for their help and guidance. To my colleagues Liz Valdes, Rafael Tejero, and Gabriela Tristan, who through the years always kept me abreast of new developments, as well as Linda Rozo, Veronica Molina, Lucia Burga, and Tania Ordaz Rues, thanks for your continued assistance, research, and phone calls. Christopher Robinson, thanks for making sure our map was consistent with the facts.

Esther Chávez Cano and Oscar Maynez, without your input, cooperation, resources, and support, *The Daughters of Juárez* would never have been so complete and timely.

To the mothers, fathers, sisters, and brothers of the murdered women, who invited us into their lives and shared their pain, it is our sincerest hope that you find closure and peace.

To my dear friend and gifted writer, Alex Hadad, your suggestions were invaluable. Thanks for always asking and caring about this project. Thanks to my close friends Lazz, Omi, Ana Margarita, Carmen, and Tillie, whose patience and understanding I will forever cherish. And, Mirian and Edith, knowing I could count on you to take care of the family while I was away made my job that much easier.

My loving sons, Victor and Julian, as you read these pages I hope you'll understand why my assignments took me far from home. There was so much to chronicle, so much to report, and yet so little time in which to do it. I hope I've been an example in your lives and shown you the difference between right and wrong. I hope I've shown you to stand up for your beliefs and defend your rights.

To Miguel Angel, you are indeed my guardian angel. Your understanding, love, and willingness to listen, read my drafts, and share my tears are only a few of the reasons why you hold a special place in my heart.

For you and all the others I failed to mention, fate has brought us together. I hope today you share with me the pride and sense of accomplishment I feel in seeing this labor of love come full circle.

Individually, Lisa Pulitzer would like to express gratitude to researcher Joan Bonina for her hard work and dedication to this project, and to literary agent Madeleine Morel for her support and encouragement. She would also like to extend a special thank-you to her stepfather, Gilbert Matthews, for always believing in her, lots of hugs to her husband/editor, Douglas Love, for his undying devotion, understanding, and editorial input, and "butterfly" kisses to her two young daughters, Francesca and Juliet, for letting their mommy tell this important story. It is Lisa's sincere hope that through the efforts of activists such as Esther Chávez Cano and others who are fighting for justice in Ciudad Juárez and in countries around the globe, Francesca and Juliet will one day enjoy a world in which women everywhere receive equal treatment.

Index

Acosta Ramírez, María de los Angeles (victim), 186
Acosta, Rodolfo, 274–75
activists: as advocates for families, 228; continuing activities of, 292; criticisms of police by, 101, 102; demands for Ponce's resignation from, 166; and drug violence, 93–94; and Escobedo murder, 219; and Kiecker-Perzábal case, 246; and Luna case, 181; and number of murders, 41; protests/demonstrations by, 58, 70, 82, 89, 93–94, 146, 149, 163, 166, 179–80, 181, 223–24, 233–34, 261–62; reaction of authorities to, 149; and Rebels case, 271–72; Sharif requests meeting with, 104; and wait time for missing person's report, 80. *See also specific person or organization*
Alejandro (factory worker), 22
Altolaguirre, Marta, 235–39
Alvarez Cruz, Edgar, 284–85, 286–88, 289
Alvídrez Barrios, Violeta Mabel (victim), 247
Amber Alert, 268

Amigos de Mujeres (Friends of Women), 295
Amnesty International, 165, 234, 240, 249–53, 261, 291, 295
Andrade de García, Norma, 160, 161, 165, 170–73, 293
Andrade, Luis, 61
Angel Loya, Miguel, 255
anonymous calls, 19, 22, 35, 105, 181–82, 195, 213, 214, 220, 222, 234
A.O. Smith (manufacturer), 137
Argentine forensic scientists, 248–49, 272–73
Armendáriz Díaz, Sergio "El Diablo," 60–61, 62, 66–68, 99, 136, 155, 191
Association of Business Owners and Professionals of Juárez Avenue, 225
Association of the Maquiladoras, 177, 178
attorney general, Chihuahua: and Argentine forensic group's findings, 273; and businessmen theory of murders, 225; calls for resignation of, 227–28; and computer school theory, 248; crime statistics released by, 258; and drug trafficking, 257; and